AQA Economics

AS

Exclusively endorsed by AQA

Alasdair Copp
Jim Lawrence
Steve Stoddard

 Nelson Thornes

Published in 2008 by:
Nelson Thornes Ltd
Delta Place
27 Bath Road
CHELTENHAM
GL53 7TH
United Kingdom

10 11 12 / 10 9 8 7 6 5 4

A catalogue record for this book is available from the British Library

ISBN 978 0 7487 9964 0

Cover photograph by Corbis
Illustrations by Fakenham and Angela Knowles
Page make-up by Fakenham Photosetting, Norfolk

Printed and bound in Spain by Graphycems

The authors would like to thank the following for permission to reproduce photographs and other copyright material:

piv Getty; p4 © Bildagenhur Hamburg/Alamy; p5 © Hoberman Collection UK/ Alamy; p20 © D. Hurst/Alamy; p23 © Aardman Animations Limited. 2005. All Rights Reserved; p35 © TravelStockCollection – Homer Sykes/Alamy; p44 © Photo-grafix/ Alamy; p52 D. Hurst/Alamy; p58 © IPC/Alamy; p61 © Gareth McCormack/Alamy; p73 © toy Alan King; p90 © Bubbles Photolibrary/Alamy; p94 © Sally and Richard Grenhill/Alamy; p105 © ICP/Alamy; p109 © Sue Cunningham Photographic/Alamy; p110 © Alvey & Towers Picture Library/Alamy; p112 © David Preston/Alamy; p127 © Photofusion Picture Library/Alamy; p134 Blend Images/Alamy; p142 © Nikreates/Alamy; p145 © Marc Hill/Alamy; p164 © Vahan Shirvanian; p183 Brian Harris/Alamy; p196 Horizon International Images Limited/Alamy; p205 © Alex Segre/Alamy; p218 © Brian Harris/Alamy; p219 Peter Webb/Alamy.

The authors and publisher would like to thank Tutor2U Limited for their kind permission to reproduce copyright material on the following pages:

p78, p82, p84, p87, p89, p91, p92, p93, p95, p96, p99, p102, p103, p104, p111, p112, p113, p119, p205, p206, p209, p210, p222, p226, p227, p230.

Contents

AQA introduction

Nelson Thornes has worked in partnership with AQA to ensure this book and the accompanying online resources offer you the best support for your A Level course.

All resources have been approved by senior AQA examiners so you can feel assured that they closely match the specification for this subject and provide you with everything you need to prepare successfully for your exams.

These print and online resources together **unlock blended learning**; this means that the links between the activities in the book and the activities online blend together to maximise your understanding of a topic and help you achieve your potential.

These online resources are available on  which can be accessed via the internet at www.kerboodle.com/live, anytime, anywhere. If your school or college subscribes to this service you will be provided with your own personal login details. Once logged in, access your course and locate the required activity.

For more information and help visit **www.kerboodle.com**

Icons in this book indicate where there is material online related to that topic. The following icons are used:

💡 Learning activity

These resources include a variety of interactive and non-interactive activities to support your learning.

☑️ Progress tracking

These resources include a variety of tests that you can use to check your knowledge on particular topics (Test yourself) and a range of resources that enable you to analyse and understand examination questions (On your marks…).

🔎 Research support

These resources include WebQuests, in which you are assigned a task and provided with a range of web links to use as source material for research.

▎ How to use this book

This book covers the specification for your course and is arranged in a sequence approved by AQA.

The book content is divided into chapters that match the AQA Economics specification for Units 1 and 2 – Markets and market failure and The national economy. Chapters 1–10 cover Unit 1 and Chapters 11–20 cover Unit 2.

The features in this book include:

Learning objectives

At the beginning of each chapter you will find a list of learning objectives that contain targets linked to the requirements of the specification.

Key terms

Terms that you will need to be able to define and understand.

Case study

A mixture of real-life and devised case studies contextualising and exemplifying the core concepts.

Activity

Activities that will help you to test your knowledge and understanding. Stretch and challenge activities, designed to stretch the most able student, also appear in some chapters.

Links

This highlights any areas where topics relate to another part of this book, or to the A2 specification.

Skills

Explanations and advice on commonly used skills in Economics.

AQA Examiner's tip

Hints from AQA examiners to help you with your study and to prepare for your exam.

AQA Examination-style questions

Questions in the style that you can expect in your exam appear at the end of each chapter.

AQA examination questions are reproduced by permission of the Assessment and Qualifications Alliance.

Learning outcomes

A bulleted list at the end of each topic or chapter summarising the content in an easy-to-follow way.

Web links in the book

As Nelson Thornes is not responsible for third party content online, there may be some changes to this material that are beyond our control. In order for us to ensure that the links referred to in the book are as up-to-date and stable as possible, the websites are usually homepages with supporting instructions on how to reach the relevant pages if necessary.

Please let us know at **kerboodle@nelsonthornes.com** if you find a link that doesn't work and we will do our best to redirect the link, or to find an alternative site.

Markets and market failure

Introduction

This unit introduces students to microeconomics and to some key elements of the 'economist's toolkit'. You will be required to acquire knowledge and understanding of some basic microeconomic models and to apply these to current problems and issues. Basic microeconomic models such as demand and supply, the operation of the price mechanism, and causes of market failure are central to this module. This book provides plenty of opportunities to use these basic models to explore current economic behaviour. You should look to apply the knowledge and skills you learn in your AS Economics course to a wide variety of situations and to different markets and examples of market failure, including environmental market failures. You should also aim to develop a critical approach to economic models and methods of enquiry. By the end of the course you should also be familiar with the various types of statistical and other data commonly used by economists, e.g. data presented in the form of index numbers.

Chapter 1 will outline the purpose of economic activity and clarify the basic economic problem affecting societies the world over. You will learn how economic resources are categorised and allocated and how to analyse some fundamental concepts with the use of production possibility diagrams.

In Chapter 2, you will be introduced to the concept of demand and to the factors that determine the extent of effective demand for individuals and the market. You will learn how to represent demand in diagrammatic form and subsequently how to analyse changes in the conditions of demand.

Chapter 3 focuses on supply and the factors underpinning how much firms are prepared to supply at a given price. Similarly, you will learn how to draw a supply schedule and analyse changes in the factors affecting supply.

Chapter 4 brings supply and demand together to illustrate equilibrium and disequilibrium in markets. It also introduces some early applications of supply and demand analysis in the form of price intervention. By this point you will have developed an understanding of a very powerful analytical component of the economist's 'toolkit'.

Chapter 5 introduces the concept of elasticity, or responsiveness, of demand and supply to changes in price and income. You will learn how to represent these concepts diagrammatically as well as understanding the significance of different statistical values. The chapter also highlights the real-world application of these fundamental concepts for households, firms and governments.

Chapter 6 presents a useful set of case studies demonstrating how the concepts covered in the previous five chapters can be applied to real-world scenarios including agricultural markets, the housing market and markets for sports and leisure.

Chapter 7 introduces the concepts of production, productivity and efficiency, underpinned by some economic ideas, including specialisation and division of labour, that were introduced by Adam Smith over 200 years ago in his famous book *The Wealth of Nations*. The chapter also introduces business costs and a comparison of the likely efficiency of competitive and monopolistic firms.

In Chapter 8, students are introduced to the idea that the free market system, as outlined in previous chapters, may, in fact, fail to generate the best allocation of economic resources. Such instances of market failure include merit goods, demerit goods, public goods, externalities, market dominance by a limited number of powerful firms, and unequal distribution of income.

Chapter 9 outlines the justification for, and methods used by, governments to try to attempt to correct the instances of market failure outlined in the previous chapter. Methods of intervention include taxation, regulation, pollution permits/carbon trading, subsidy and improving information. The idea that governments may fail to improve resource allocation and thus contribute to 'government failure' is also introduced.

Finally, in Chapter 10, the themes explored in the previous chapters in this unit are brought together in a series of case studies focusing on attempts by governments to correct some of the instances of market failure outlined in Chapter 8. The chapter considers intervention in commodity markets, policing and national defence, health care, tobacco markets and the establishment of a market in emissions trading.

Having completed this unit, you should be well equipped to tackle questions on markets and market failure, testing among other things: your knowledge of key terms and concepts; your ability to apply these terms and concepts; your ability to analyse situations diagrammatically and numerically; and your skill at commenting and evaluating upon attempts by governments to correct instances of market failure.

1 The economic problem

As you begin your studies of this subject you will find that there are a number of ideas that act as foundations to the subject. In this chapter we explore a number of these foundation concepts. In particular, we will begin to consider the role of incentives in making us behave the way we do that help us explain how economic agents react to different information and situations. We will also consider the idea that we have choices but in exercising those choices we incur costs and so it is worth being mindful about these costs when making decisions about how to spend our time, money or other resources.

The nature and purpose of economic activity

When starting to study Economics it is important to get a broad overview of the subject. This chapter will attempt to get you familiar with the main ideas and the main players (agents) that make an economy work. Some of the ideas are crucial and later on you will need to come back to them or at least remember them when dealing with new concepts.

As human beings we all have some basic needs, and as more sophisticated and wealthy individuals we increasingly have a range of wants too that go beyond the purely simplistic survival-based needs. These may vary from something to eat for lunch to a new pair of shoes we want to buy. Our range of needs and wants is pretty extensive, from concert tickets to pet food, from drugs for diabetes to iPods and computer games.

Have you ever stopped to consider what you need and what you want? Isn't it amazing that our economic system seems to provide it even though nobody asked you directly? An economy and the central purpose of economic activity is to produce **goods and services** to provide what we need and want. If we could organise a system that would meet wants and needs more efficiently and effectively then we would see overall **economic welfare** for the citizens increase. The purpose of this subject is largely to see how the system works best to do this. As you study the subject it is worth asking what is the effect of somebody's actions on overall welfare. If the answer is positive and welfare rises then this activity is potentially worth doing. But before you rush forward to do that activity you will need to consider a range of other options available too, to see if we have achieved the most welfare possible.

So what problems or questions does an economic system attempt to solve?

There are three key questions:

1. What should we produce?
2. How should we produce it?
3. For whom should it be produced?

Economics attempts to provide a logical way of answering these three questions.

There are millions of different products and services that are produced. However, are we producing them in the right quantities, using the best methods and getting to the people who value them most?

Figure 1.1 *A large shipping port*

When considering the idea of economic activity we tend to see it as a definite range of activities where we interact with other groups or individuals, for example at work or in the shops. We assume that it involves money changing hands, but this is a bit of a narrow view. Economic activity can include trade between nations or individuals in shops, between providers of goods and services who aim to make profits. But economic activity also includes charity work, DIY, subsistence farming, as well as car boot sales, barter (trading goods and services without using money) or illegal trades such as those in drugs. These are all goods and services provided that satisfy needs and wants and so come under the category of economic activity, as does the 'consumption' of the natural environment for leisure and recreation. So economic activity covers both the legal and illegal, formal economy (measured) and the informal (which is largely unmeasured), for example DIY, etc.

■ The fundamental economic problem

Despite all our wants and needs there simply are not enough resources to meet these needs. There is *scarcity*. And as resources are scarce (finite or limited) then we must decide on the best way to allocate them to get the maximum benefit for society as a whole. Therefore choices need to be made and one of the fundamental areas of economics is to study the range of choices that are made and to question whether they are in fact the best choices. The answer to this may depend on your point of view and makes the subject more intriguing.

The fundamental economic problem, therefore, is that there are infinite wants and yet limited resources. Each choice will carry with it a cost, the alternative that is given up as a result. So in nearly all circumstances the use of resources for one thing means that you cannot use those resources elsewhere. This is called **opportunity cost.**

For example, if you have only £2.50 to spend you could spend it on a magazine but you would have to give up the idea of a sandwich that you would have bought instead. Deciding on your AS Levels presumably involved you making a series of choices – did you consider the opportunity costs?

Economic goods are goods that are scarce and therefore they involve opportunity cost, whereas **free goods** are goods which have no opportunity cost. In reality nearly all goods and services are economic goods, even clean air these days seems to be an economic good because the world's population has grown so fast and pollution has increased so that clean air is now scarce.

Therefore, when we ask whether an activity increases economic welfare of society as a whole we should also ask is there another use of those same resources that would make an even bigger overall contribution to society's well-being. What is the opportunity cost of making that decision? Economics sees these opportunity costs as very real and at AS Level it will be important you recognise them throughout.

■ The economic resources

There are a number of different resources available for production but economists classify them into four main types that they call the factors of production. They are:

■ *Land* This refers to goods like minerals, land itself, and all the resources we take from the world, for example fish, forestry and even the air.

■ *Labour* This includes all the potential workforce, but includes not just the physical people but their skills and abilities and intelligence.

■ *Capital* This is defined as the stock of goods used to make other goods and services, so would include machines, tools, computers, roads, railways, buildings, etc. It is worth noting the distinction here between money as capital and actual machines as capital because often there is confusion. Businesses often need to raise capital – this word is used in a financial sense as money. But it is what the money is used for that is the real capital – the firms buy machinery, stocks of raw materials, etc. (the fixed and working capital) used to make goods and services.

■ *Enterprise* This is more difficult to define but crucial in a modern economy. Enterprise refers to risk takers who are prepared to work to bring the other three factors of production together to make goods and services. Entrepreneurs are the movers and shakers that organise and make production happen. They are catalysts for action and it is the fact that they take risk that distinguishes them from ordinary workers.

💡 Each of these economic resources or *factors of production* attracts payments for their use. It is important you give them the correct terms.

■ The reward or payment for land is *rent*.

■ The reward or payment for labour is *wages*.

■ The reward or payment for capital is *interest*.

■ And lastly the reward or payment for enterprise is *profit*.

So the factors of production give rise to *factor incomes* – the owners of the factors of production can sell or loan them and in return receive these payments. Later on in the book we will use the term **factor market**, which will refer to the markets where these factors of production are bought and sold, for example the labour market. Those of you interested in the City will be aware of the 'stock markets' where ownership of capital is traded.

These headings are slightly abstract and do not mean much in the real world at times. We do need to be aware of the wide range of resources. For example, a landscape, the countryside or a lake are all resources and can be exploited for leisure and pleasure. We often do not think of our wider environment as a resource and that is a big danger, many people want to live in the countryside because they get pleasure from it, others want to live in the city because they enjoy the architecture and community resources available to them. The wind is a resource, as is the sun. Some resources are **renewable** (they can be replenished) such as fish stocks (if we do not over-fish them), as are forests. Others, such as oil and coal, however, are not and once used we cannot replace them – these are non-renewable resources.

In the same way, time is a resource (certainly for us it is non-renewable), as are our skills and abilities. Much of modern business management now is about exploiting these often under-used resources effectively. Anyone studying Business Studies will be looking at practical ways in which organisations can save time in their processes and also how they can harness the skills and ideas of their employees more effectively. Nearly all political parties talk about developing an entrepreneurial

■ **Key terms**

Factor market: the market for the factors of production that make others goods and services such as labour or raw materials.

Renewable resources: resources that are able to be replenished over time, whereas non-renewables such as oil and gas are likely to run out.

Figure 1.2 *City traders*

culture in our country that will encourage us to take risks, use our initiative and organise and mobilise other factors of production.

The economic objectives of individuals, firms and government

In an economy we have a number of different players, some have more than one role. There is government, individual consumers, firms and workers. We assume that each agent tends to act in its own interests – the first of very many assumptions in the subject. Many of these interests are competing.

Consumers

These are people like you and me who have a limited amount of income and therefore need to make choices. Their objective is to maximise their own well-being or economic welfare. We ask is it worth it? Is it worth giving up our hard-earned money to buy a product? Will I get sufficient satisfaction from the purchase to make it worthwhile?

When you go into a newsagent and feel like buying a chocolate bar your sophisticated brain when faced with the huge range of choice starts to make a number of decisions – would I prefer the Mars Bar or the Snickers? The Mars beats the Snickers but the Crunchie beats the Mars, the KitKat is as good as the Crunchie but is 2p more. The Yorkie is preferred to both the Crunchie and the KitKat and so on. A possibly unconscious set of thoughts but nonetheless a set of thoughts honed to help you select the choice that ultimately gives you the most satisfaction, or 'utility' as they call it in economics.

Most of economic theory is based on the idea of rational (sensible) consumers who make decisions based on attempting to maximise their own welfare. This does not mean that we cannot give to charity or do things for other people. It may mean, though, that we get satisfaction from doing it, which makes it worthwhile for us.

Workers

We assume workers want to maximise their gains from working. They typically want higher wages and better working conditions, and job security. Our general starting point is to start with looking at the monetary reward – wages. But it is important to note that workers often want other things too and will accept lower pay if other benefits emerge, such as a company car or health care, etc.

Firms

Similarly, we expect a firm's objective is to maximise **profits**. This is especially true in modern Western capitalist economies such as the USA and UK where the businesses are often owned by private individuals who want to maximise their returns on their investment. This view, though, does change when you look at different economic models where owners of industry are simply one of many different stakeholders and the needs of these different stakeholders are considered when making business decisions.

Governments

They are supposed to represent the people and therefore act in their best interests. However, as you may well be aware the interests of some

Key terms

Profit: when total income or revenue for a firm is greater than total costs.

people are not always the same as others and so a balance must be struck. Should we build a new fast rail route to the English Channel? The answer may appear obvious to some but to others it means noise from construction, the government purchasing their homes and those near the line complaining of noise and damage to the environment.

It is also the case that governments often have a political objective and motive to their actions too. Decisions made affect their own chances of being re-elected and this again may be a factor to consider.

So decisions about the allocation of resources will need to take account of the influence of these different agents and recognise that often the answer is not obvious. It is perhaps a good starting point to assume that each group has a welfare maximising objective based on the money or financial reward and then develop your thinking by asking what happens when that objective changes and becomes distorted by other motives that might not be financial, such as holiday entitlement or job satisfaction.

In the case of government involvement we will need to investigate whether we need government to intervene in the market or whether the market will allocate resources in such a way as to maximise economic welfare or well-being. We will be referring to a **free market economy.**

We have also introduced the idea of *assumptions*, for example that consumers want to maximise their own satisfaction or firms want to make maximum profit. We use assumptions because as a behavioural science we need to get some consistency so as to establish a pattern of behaviour. Assumptions are important but throughout your study of Economics you need to get into the habit of questioning the assumptions that lie behind the models and concepts and as the assumptions break down we can see the effect and explain the behaviour of the different agents or groups in an economy.

> ▮ **Key terms**
>
> **Free market economy:** one in which there is very limited government involvement in providing goods and services. Its main role is to ensure that the rules of the market are fair so that, for example, people cannot steal each other's property.

▮ Scarcity, choice and the allocation of resources

Because resources are scarce and choices need to be made we need to briefly examine what actually determines how the resources are allocated. What are they used for? What is going to be produced and for whom?

The answer lies in the last section on what people's incentives are. Remember the agents or players in the economy. Individuals who own the factors of production, for example labour, will sell their labour to the highest bidder who wants to use them – the entrepreneur. The workers will achieve their goal of maximising their own welfare by getting paid the highest possible wage rate. The entrepreneurs will use them to produce things that consumers want and need and are prepared to pay the most for, in this way they achieve their maximum profit objective. The consumers, faced with a range of choices on which they can spend their money, will buy the goods or combination of goods that maximises their satisfaction given their limited income.

What drives the whole system is the incentive to maximise. When the profits fall because consumers change what they want, so the entrepreneur(s) changes their behaviour to produce the new products and services needed and thereby increase profits again. The workers must therefore change what they do too, to meet the new requirements of the entrepreneur, if they do not their wages will fall to reflect the lower levels of profit that are earned.

In this way resources are allocated to meet the new choices that consumers want. The consumer in theory drives change although in reality new inventions and clever marketing enable firms to take a powerful role in influencing consumer wants and their perceived needs. Did we really need or want an iPod until Apple developed the technology?

A key signal in the whole system is price – if prices change it alters the choices made by all the agents and they therefore re-allocate themselves to new activities.

Case study

An illustration: moths and lights

Imagine a system where moths represent resources, they are allocated to a particular use and therefore in a state of equilibrium. The light, when it comes on, represents more profit, rent, interest or wages for the individual agent, in another activity than they are receiving at present in their current use. Currently the light is switched off. Then consumer desires change (a light comes on) and one of the moths recognises an opportunity exists to achieve more welfare than they are currently achieving if they can meet the consumers' new needs. They move immediately towards the light, this new centre of potential gain. Other moths (resources) will immediately follow suit. The more moths that arrive the dimmer the light becomes and the less attractive it becomes to other moths. Eventually when the brightness of the light is so dim no more moths will move and everything will be still – until a new light comes on as consumer wants change again.

In the same way a free market economy, which allows resources to flow between different uses unrestricted, will allocate resources to areas of highest profit or the brightest light. Where a light burns brighter than your current position there will be an incentive to move. When all areas are equally bright the incentive to move will not exist.

In this way you can see that the maximising objectives of the agents, combined with the signals sent out by prices (rewards for the factors of production) will help allocate resources to where consumers want them most.

Adam Smith, the founding father of modern Economics described this as the invisible hand of the market moving resources to their best use. Profit or higher reward acted as a magnet to new resources, pulling them from their current use to new uses that consumers value more highly.

Activity

1. If you were a clever moth what would you do having found an area of profit?

2. Consider what assumptions lie behind these ideas?

The role of prices and profits in a free market economy

So far we have considered the fundamental economic problem and the notion of *scarcity*. You will recall that scarcity means we tend to value things more highly when they are both sought after and rare (scarce). Typically diamonds are scarce and sought after and so they tend to have high prices. Similarly, so are World Cup Final tickets or Wimbledon

Finals day tickets scarce. Their limited supply and the strong demand make them rare and highly valued. We have developed a notion of their value and we use money to measure their value. Perhaps £1,000 for a ticket for a prime seat. The higher the price the more attractive it is for entrepreneurs to supply the good or service. The price therefore creates an incentive for suppliers to offer goods for sale, provided they can cover their costs. But increased prices mean the money consumers have will buy proportionately less and they will therefore have to ration their choices, cutting back on those items they consider to be the poorest value for money.

High prices also indicate potential profits for producers and therefore send a signal to firms to increase output or for new firms to enter the market.

Thus prices and profits have three key functions:

■ incentive function
■ rationing function
■ signalling function.

When you see prices in any market change you will need to consider how this may affect the allocation of resources.

A good example has been the recent rises in oil prices, which has made it more expensive for those of us who own and drive vehicles. In theory, we will then spend more money on petrol and we will be tempted to limit or ration the number of journeys we take, cutting back on demand for petrol. Secondly, higher oil prices are making the development of new, harder to access oilfields such as those in the Arctic Circle in northern Canada and Alaska potentially viable. Firms like BP and Shell will need to be sure that the price will remain high given the huge cost of developing those oilfields. So we see the incentive function at work – high prices create an incentive to increase supply. In addition, other known oil reserves in Canada in the form of bitumen (a 'tar'-like substance), which are known but expensive to exploit, are now viable in the market when before they were not. The high market price has signalled that new firms should enter the market and exploit these resources.

In summary, when prices rise consumers tend to ration (cut back) their demand, when prices rise it sends a signal to producers that there is a shortage or scarcity, and when prices rise it creates an incentive to suppliers to increase supply as more profit is potentially available.

Similarly, when prices fall consumers extend their demand, there is an end to rationing, a signal is sent to producers that there is the opposite to scarcity and too much supply, and finally it creates an incentive for producers who see profits falling to leave the market.

💡 The production possibility boundary (PPB)

If we view an economy as a range of agents and resources that exist in a particular region, for example a country like the UK, it is possible to say that given a particular set of resources there is a maximum amount of goods and services that the economy can produce.

We tend to show it diagrammatically, showing only two possible goods or services being produced, let's say financial services such as banking and computer software. This allows us to see the choices that an economy can make – should it produce more financial services or more computer

Activity

1 Identify prices of a specific good or service that may be rising in the economy.

2 Try to identify the reasons you think prices are rising.

3 How would you expect this to impact on:

a consumers

b firms currently operating in that market

c firms operating outside that market?

software? If it produces more financial services, it must allocate fewer resources to computer software. As you can see from Fig. 1.3, if all resources were used in financial services *OA* on the diagram, then clearly none could be used in developing computer software. And likewise if all resources were used in the computer software market, at point *OB* on the diagram, then there would be no production of financial services. It is possible to use some resources for both industries, for example in the case below we could produce *OC* computer software and *OD* financial services.

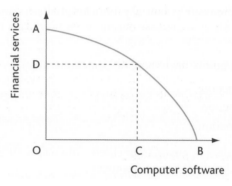

Figure 1.3 *The production possibility boundary*

Key terms

Production possibility boundary: the PPB indicates the maximum possible output that can be achieved given a fixed set of resources and technology in a particular time period.

Productive efficiency: when a firm operates at minimum average total cost, producing the maximum possible output from inputs into the production process.

Allocative efficiency: this is achieved in an economy when it is not possible to make anyone better off without making someone worse off, or you cannot produce more of one good without making less of another.

In each of the above cases we have shown a level of output that is using all the resources to their maximum potential and see these points are on the **production possibility boundary (PPB)**. We would describe any point on the PPB as using resources efficiently, i.e. producing as much as physically and technologically possible given the technology at the time. Note: the points on the PPB do not indicate whether we have chosen the right combinations of resources that maximise economic welfare but do show that the combination chosen is not wasting resources or under-using them – this is **called productive efficiency**. A firm not operating at its lowest possible costs would be wasting resources that could be used elsewhere in the economy to produce more. So any point on the PPB is described as being productively efficient.

Allocative efficiency is also achieved at points on the PPB because it is not possible to make anyone better off without making someone else worse off. In order to produce more financial services it would be necessary to reduce production of computer software. It is not possible to produce beyond (to the right of) the PPB.

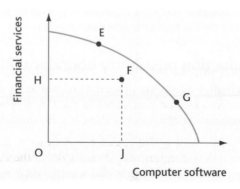

Figure 1.4 *Allocative efficiency*

In Fig. 1.4 at all points that lie on the PPB it is impossible to produce more of one without reducing the production of the other. So any desire to increase output of financial services must mean that resources that were allocated to computer software must change use and output is reduced in that industry.

Any point that lies within the PPB indicates that some resources are not being fully utilised (used). In this case at point *F* there are *OH* financial services produced and *OJ* computer software. However, it is possible to produce more of either good without reducing production of the other. This must mean, therefore, that some resources at point *F* were not being used and therefore we can claim that there was an inefficient use of some resources. Society could be made better off by using those resources more effectively.

The PPB diagram can therefore show the potential range of choices achievable within the economy. We cannot be sure which is the best set of choices at this stage but, if all resources are used to their maximum capability then the best level of output we could achieve would be a point on the PPB.

The PPB and opportunity cost

The PPB can also be used to illustrate the idea of choice and opportunity cost (the next best alternative forgone). If we have an economy operating on its PPB then in order to increase the output of one type of product we must reduce the output of the other. In this case if we want to move from point *X* to point *Y* on the diagram then we can examine what the cost of the decision is.

As can be seen in Fig. 1.5, at point *X* we were producing *OA* financial services and *OB* computer software. By shifting output from *X* to *Y* we would now be producing *OC* financial services and *OD* computer software. This means we have reduced output of financial services by the quantity *AC* but increased computer software output by *BD*. Therefore the opportunity cost of the decision to increase output of computer software is lost output of *AC* financial services.

Summary

■ All points that lie on the PPB must be productively and allocatively efficient.

■ It is not possible to achieve output levels beyond the PPB.

■ Points within the PPB are not using all the resources to full capacity.

■ And therefore it is possible to increase output and welfare without any changes in the level of resources or technology.

■ Shifts between two points on the PPB will always carry an opportunity cost.

Shifting the PPB

As we have already said the PPB represents the maximum possible production capability of an economy at a given moment in time and given a state of technology and know how. It implies all resources are used to their very maximum.

Figure 1.6 shows that the capacity of the economy to produce goods and services has risen. This is represented by the shift in the PPB, so that it can produce more of any combination of goods.

In order to shift the PPB outwards, either new resources need to be found,

AQA Examiner's tip

This is frequently used in objective test questions. What output must be given up of one good if you want to increase the output of another?

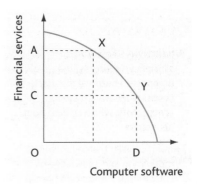

Figure 1.5

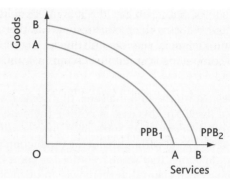

Figure 1.6 *Capacity of the economy to produce goods and services*

technology and understanding need to improve or the quality of the resources needs to improve. Let us examine each of these areas.

- Finding new resources: when we consider the term 'resources' we mean the factors of production, land, labour capital and enterprise. If we were to discover new 'land' it might be in the form of mineral deposits or a new oilfield. Going back in history it might be the discovery of a new continent like Australia or America, bringing new possible production capabilities into play. In terms of labour in an economy it might be through increases in the population through migration or increases in the birth rate. In the UK, for example, net migration into the UK has been estimated to be between 400,000 and 600,000 per year for the last few years; this in effect increases the quantity of labour available in the UK economy and enables us to potentially produce more.

- Improving technology: if we can find new and more efficient ways of producing goods and services then fewer resources will be required to produce each unit of output. This must mean that resources are now freed up to be used in other areas. For example, by developing new production methods in the car industry where robots take the place of people in production those people could be redeployed elsewhere to make other goods and services. By making output quicker we free up the resource 'time' so other things can be made as well.

- In effect new technology helps raise our **productivity** and as such workers can produce more output with the same number of inputs. The investment in *capital goods* will potentially increase an economy's production potential for the future.

Improving the quality of existing resources

One key area here is labour. When we defined labour earlier in the chapter we said that it was not simply the quantity of people available to work but also their skills and abilities. Clearly, if we improve the skills and abilities and to some extent the motivation of those workers then output can increase using the same number of workers and the same amount of time.

How can this be achieved? The answer is through training, education and good management that motivates staff. This in reality takes investment in **human capital.**

In recent years in the UK the government has encouraged the extension of higher education. Gordon Brown has recently announced plans for the extension of compulsory education to 18-year-olds. Why? It is probably something to do with raising the possible potential output of the workforce for the future with a view to extending the PPB for the UK economy.

Key terms

Productivity: a measure of efficiency, measuring the ratio of inputs to outputs; the most common measure is labour productivity, which is the output per worker.

Human capital: the skills, abilities, motivation and knowledge of labour. Improvements in human capital raise productivity and can shift the PPB to the right.

Better organisation and management of existing human resources can lead to efficiency gains. Adam Smith famously wrote about a pin factory he observed and how when production was divided into specific and specialised tasks he observed that output rose quite dramatically. He gave these ideas names: the **division of labour** and **specialisation**. Division of labour refers to dividing up the production process into clearly separate roles and then encouraging workers to specialise in a particular role. The workers, by specialising, develop particular skills in that area and thus increase their productivity. Therefore the PPB could shift outwards, allowing more to be produced. In addition, division of labour tends to make it more effective to provide machinery for specialised workers, such as forklift trucks for warehouse staff, which increases productivity of labour.

If efficiency and productivity increases in the production of one good rather than all goods it will be represented on the PPB as below. In this case investment has occurred in the technology of developing computer games and therefore there is an increase in productive potential of computer games form OB to OC but there has been no change to possible maximum output of financial services OA. The PPB shifts as shown in Fig. 1.7.

Key terms

Division of labour: breaking the production process down into a sequence of tasks, with workers assigned to particular tasks.

Specialisation: the production of a limited range of goods by an individual factor of production or firm or country, in cooperation with others so that together a complete range of goods is produced.

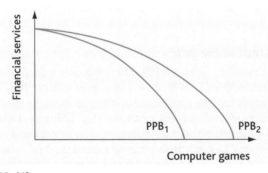

Figure 1.7 *PPB shifts*

Activity

Dunlop Slazenger is just one of a number of companies involved in the making of a tennis ball. All over the world there are ships chugging across oceans towards Dunlop's new factory in the Philippines. They are carrying an amazing variety of ingredients. Clay from South Carolina, sulphur from Korea, silica from mines in Greece, magnesium carbonate from Japan and zinc oxide from Thailand are a few of the substances used to give the ball the right amount of stretch and bounce. The tins are from Indonesia and the distinctive yellow dyes from the UK.

The balls used to be produced in Dunlop's Barnsley factory in the UK. The decision to close the factory here in the UK and move production to the Philippines illustrates how changes in international specialisation and the division of labour affect both businesses and workers. The company will benefit from falling production costs and increased competitiveness (its ability to compete with other firms). Although workers in the new plant earn typically 65p per hour, job insecurity

is still a concern for Philippino workers as much as for UK workers. They fear competition from even cheaper workers in China. UK workers might find it difficult to get new jobs as labour is not as internationally mobile as capital because of language and cultural issues.

The closure of manufacturing plants in the UK is just one of many factors contributing to social problems and the growth of income inequality in the UK.

Source: adapted from Fran Abrams, 'New Balls Please', *Guardian*, 24 June 2002

1 Explain the meaning of the terms 'division of labour' and 'specialisation'.

2 Explain how the division of labour might reduce costs and increase competitiveness.

3 Analyse the factors that would have encouraged Dunlop to relocate production to the Philippines. You may wish to consider the assumptions you are making about the objective of the firm.

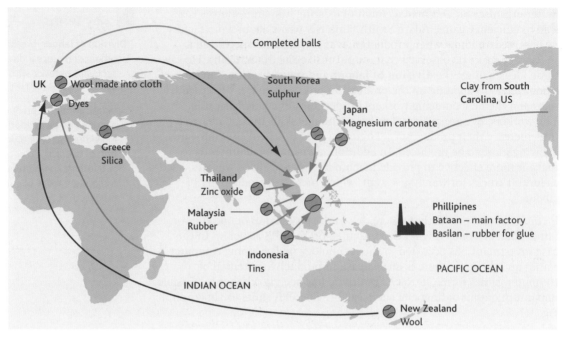

Figure 1.8 *The journey of a tennis ball*

Activity

China has seen rapid economic growth in the past decade with average annual changes in output of around 10 per cent. Investment in new production capacity has been one of the main reasons for such increases in growth and has allowed up to 400 million people to be freed from poverty. Estimates suggest that investment makes up nearly 40 per cent of all spending in the economy. China is continuing to invest in both physical capital but also in human capital and growth rates look set to continue for some time. However, the impact of such growth is plain to see on the streets of China's rapidly growing cities as pollution and inequality grow.

1. Explain what is meant by the term opportunity cost.

2. Explain the effect of high levels of investment on the production possibility boundary.

3. Consider whether China should continue to spend such a high proportion of their GDP on investment or switch production towards more consumer goods?

Can the PPB shift to the left?

Similarly, it is possible to see a PPB shift inwards – total possible production can decline. This is shown by a shift from $PPB2$ to $PPB1$ in Fig. 1.6. This is far less common but a recent example might be Zimbabwe where there has been a dramatic fall in living standards as the economy's infrastructure has collapsed. The emigration away from Zimbabwe of many farmers with years of experience and know-how following government reclamation of farms as part of the land reform programme has left the agricultural industry without either capital or knowledge. Existing machinery has not been maintained, investment in agriculture and other sectors of the economy has declined rapidly and as machinery has aged it has not been replaced, leaving the PPB shifting to the left. The problems have been exacerbated by HIV and malnutrition that have reduced average life expectancy to below 40 years old. In addition to the emigration of the farmers, hunger and poverty has driven an estimated 3 million Zimbabweans over the border to neighbouring countries such as South Africa.

The factors that shift the whole PPB curve to the right are:

- investment in new technology
- introduction of new resources such as minerals
- increased supply of labour through increases in population and migration
- improvements in human capital through education and training
- better management of resources via division of labour and specialisation
- changed attitudes encouraging entrepreneurialism.

Activity

Assume an economy makes only two types of goods, consumer goods and capital goods, and is producing at a point *D* on its PPB as shown below.

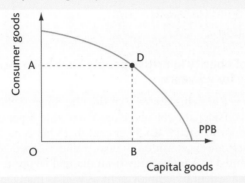

Figure 1.9 *PPB of an economy making consumer goods and capital goods*

Explain, using a diagram in each case, the likely effect of the following on the PPB:

1 An improvement in the available technology for producing consumer goods only.

2 A hurricane that destroys approximately 5 per cent of all factories and production facilities.

3 A decision by individuals to allocate more resources towards producing consumer goods at the expense of producing capital goods.

Value judgements, normative and positive statements

The government should spend more on education.

Businesses ought to take much more account of the environment than they do.

We should ban smoking completely.

Britain should adopt the Euro.

These are all statements that one could argue have real validity and there is a strong case for each one. There are considerable benefits to society to be derived from more education or a reduction in smoking. However, these statements are based on an opinion or viewpoint and called **value judgements**, judgements about the role of government or what the purpose of businesses should be. They might not be shared by everyone. Whilst it may be possible to calculate exactly the implications of carrying out these policies, although it would be difficult, all these ideas are opinions and as such we describe them as **normative statements**. They cannot be proven or tested.

In contrast, **positive statements** are statements that can be tested. For example, if the government increases taxes then total demand for consumer goods will fall. Whilst this might not be the case every single time it is possible to claim it to be broadly the case. Positive statements are more objective and scientific and as such tend to be given a lot of weight in arguments.

It is worth taking time to consider how many of your statements carry value judgements and how many can be supported by scientific

Key terms

Value judgements: statements or opinions expressed that are not testable or cannot be verified and depend very much on the views of the individual and the values they hold.

Normative statements: opinions that require value judgements to be made.

Positive statements: statements that can be tested against real-world data.

reasoning. Many students like to make value judgements that in themselves are fine and interesting but be aware that they may lack the authority that more scientifically tested or testable statements have when building arguments.

Case study

Cases of obesity in British people have been increasing steadily for 25 years

Obesity is a growing problem in the UK. Since 1980 the proportion of men considered to be obese has risen from 6 per cent to 22 per cent and for women from 8 per cent to 23 per cent. This explosion in obesity rates is common to nearly all developed countries and can be attributed to a move away from manual labour to more office-based and sedentary employment as well as many labour-saving devices in the home that reduce the level of physical effort required. Amongst younger age groups, too, many teenagers are watching too much television and playing computer games for too long, say campaigners. It is also the case that with increasing wealth comes the opportunity to consume more; however, data examining calories consumption suggests that additional calories consumed is not the main cause, it is the lack of calorie expenditure that is the principal cause of the problem.

Government has a role to play and some pressure groups are arguing for stricter government intervention in food labelling and advertising, especially that which is aimed at children. Information is important in consumer decision making and clear labelling will help parents make more informed choices as to which products to buy. However, the government should be developing many more social facilities that encourage children to play outside and burn more calories. Local Education Authorities ought to re-establish more playing fields for school children and ensure more sport and activity in the curriculum.

It is hoped the Olympic Games in London in 2012 will provide a catalyst for change and reverse the trend where too many people do too little exercise.

AQA Examiner's tip

Quite often normative and positive statements are tested in the objective test part of the exam. Look out for words such as 'should' and 'ought to', these often indicate (although not always) potential value judgements or normative statements.

Activity

Read the case study and identify the positive and normative statements.

After completing this chapter you should:

- understand the world's resources are scarce and our wants and needs cannot all be met
- understand that scarcity means choices need to made and each choice carries an opportunity cost
- understand that the economic system attempts to allocate resources
- appreciate that a market-based system will tend to do this through using prices and profits as a way to attract resources to be allocated to their best use
- remember that land, labour, capital and enterprise are the four economic resources
- understand that agents in the economic system try to maximise their own welfare

- appreciate that the amount of possible output an economy can produce is limited by the amount and quality of its resources and this can be shown by the production possibility boundary

- understand the basic concept of productive efficiency for an economy is the degree to which output is maximised using the potential economic resources available – as shown by a point on the PPB

- know that it is possible to shift the PPB outwards (to the right) via improvements in the quality and quantity of resources or increases in technology

- recognise how to identify the difference between normative and positive statements.

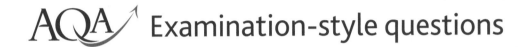

AQA Examination-style questions

1 One reason why specialization raises labour productivity is because
  (a) specialization shifts the production possibility boundary to the left.
  (b) labour replaces capital to produce goods and services.
  (c) specialization allows an economy to produce on its production possibility boundary.
  (d) the division of labour makes it cost-effective to provide workers with specialist equipment.
  (AQA, 2006)

2 Choice is an important element in the basic economic problem because
  (a) wants increase with income.
  (b) resources are distributed equally.
  (c) limited resources have alternative uses.
  (d) high demand leads to high prices.
  (AQA, 2006)

3 Five years ago Emma bought a guitar for £150 but has never learnt how to play it. The price of a new guitar is now £300. Emma could sell hers for £120. What is the present opportunity cost of keeping the guitar?
  (a) 0
  (b) £120
  (c) £150
  (d) £180
  (AQA, 2006)

4 Which of the following statements is a value judgement?
  (a) In 2012 it is likely that London will see a big rise in the number of tourists.
  (b) A fall in the price of the iPhone should lead to an increase in demand in normal circumstances.
  (c) Spending on education could cause an increase in productivity.
  (d) Economic decisions should not be made by politicians

2 Demand in a market

Key terms

Demand: the amount that consumers are willing and able to buy at each given price level.

Effective demand: demand supported by the ability to pay for a good or service.

Market demand: total demand in a market for a good, the sum of all individuals' demand, at each given price.

The focus of this chapter is the concept of demand – what constitutes real demand rather than simply our dreams or desires and wishful thinking. It will investigate another foundation concept that will help us to understand how we are affected by prices and what other influences there are on how much of a good or service we want to buy at different price levels.

💡 The individual demand curve for a good and market demand

Often we desire certain things such as luxury cars or jewellery but do not have the ability to afford them and so they are not part of what economists consider **demand**. **Effective demand,** as it is called, is backed up by real purchasing power.

The demand curve shows the relationship between the price and the amount consumers intend to buy at each given price. Note that *intended* or *planned demand* may actually differ from how much is actually bought at that price – *realised* or *actual demand*. It is the case for most goods that as prices rise then the level of demand will tend to fall. Therefore it is likely that when shown in Fig. 2.1 there will be an inverse or negative relationship between these two variables, so that as price rises from P_1 to P_2 the quantity demanded falls from Q_1 to Q_2 and vice versa.

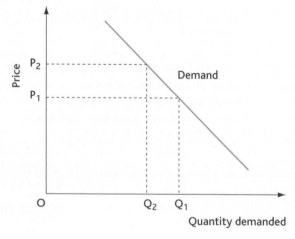

Figure 2.1 *A demand curve*

Individual and market demand curves

Each consumer will buy as much of a product they deem as worth it at each given price level. This is an individual choice based on each person's preferences and income. Therefore we can plot a demand curve for each individual based on the satisfaction or utility they get from each unit of a product.

To identify the **market demand curve** for a product or service we must calculate the sum of demand from all individuals together. One

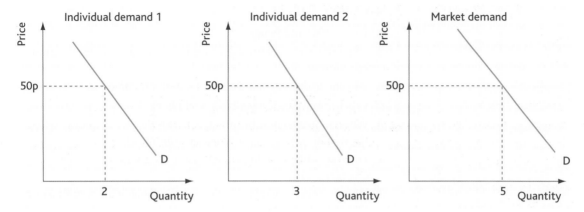

Figure 2.2 *Demand curves for Coke*

person may wish to buy three cans of Coke per week at a given price of 50p, another may wish to buy only two cans at the same price. The two individual demand curves can be added together to get the overall demand for Coke or the market demand curve of five cans of Coke as shown above.

AQA Examiner's tip

Be careful to pay attention to whether the demand is intended or actual /realised, the demand and supply curves show market plans, not necessarily what actually happens.

The shape of demand curves

The demand curve as we have illustrated typically is downward sloping from left to right so that as price falls more is demanded. There is a negative relationship between price and quantity (as one variable goes down the other goes up). The explanation behind this goes back to our underlying assumptions about consumers. We assume they want to maximise the benefits they can receive with their limited income, their own economic welfare. If price is high then consumers need to give up much of their limited finances to pay for the good. Therefore they consider how much satisfaction or utility they might receive in return. They will only buy something if it is worth it, so that the benefits received from purchasing it outweigh the opportunity costs of using the money for something else. It would be irrational to buy something that you did not consider was worth the price being charged. The laws of economics state that as we buy more and more of something then the benefit we receive from each extra unit will begin to diminish or fall. Thus, as we buy more of a good with each extra unit it gives us less satisfaction and so becomes less valuable. Therefore we will only buy more if the price falls. For example, if you were to buy chocolate your first chocolate bar may seem delicious and certainly be worth buying, your second might still be nice but not be worth as much as the first, your third may give less satisfaction still and ultimately you might not be prepared to pay as much for it. Eventually if you keep eating chocolate you might find you get no satisfaction or utility at all and in such circumstances, if you were rational you would not buy it at all. This is true with all products although the point at which the value falls will vary from person to person and product to product.

Skills

Drawing diagrams is an essential requirement at AS (and A2 Level) and it is critical that you use this skill – many marks are awarded for it. However, common errors occur that cost marks.

Some tips:

- ■ Use a ruler and pencil
- ■ Label the axes, quantity goes on the x axis as standard form in economics
- ■ We tend to draw demand curves (and supply curves) as straight lines
- ■ Label the curves (typically D_1 and D_2, etc.)
- ■ When plotting equilibriums label both the axes carefully where the equilibrium cuts the axis, for example Q_1 or P_1
- ■ Draw the diagrams big enough so it is easy to see any labels changes clearly
- ■ Do not forget to explain what you are showing in your diagram – there are more marks for this!

Activity

Figure 2.3 *An iPod*

A student who likes music is keen to download a number of favourite songs from the internet in preparation for a party she is having. She must pay for each individual song. At a price of £1 each she wants to buy a total of 20 songs. However, if the price was at only 80p each she would buy 25 songs. If the price was 60p her demand would be 30 songs.

1 Construct a demand curve to show how much she would purchase at each price level.

2 If she bought 40 songs on the basis of the demand curve what price level would you expect her to pay for each song?

3 If there is a rise in the price of drinks she plans to provide for her friends at the party her remaining income is limited. She will now buy 20 per cent less at each given price level. Plot a new demand curve to show this.

💡 Movements along the demand curve

When price rises this always causes movement *along* the demand curve, which is called a **contraction in demand**. Likewise a fall in prices will cause an **extension in demand** as the quantity increases. It is important to note that a change in the price of a good does not shift the demand curve but causes movement along the demand curve. When firms decide to reduce prices to stimulate demand, as they do at times, they bring about extensions in demand. In Fig. 2.4, a rise in the price from P_1 to P_2 causes a contraction in demand, whilst a fall in price from P_1 to P_3 brings an extension in demand.

■ Factors shifting the demand curve (the conditions of demand)

So far we have identified that changes in price cause movements along the demand curve. Now we need to consider what causes shifts in the whole demand curve. Consider what would make someone want to buy more of a good or service at the same price. Take an example of holiday villas in Spain for a week's rental. What would make the demand for this service rise even though prices of the actual rental did not change? There are plenty of possible answers but here are a few.

■ Key terms

Contractions in demand: falls in the quantity demanded caused by rises in prices.

Extensions in demand: increases in demand caused by changes (falls) in price.

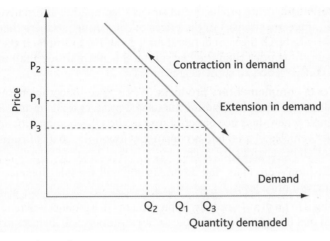

Figure 2.4 *A demand curve*

First, incomes – if average incomes rise then it is likely that demand for more holidays will rise, the extent to which demand changes will depend on income elasticity of demand which we will examine later, but in the first instance for most people more income is likely to mean more holidays. Secondly, there is the cost of flights, which in this case are complementary goods to renting an overseas holiday home. If flights become cheaper due to more competition then more people will consider holidays in Spain. Thirdly, if UK holidays or other European holidays become more expensive then individuals will consider substituting to the relatively cheaper Spanish villas, again demand at the same price would rise. Fig. 2.5 shows how demand would shift from D_1 to D_2.

In the above example three factors are used as examples but there are many more. The most common factors that shift the demand curve are:

■ Changes in income – rises in income typically will mean more demand at the same price level, although this is only for **normal goods**. There are circumstances when rises in income actually cause falls in demand; this is when consumers prefer to 'trade up' and buy better products as their incomes rise – an example might be cheap white bread. These goods are called **inferior goods.**

■ Advertising and publicity – successful advertising and promotional activity will usually mean rising demand at each given price level. This is because as consumers become more aware of the benefits of a product, or simply feel more confident about a product they tend to buy more of it assuming all other things remain the same.

■ **Key terms**

Normal goods: goods or services that will see an increase in demand when incomes rise.

Inferior goods: goods or services that will see demand fall when income rises.

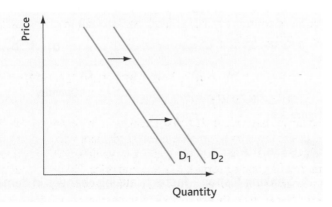

Figure 2.5 *Shifts in demand*

■ Prices of substitute products and services (competing alternatives) – when there are changes in the prices of competing products then there is likely to be changes in demand for a good. For example, if the Xbox 360 drops its price then the Playstation 3 is likely to see a fall in sales as a consequence, to some degree at least.

■ Prices of **complementary products.** When prices of complementary goods go up, then demand for the related product tends to fall. So for example when the price of petrol rose in the USA demand for sports utility vehicles (4×4s) fell as consumers found the costs of running cars with big engines too high.

■ 💡 Fashion – products that are in fashion will see sales increase at each given price level.

■ Changes in quality – similarly, improvements to a product will tend to mean that if the price remains the same consumers will increase demand.

■ Weather conditions – some products are seasonal and demand is closely linked to the weather. Cider is typically a summer drink, skiwear is demanded in the winter. So demand may be influenced by weather patterns.

■ The law – changes in demand can result from legal changes. In October 2007 initial results from the ban on smoking in public places showed an 11 per cent drop in demand for cigarettes. Likewise if governments make the use of an item compulsory, for example cycle helmets, sales will rise.

■ Uncertainty over future prices – if consumers expect future prices of goods to rise sharply they might demand them now and increase demand at the current price – this is often the case in commodity markets such as oil and gas.

In each case if any or more than one of these factors change then it is likely that the demand curve will shift. We tend to draw the shift in the curve as parallel but this need not be the case in reality. If demand falls at each given price then the demand curve shifts to the left at D_2 (see a lower quantity Q_2 at that same price P_1).

Key terms

Complementary products: goods that are consumed together, for example bread and butter, or DVDs and DVD players.

AQA Examiner's tip

When explaining the cause of shifts in demand try to use the technical language such as 'prices of complements or substitutes changed' rather than simply saying that flights have become cheaper or other holidays are more expensive. Identify the factor and then add the detail. Whenever possible draw diagrams to illustrate.

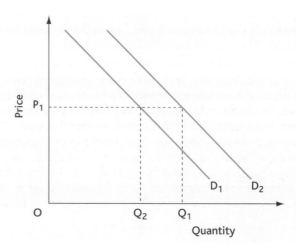

Figure 2.6

Case study

Stinking Bishop – factors causing changes in demand

The movie *Wallace and Gromit* has caused a surge in demand for the hitherto little-known cheese Stinking Bishop. The movie featured the cheese and since then the Gloucestershire businessman who makes it has been almost overrun by demand for his cheese. Most businesses would be thankful for such positive publicity but it would seem that the businessman concerned does not want to expand his business and was very happy with life before his Stinking Bishop cheese became famous.

Figure 2.7 *Wallace and Gromit*

Composite demand

Composite demand applies to products that are used for more than one purpose. An increase in demand for one use will reduce the availability of the good for the alternative use. Consider land, it can be used for residential housing or commercial property. If it is used for housing then there will be a reduction in the supply of land for commercial purposes and therefore the price of commercial land will rise as it becomes more scarce. Likewise milk is used for cheese, yoghurt and butter. Increases in demand for cheese and yoghurt might cause rises in the price of butter as the available supply of milk is used in the other products.

■ Case study

Italians protest as pasta prices rise

Pasta prices in Italy are expected to rise by up to 20 per cent and angry Italians have taken to the streets in protest as a result. They are concerned about the rapid rise in prices of their much loved spaghetti and fettuccine as manufacturers push up prices. The cause is that durum wheat, the main ingredient in pasta, is becoming increasingly expensive. Manufacturers blame the price rises on the fact that durum wheat is also being used as bio-fuel and despite increased output in Canada of durum wheat the growing demand for bio-fuel means there has been a growing shortage in Italy.

Source: adapted from © bbc.co.uk/news

The changes in demand we have been considering have mainly been in goods markets. However, it is worth considering factor markets too. Factor markets are the markets for factors of production such as labour but to some extent include commodities such as oil, gas, steel, rubber and cocoa. These are ingredients in the production process. The same principles apply here too. Demand in factor markets is often

■ Key terms

Composite demand: a good that is demanded for more than one purpose so that an increase in demand for one purpose reduces the available supply for the other purpose, typically leading to higher prices, e.g. milk used in butter and cheese.

■ Activity

Oil is an essential commodity in world economy. It is used for a huge variety of things from producing power and energy to use in plastics, paints and also in transport. In recent years the demand for oil has been rising strongly on the back of industrialisation in countries like China and India and growth in economies such as the UK and USA where average incomes have been rising. At the same time rising concern about the environment and regulations by government to reduce the emissions of greenhouse gases like carbon dioxide have led to the development of policies that aim for carbon-neutral homes. This has led to rising demand for clean energy sources to power our homes and offices such as solar energy.

Identify the factors that have contributed to the changes in demand for (a) oil, and (b) solar panels.

Derived demand: when the demand for one good or service comes from the demand for another good or service. The demand for cars stimulates the demand for steel, therefore the demand for steel is derived demand.

derived demand. Its demand comes from the demand for the good or service that the factor of production makes. So increases in demand for health care lead to increasing demand for doctors. Growth in global output leads to growth in the demand for energy and therefore the raw materials that make energy, gas and oil mainly.

■ **Activity**

Stretch and challenge

It is argued that the demand curve indicates the benefit that consumers expect to receive from a product. To what extent does the demand curve accurately reflect such benefits received from a purchase?

☑ *After completing this chapter you should:*

- understand what is meant by effective demand

- be able to explain why the demand curve has a negative slope (slopes downward from left to right)

- be able to identify the factors that shift the demand curve

- understand the terms extension in demand, contraction in demand, composite demand and derived demand

- be able to distinguish between shifts and extensions/contractions in demand

- draw correctly labelled demand curves

- understand the distinction between individual and market demand curves.

 Examination-style questions

1 **Extract A**

Coke on the Rocks

In recent years, soft drinks giant Coca Cola has been under pressure. There have been some significant changes in the market for soft drinks and Coke is having to respond. Firstly there have been growing concerns on both sides of the Atlantic about the rising levels of obesity and increasingly parents and young people are turning to healthier options. In addition there have been changes to the law in California by Governor Arnold Schwarzenegger who has banned the sale of carbonated drinks in schools across the state. There are growing calls for more bans across America and also in the UK. This is of real concern to Coke whose main target audience is young people. To make matters worse, there have been a number of new innovations such as fruit juices and smoothies in the market from firms like PJ Smoothie and Innocent Drinks. The picture is not entirely bleak though; sales are rising in newly developing countries where incomes are rising fast.

Coke is having to fight back with a range of new products and move away from its reliance on Coke, which represents about 80% of its sales in the US. They have launched Minute Maid in an attempt to catch up with rival Pepsi who own the very successful Tropicana brand. Will this belated move into new markets be enough to compensate for changes in the cola market?

Extract B

Intensified Competition from Other Beverages Results in Unprecedented Volume Decline

For the first time in decades, US carbonated soft drink volume declined in 2005. Although the category had been growing slowly in recent years, it had grown volumetrically in every year since at least 1960 – the earliest year for which Beverage Market Corporation has data on the market. While carbonated soft drinks remain the largest beverage category in the country, and the leading brands rank as the most popular refreshment beverages, consumers are increasingly including other types of beverages in the refreshment routines. Generally, these are products, such as bottled water, which are perceived to be healthier than carbonated soft drinks.

Total carbonated soft drink volume declined from 1.24 billion cases (1.54 billion gallons) in 2004 to 1.18 billion cases (1.53 billion gallons) in 2005. The 0.6% decline followed growth of 0.7% in 2004 and 0.4% in 2003. The US soft drink market has not seen annual volume growth greater than 1% since the late 1990s.

Source: Beverage Marketing Corporation. US market report April 2006

(a)	What factors have influenced demand for Coke?	(*6 marks*)
(b)	Draw a diagram to show the effect on demand for Coke	(*3 marks*)
(c)	How would a decision to drop the prices of Coke affect the demand curve for it?	(*3 marks*)
(d)	Analyse two different strategies Coke might adopt to boost sales volumes of its cola.	(*8 marks*)

3 Supply in a market

Key terms

Supply: the amount offered for sale at each given price level.

Planned supply: the amount producers plan to produce at each given price.

Actual supply: the amount that producers in fact produce. This may differ from planned supply for a variety of reasons such as breakdowns in production, staff absences, etc.

This chapter develops the analysis of supply of goods and services and explains how firms behave with regard to decisions on how much firms will plan to produce. As with the previous chapter it will explain how supply curves are derived and explain their shape.

A firm's decision to supply a good and market supply

Supply is the amount of goods or services producers plan to offer for sale at each given price level. This is a critical topic in economics and once you have mastered its basics it will help you enormously to understand the behaviour of firms and individuals. Note **planned supply** may be different from **actual (realised) supply** because if consumers do not want to buy as much as producers are prepared to sell they will limit their output.

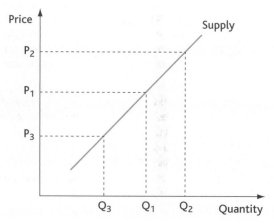

Figure 3.1 *Supply curve*

The supply curve will therefore show the relationship between the amount offered for sale and the price. We assume in economics that firms have one main objective that is to *maximise profits*. When they are working out how much to produce they will consider their costs of production and the price they think they will receive for each unit they sell. As prices rise producers will recognise that potentially there is more profit to be made and will want to increase their supply to take advantage of this. However, one of the laws of economics suggest that as firms produce more the cost of producing an additional unit of that good will eventually begin to rise; therefore in order to make it worth their while supplying more there needs to be a higher price potentially on offer. So when prices rise it does attract additional supply into the market. The increase in price on offer convinces existing firms to extend production and may attract new, less efficient firms into the market.

You could also use the concept of opportunity cost – the opportunity cost of remaining out of the market is higher if more profit is possible due to an increase in price. This will increase the incentive to enter that market and supply more. As the price rises the incentives and signals that higher price sends to other resources (remember the signalling and incentive functions of price) attracts additional resources.

Put another way still – if the most efficient producers enter the market first they are prepared to offer supply at a lower price, less efficient producers will only be attracted to the market if the price is higher and they can now make a profit and so supply will only increase if prices rise.

Supply can be both in goods and service markets and also in factor markets (e.g. markets for the factors of production such as labour) – in essence the principles are the same.

Imagine members of your class have been asked to babysit. How many of you would offer babysitting services at £1 an hour? I suspect probably not many will. As the price level offered increases (in this case the wage rate) more of you will be prepared to supply your labour at £3 per hour, there may be more hours of babysitting supplied, at £4 an hour still more and so on. As the price rises the amount of hours of babysitting services offered for sale will rise. The same is true of other goods and services – the higher the price the stronger the incentive to move resources from an alternative use into that particular market. The supply curve will show this relationship. Whether your teacher can afford them is another matter – that is demand!

At price level P_1, Q_1 is offered for sale as the price is low and few firms are attracted to the market. As price rises from P_1 to P_2 more is supplied, increasing the quantity supplied from Q_1 to Q_2 and so on referring to Fig. 3.1.

■ Case study

Plumbers required!

An interesting recent example has been in the supply of plumbers in London. The relative shortage of plumbers had seen the price of plumbing services rise. Some plumbers were reputedly earning up to £90,000 per year. As this happened the number of people willing to give up their current employment to become a plumber increased. They were responding to the higher price on offer and therefore willing to become plumbers (supply plumbing).

The difference between individual supply and market supply

Each individual firm will have a trade-off to consider. How much are they prepared to offer for sale at each price level – think of the babysitter – as the price rises they may be prepared to work longer. However, as their leisure time becomes more scarce they value it more highly and so will need an even higher price to attract them to work longer. This is true of all individuals providing babysitting services – each one forms an individual supply curve but added together we have the market supply of babysitters.

The individual supply plans of firms at each price level can be added together to form the **market supply** curve. So if a firm selling cakes is prepared to supply 20 cakes at £3 each and a second firm is prepared to supply 30 cakes at the same price then market supply is a total of 50 cakes at £3.

■ Key terms

Market supply: the sum of all individual firm's supply curves at each given price.

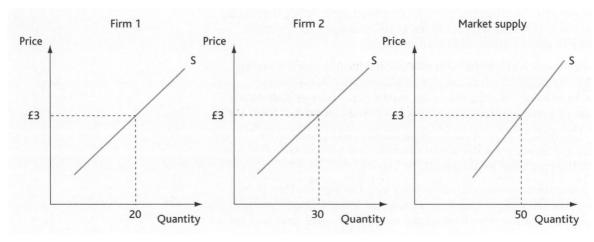

Figure 3.2 *Firm 1 and 2 and market curve*

■ The slope (shape) of the curve

As you will no doubt notice most diagrams in Economics talk about curves but in fact draw straight lines. This is purely to make life simple but in real life the 'curve' may not be a curve at all, or a straight line either but a plotted graph that demonstrates a relationship, which may not be consistent, between two variables.

Typically, though, economists will draw a supply curve as upward sloping in the main – showing a **positive** relationship between price and quantity supplied – the higher the price the more is offered for sale at each given price level and vice versa. As seen in Fig 3.1, if the price level is P_1 then Q_1 will be the planned level of supply; at P_2 supply will rise to Q_2, etc.

The explanation behind this positive relationship is that in order to attract new suppliers into a market there needs to be sufficient incentive. Producers who are in the market will need to purchase additional resources; these resources may be less suitable or less productive, meaning increased costs of production per unit. Therefore the supplier will need a higher price in order to make a profit.

💡 A movement along the supply curve

Remember, this relationship seen in the supply curve is based on the assumption that only price is changing and all other things (variables) remain the same. Therefore any movement *along* the supply curve is caused only by an increase in the price level. This is called an **extension in supply** when the quantity supplied increases as price increases. It is a **contraction in supply** when the reverse happens; as price falls the quantity supplied falls.

■ Links

We will see how much supply increases when price rises when we tackle the concept of price elasticity of supply on p60 in Chapter 5.

■ Key terms

Extension in supply: when there is an increase in supply because the market price has risen.

Contraction in supply: when the amount offered for sale is reduced because the price level has fallen.

■ Activity

1 Using the information below plot a supply schedule (curve)

Price £	20	18	16	14	12	10	8	6
Quantity	40	35	30	25	20	15	10	5

2 If the price was expected to rise to £26 estimate the likely level of supply.

3 Briefly explain the cause of changes in supply you have plotted.

💡 Factors causing shifts in supply (the conditions of supply)

We have just established that changes in the price of a good cause movement along the supply curve, so what shifts the whole supply curve? Well the answer is things other than price. The supply curve is very closely related to the costs of production and it is useful at AS Level to consider that anything that either reduces or increases costs might impact on the quantity supplied *at each given price level*.

It is critical that this last phrase, 'at each given price', becomes part of your thinking. Remember the definition of supply: the amount offered for sale at each price level. Now ask yourself would there be more or less incentive for a business to be in the market if costs rose but the price in the market was the same. In this instance firms would make less profit and the least efficient firms would possibly leave the market, recognising that profits in that market are minimal or even negative.

We can see the effect below – there would be lower supply at the same price. This is shown by a point to the left of the original supply curve at each given price level. If this relationship is then true at all price levels we have a new supply curve to the left – *a shift in supply*, in this case caused by rising costs of production as a result of, perhaps, increased wage rates for staff.

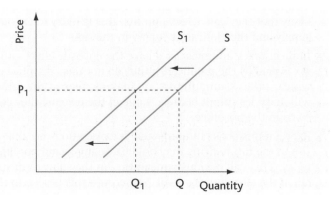

Figure 3.3 *Shifts in supply (a reduction in supply)*

■ Case study

Supply fears in US petrol market

Retail prices of petrol, or 'gas' as the Americans call it, were driven up by the closure of a number of petrol refineries in the southern United States. Up to a third of refining capacity was closed as the latest storm threatened to lash America's southern states. This has left petrol retailers concerned that they are going to run out of supplies in the coming days.

The factors that shift the supply curve are:

■ Changes to raw materials prices: If raw material prices rise then the costs of production rise, thus meaning that firms that continue to supply at the same price will make less profit. This reduces the incentive to supply and consequently shift the supply curve to the left.

- 💡 Technology improvements: If we see improvements in production technologies it is likely that firms will be able to produce more efficiently and therefore at a lower cost. If firms continue to sell at the same price profit margins are bigger and there is a stronger incentive to increase output at that price, shifting supply to the right.

- Increases in labour productivity (more output per worker/time period): If, on average, workers' output rises, all other things remaining the same, then unit costs of production fall and so, as above, profits can potentially rise, increasing the likely level of supply.

- Regulation and bureaucracy: Governments often impose regulations on firms, which generally add to costs, for example additional environmental controls mean that firms must take more care when dealing with waste and pollutants. The extra costs incurred are often additional investment and infrastructure to meet the new laws and also the extra administration costs of checking that the firms have actually met and continue to meet the new standards. These are called compliance costs.

- Wage rates: If wage rise, *ceteris paribus* (all other things remaining the same) then production costs will rise, again driving down profit margins and thus possibly forcing those firms that are least efficient out of the market causing the supply curve to shift to the left.

- Subsidies offered by government to producers: Subsidies are payments made by government usually to promote and encourage production. They in effect reduce the costs borne by the firm and make it more likely that they can achieve profits; this is likely to encourage greater supply and therefore shift supply to the right.

- Indirect taxes: Indirect taxes have the opposite effect – the indirect tax is paid by the producer; if they do not raise the price of the good, which is the assumption we are making, then at the same price they will make less profit because some of the revenue they collect will be owed to the tax office.

- Expectations about future prices: If expectations are that prices will rise in the future firms may hold back supply and not offer it for sale today. This will obviously mean that in the short term supply will fall at the current price level. Sometimes this is seen in the housing market when home-owners are reluctant to sell in a rising market. The opposite is also true: if we expect prices to fall next month or next year we might try to sell now, this is especially true in the stock markets and currency markets.

- Objectives of firms: We have assumed that firms aim to maximise profit in the short run, this is not always the case. Some firms might have other objectives such as increasing market share or simply selling more output. In these cases it is likely that they may attempt to increase supply at the current market price.

- The number of sellers in the market will increase the available supply (assuming all other things remain the same) so if new firms enter the market then supply will increase, shifting the supply curve to the right.

These are a few of a number of different factors. Other examples of how supply might be affected include a bumper harvest, which would increase the supply of agricultural products, new discoveries of oil or precious metals will increase the supply of a commodity like gold or platinum.

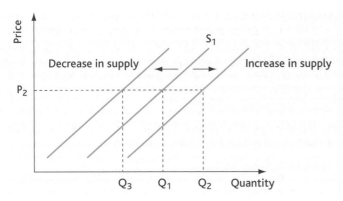

Figure 3.4 *Shift in supply*

When drawing or plotting diagrams it is important to look at the bottom (*x*-axis) of your graph when plotting the new supply curve. Ask yourself would they want to supply more or less in this market at the same price. If costs have risen but all else remained the same then firms will have less incentive to be in the market = less supply and a shift to the left of the supply curve. If on the other hand costs have fallen then the incentive rises and more firms will want to join the market = increased supply and a shift to the right of the curve supply.

■ Case study

Queues at Waterstone's as last Harry Potter novel hits the stores

It is unusual to see people queuing outside bookstores these days but Harry Potter fans have been doing just that as they await the release of the final book *Harry Potter and the Deathly Hallows*. The publishers have decided to restrict the first print run of the book and the limited supply available has seen fans prepared to stand outside shops for several hours in order to secure a copy. In fact it is an increasing phenomenon amongst marketing departments on the release of new products. Limiting the initial supply of eagerly awaited products has allowed manufacturers and retailers to charge higher prices initially. Playstation and Xbox both only supplied limited amounts to the UK market at their initial launch partly due to their inability to increase supply.

■ Activity

Show on a diagram and briefly explain the effect on supply of hotel and restaurant services of the rise in the minimum wage from £5.35 to £5.80 per hour paid to employees such as bar staff and waitresses.

AQA Examiner's tip

Often students confuse a shift to the right as being a fall in supply (because visually the supply curve looks to be lower down on the diagram). This is not true. Look at the *x*-axis, you will see *Q* has increased at the same price level and so it is in fact an increase in supply.

■ Activity

Using a diagram in each case explain how the following factors might affect the supply of wine produced in France:

1 A sharp frost that destroys 20 per cent of the grape harvest (the raw material in wine).

2 The introduction of new machinery that can take the place of the grape pickers, picking the harvest in a fraction of the time.

3 A rise in the price of French wine on the market.

Figure 3.5 *Leather goods*

Joint supply

Joint supply often occurs when a product is made as a by-product of the manufacturing or production process and is a common feature of the chemical industry. Beef and leather provide a different example, where an increase in the demand for beef and the subsequent extension in supply also increases the supply of leather.

Therefore if goods are in joint supply there might be a change to the price of one of those goods caused by changes in demand for the other.

The increase in demand for refined crude oil has led to an increase in the supply of asphalt, or bitumen as it is often called. Bitumen/asphalt is a by-product of the refining process. It is used in road construction and so this should lower the costs of construction assuming all other things remain the same.

Key terms

Joint supply: when the production of one good also results in the production of another.

Activity

Stretch and challenge

The shape of the supply curve is determined to a large extent by costs of production of a good or service. Consider the impact on the supply curve if not all the costs of production were fully accounted for.

What costs might a firm not consider in its decisions about supply?

☑ *After completing this chapter you should:*

■ understand the concept of supply and that planned supply is not necessarily the same as actual supply

■ be able to explain why the slope of the supply curve is positive

■ recognise that the supply curve is predominantly determined by the costs of production

■ be able to identify and explain the factors that shift the supply curve to the left or right

■ understand that changes in price cause extension or contractions along the supply curve

■ understand the concept of joint supply.

AQA  Examination-style questions

1 Figure 1 shows a shift in the supply curve for computers.
The shift in the supply curve for computers from S1 to S2 can result from
(a)   a decrease in the demand for computers.
(b)   increased economies of scale in the computer manufacturing industry.
(c)   a decline in the price of computers.
(d)   an increase in wages in the computer manufacturing industry.

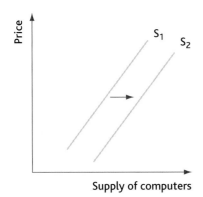

Figure 1 (AQA, 2006)

2   The quantity supplied of a product onto a market increases when the price of the product increases. This shows that
(a)   wants are infinite.
(b)   the product has few substitutes.
(c)   the supply of the product is price inelastic.
(d)   prices perform an incentive function in resource allocation.   (AQA, 2006)

3   Which one of the following could explain a shift to the right of the supply curve for a good?
(a)   The imposition of a tax on the good
(b)   A new supplier entering the market
(c)   A rise in firms' wage costs
(d)   A rise in the price of the good   (AQA, 2006)

4   Nickel Prices
Study Extracts A and B, and then answer the questions that follow.

Extract A: Index of metal prices, 2003 (1995 = 100)*
Table 1

February	74.5
April	69.3
June	71.9
August	76.9
October	82.9
December	91.3

* Note: The figures are taken from *The Economist* Metal Price Index, which measures the average price of metals, such as iron and nickel, but excludes precious metals such as gold.

Extract B Nickel Prices

During 2003, the price of nickel rose from under $8000 to over $14 000 a tonne. Two thirds of the world output of nickel goes into the production of stainless steel, used for products such as cutlery and kitchen sinks. The factors that influenced the price of nickel included:

A strike by workers at a large nickel mine in Canada. The mine normally produces 9% of the world output of nickel. 9000 tonnes of nickel production was lost each month for several months.

Early in 2003, Russian producers sold 36 000 tonnes of nickel from their stockpile, which was the largest in the world. In June 2003, the Russians sold a further 24 000 tonnes to offset supply concerns caused by the strike in Canada.

Output of manufactured goods grew throughout the world in 2003. In China, surging output of stainless steel affected the nickel market.

Speculative demand also affected the market. When speculators believe prices are going to rise, they buy the commodity in order to make a profit by selling at a higher price in the future. In the nickel market, changing demand conditions and running down of stocks led to speculative activity in 2003. Stocks had been the only buffer in the market stabilising the price of nickel.

Market traders expect the price of nickel to grow in 2004, as the world economy continues to grow and production falls due to the lack of new mines and dwindling supply from existing ones. In the 1990s, mining companies bet on new technology lowering the cost of extracting nickel from ores found in tropical soils. But innovation failed to live up to expectations and the new mines in developing countries are not expected to start production for at least another two years, leaving the market short of nickel in 2004 and 2005. Steel makers are also seeking alternatives to nickel in an effort to deal with rising prices and undersupply.

Source: adapted from Kevin Morrison, *Financial Times*, 14 June, 23 August and 18 December 2003

(a) Using Extract A, calculate the percentage change in the price of metals:
   (i)   from 1995 to December 2003;   (*2 marks*)
   (ii) from February 2003 to December 2003.   (*2 marks*)

(b)   With the help of diagrams and the information in Extract B, distinguish between those factors: affecting demand for nickel and those affecting supply of nickel.   (*6 marks*)

(c)   Analyse and explain the possible effect of steel producers finding alternatives for nickel on the production of nickel.   (*10 marks*)

4   How a competitive market functions

'It is all about demand and supply'. Many of you might have heard someone say this when discussing changes in prices. In this chapter we will bring together the supply and demand curves studied in the previous two chapters to explain how the market establishes an equilibrium price. This chapter really begins to get to the heart of how a modern functioning market economy operates. The operation of a market is sometimes referred to by economists as the price mechanism or market mechanism. We will then go on to consider how the firms and consumers respond to the signals sent out by the levels of prices and profits to restore equilibrium in the market. We will then consider how markets for different goods and services might be linked. Finally, we will begin consideration of what happens when governments or other bodies intervene in the market with regulations regarding maximum, minimum and zero prices.

💡 Bringing market demand and supply curves together

Bringing buyers (demanders) and sellers (suppliers) together creates what economists refer to as a market. While the popular conception of a market is a street market with market traders selling from their stalls, economists see markets existing in any situation where buyers and sellers interact. This means that we can split up markets into factor markets, where the factors of production are bought and sold and goods (and services) markets where consumer or capital goods are traded.

Figure 4.1 *A traditional market scene*

Markets do not require buyers and sellers to physically meet because transactions can be carried out by phone, mail order or over the internet. The purpose of a market is to set a price that is acceptable to both buyers and sellers. In some cases, for example a fish and chip shop, the prices have already been set and are usually displayed and if the buyers find the price unacceptable they have the alternative of going elsewhere to purchase their fish and chips. In other markets, for example in the purchase of a second-hand car, there is the possibility of haggling taking place until a price that is acceptable to both parties is reached.

There is a degree of inter-relationship between both goods and factor markets. For example, an increase in the demand to study Economics will increase the demand for Economics textbooks, the goods market, and the demand for economists who write economics books, the labour market. Note that in order to satisfy the increased demand not only will the labour market be affected but if the printing company requires extra printing machinery the market for capital goods will be affected as well.

In order to analyse how a market works we bring the demand and supply curves together on the same diagram. The demand curve slopes downwards, indicating that more will be purchased as price falls, while the supply curve slopes upwards, indicating that more sellers enter the market as prices rise.

The equilibrium

The price system should produce **equilibrium** where demand and supply are equal and there is no immediate tendency for the market to change. In Fig. 4.2 this occurs at price OP_1 and quantity OQ_1. The term equilibrium suggests a condition of stability and market equilibrium is the expected state that markets will reach.

> ■ **Key terms**
>
> **Equilibrium:** the price at which demand is equal to supply and there is no tendency for change.
>
> **Disequilibrium:** a situation within the market where supply does not equal demand.

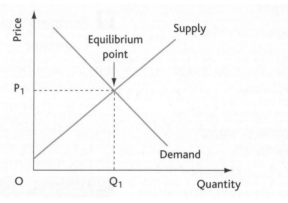

Figure 4.2 *Market equilibrium*

Market disequilibrium and eliminating excess supply

When a market is not in equilibrium or is in **disequilibrium** as it is called, then there is likely to be a further change or reaction by buyers or sellers. We explore this below.

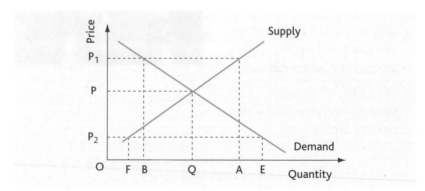

Figure 4.3 *Disequilibrium and elimination of excess supply*

At a high price, P_1, the supply OA exceeds demand OB and suppliers will not be able to sell all they have produced at this price. In economists' terms there is **excess supply** as supply exceeds demand and if suppliers want to sell the product then they will have to lower the price.

In this situation of excess supply the *signalling function* of price is operating – the market signals to suppliers that they have oversupplied the product and if they are to sell it the price must fall. The market is also performing another function, the *incentive function* – it is indicating to suppliers that too many resources have been allocated to this product as more has been produced than consumers wish to purchase. As prices fall there is less incentive for them to supply this market and a greater incentive to supply in other markets as profits are likely to be higher. This suggests to suppliers that they should reallocate their resources away from the production of this product and into areas where consumer demand is increasing.

In a situation of excess supply, often referred to as a 'glut' there is pressure on the price to fall. In the context of the diagram, as the price falls demand will extend down the demand curve and supply will contract down the supply curve until they meet at price *OP* and quantity *OQ*. At this price, demand and supply are equal and it is referred to as the equilibrium or **market-clearing price.**

Market disequilibrium and elimination of excess demand

Similarly, at a low price of OP_2, demand *OE* exceeds supply *OF* – a condition of **excess demand**. This is a disequilibrium position where suppliers will sell out of their stock very rapidly and there will be a shortage. The pressure on price is to rise in these circumstances and price is performing all three of its functions. It is *signalling* to suppliers that more of the product needs to be produced via increased prices; this is closely linked to the *incentive* function – increased prices are likely to result in more profits for firms, which creates incentives to supply more. And finally the *rationing* function of prices, as prices rise demand contracts along the demand curve as consumers ration themselves, until an equilibrium is reached at price *OP* and quantity *OQ*.

Signals sent out by prices are very important for the market to function efficiently as at low prices they inform consumers that the product is a bargain (below the expected equilibrium price) and more of it should be consumed, while in conditions of excess supply they signal to suppliers that they should produce less.

■ The effects of shifts in demand

We have thus far looked at factors shifting the demand curve in Chapter 2 and factors shifting the supply curve in Chapter 3. Now we want to consider the effects of such shifts on equilibrium prices and quantities sold. In real life many factors may be changing at the same time but we will deal with only single changes so that we can isolate the effects of the change in one variable. We assume, therefore, that the *ceteris paribus* condition is met. It is important in the next stage to go slowly and logically and build your analysis step by step. Here we are going to consider the effects of a shift in the demand curve on both the equilibrium price and quantity in a particular market.

■ *Step 1: Initial equilibrium* Take a market for DVD players at a state of equilibrium, so that demand is equal to supply. Here the market is in balance, there is enough being supplied to match demand, there is no excess or shortage. The equilibrium price of training shoes is OP_1 and equilibrium quantity of output is OQ_1, as seen in Fig. 4.4.

■ Key terms

Excess supply: when supply at a particular price is greater than demand; this should signal to producers to lower prices.

Market-clearing price: the price at which all goods that are supplied will be demanded.

Excess demand: when demand is greater than supply at a given price.

Step 2: The change in demand Let us assume there has been an increase in demand because individuals' incomes have risen and now, at the same market price, they can afford to buy more. This means a shift in the demand curve to the right. The whole curve will shift so that there is higher quantity demanded at each price level. D shifts to D_1.

Step 3: The disequilibrium Now we would have a situation where there is excess demand, demand has increased *at the original price level* but supply has remained the same, so demand exceeds supply. You can see this on the diagram where at price OP_1, demand is equal to point OQ_3 but supply is still OQ_1.

Step 4: The reaction of the market to restore equilibrium As there is now excess demand and there is a shortage suppliers recognise this and realise they can increase their prices. The increase in price will send a signal to other suppliers to enter the market (or existing suppliers to increase output). As this happens supply extends *along* the supply curve. At the same time the increasing price forces consumers to cut back (ration) some of their expenditure and demand contracts *along* the demand curve as the price level rises.

Step 5: The new equilibrium When price has risen sufficiently it will have attracted enough extra supply to have dealt with the shortage, the situation will be helped by the simultaneous movement along the demand curve caused by the increase in prices rationing demand until a new point is reached where demand is equal to supply and the market establishes a new equilibrium at $OP_2 OQ_2$.

Figure 4.4 *Shifting the demand*

■ Case study

House prices continue to rise

House prices in the UK have nearly doubled over the last decade. The average house price is now nearly £200,000 and industry analysts wonder for how much longer the market can continue to rise.

In London the average house price between April and June 2005 rose from around £290,000 to around £320,000 in the same period in 2006. Demand has been fuelled by a number of factors including strong employment, significant inward migration, investor demand from overseas for property in London as well as relatively low interest rates. This is combined with a shortage in supply, especially in places like the south-east where building restrictions are tough and there is little available spare land.

It is worth spending a moment thinking about the final outcome. Demand increased without an initial change in supply so there was a shortage. In the circumstances, what would you expect to happen to both the price and quantity? Hopefully you would expect there to be a rise in price and an increase in quantity of output. The shortage had sent a signal via the increase in price to the market to produce more. If you look at your diagram this is exactly what happens – as price rises supply extends (note that it does not shift), both output and price have risen.

Hopefully you will notice that after the initial shift in the demand caused by the rise in incomes all other changes to demand and supply are caused by price. It is crucial to recognise the difference this makes. Incomes shifted the whole demand curve, but the subsequent price changes meant movements along the supply and demand curves.

When demand falls the reverse is true, the demand curve shifts to the left, there is now a surplus, where supply exceeds demand. The price falls and suppliers will either reduce the amount they supply or leave the market altogether as a result. As price falls consumers will buy more, extending demand until a new equilibrium is reached.

■ Skills

Drawing new equilibriums

As outlined above do this methodically and you will tend to get it right. Follow the sequence each time:

1 Draw a demand and supply curve and label an initial equilibrium position.
2 Label the axes, the curves and equilibrium price and quantity.
3 Think whether you would expect price to rise or fall and similarly what would happen to the equilibrium quantity (remember that only one factor is changing).
4 Now, using the information in the question, decide which curve would shift and work out whether it is an increase or decrease in supply or demand.
5 Draw and label the new curve.
6 Mark the new equilibrium and label the new equilibrium prices and quantity.
7 Check that this is what you expected to happen to both price and quantity.

Activity

1 Changes in the law meant that in July 2007 smoking was banned in all enclosed public places including pubs and restaurants. The effect on many businesses was expected to be significant. Some local pubs where the many regular customers were smokers were expected to suffer as customers stayed away.

Draw a supply and demand diagram to illustrate the likely effect on the equilibrium price and quantity of beer consumed in such pubs.

2 The recent concerns raised about growing obesity levels have led to a number of changes in the food industry. Parents have become increasingly aware of the issue and are beginning to alter their buying habits when it comes to food in general and fast food in particular. McDonald's, the American fast food retailer, even changed its menu in response to the concerns.

Draw a supply and demand diagram to illustrate the likely effect on the equilibrium price and quantity of both healthy option foods such as salads and also that of McDonald's hamburgers following the publicity around the obesity issue.

The effects of changes in supply

As with demand there are a number of factors affecting the supply curve that we dealt with in Chapter 3. The mechanism described above for demand can be adapted to explain changes in supply.

For example, take the market for motor cars at equilibrium price and quantity OP_1OQ_1. An improvement in technology in production of motor cars has the effect of reducing the costs per unit. This means that at the same price car manufacturers are likely to make more profit. This in turn means that more suppliers will want to enter the market or existing suppliers will increase output shifting the supply curve to the right, S_1 to S_2. Additional supply with no change in demand means excess supply will exist, putting downward pressure on prices. As prices fall then demand extends and supply contracts to meet a new equilibrium OP_1 OQ_1.

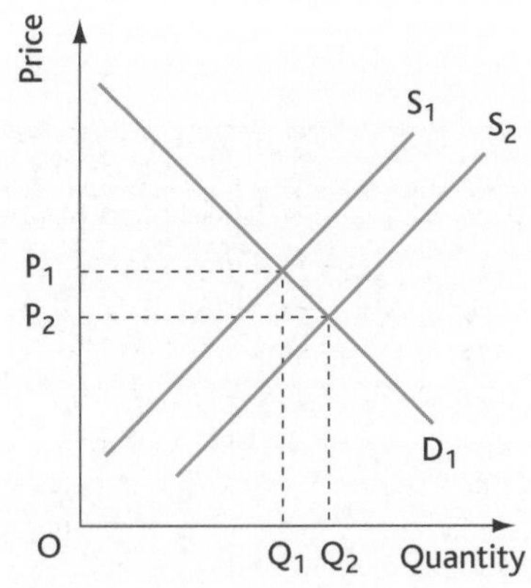

Figure 4.5 *Changes in supply*

The same step-by-step approach is necessary.

- Start by drawing the initial equilibrium and label it.
- Then decide which curve shifts (demand or supply) – usually there will only be one curve that shifts.
- Then decide which direction, is there an increase or decrease? It is important to make sure you are considering the quantity at this point as seen on the *x*-axis.
- Draw the new curve, label it and mark on the new equilibrium price and quantity.
- Check your diagram against what you would have expected. Often candidates write down what they expect to happen correctly but draw something different.
- Finally, explain your diagram making reference to the prices and quantities you have marked.

AQA Examiner's tip

- In most cases there will be a shift in either demand or supply but not both on the same diagram.
- Many candidates think that the diagrams they have drawn need no explanation. This is not true. You will be awarded additional marks for explaining them using the correct terminology.

■ Case study

Giving gas away

An excess of natural gas has resulted in some traders giving it away or in some cases paying for someone to take it off their hands.

Wholesale gas prices for immediate delivery turned negative as supplies flowed in from Norway, via the Langeled pipeline.

Britain's gas storage capacity is 96 per cent full, which means firms need a way to rid their supplies.

After trading at an average of 26p a therm through September, the spot price for gas delivered immediately fell to −5p during the course of the day, meaning traders are paying to get rid of it.

The current climate of mild weather (particularly through the winter months) is also causing plummeting consumer demand.

'There is simply too much gas flowing into the UK,' said Chris Bowden, chief executive of energy services company Utilyx.

Source: adapted from © bbc.co.uk/news

Activity

Draw a diagram and briefly explain the likely impact on equilibrium price and quantity of:

1. iPods following successful advertising campaign on television by Apple.

2. Double glazing following falls in domestic gas and electricity prices for heating.

3. BMW Minis following the successful introduction of new technology into the plant that has helped to raise productivity.

4. Short-haul air flights following the doubling of air passenger duties (taxes) by the government.

5. Sun cream used by UK citizens following the expansion in demand for foreign holidays to southern Europe.

AQA Examiner's tip

It is very important that in each diagram you label the axes clearly, label the equilibriums before and after the change (typically P_1 and P_2 and Q_1 and Q_2) and show the shift in demand or supply. There are certainly marks for this and without it your diagram is meaningless.

The impact of changes in demand and supply on associated markets

Any change in the conditions or determinants of supply or demand will interfere with the market equilibrium and create a temporary disequilibrium situation that may also affect other interrelated markets. In the diagrams below we will consider increases and decreases in supply and demand and their likely effects in both the goods and associated markets. You will get the opportunity to reinforce the demand and supply analysis done already but also see how markets for different areas are interconnected.

An increase in demand and derived demand

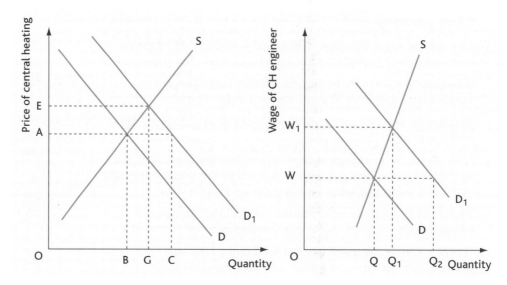

Figure 4.6 *An increase in demand and derived demand*

On the left-hand side of Fig. 4.6 it shows the *consumer goods market* for the purchase of central heating equipment. As with all market diagrams it starts from a position of equilibrium where both demand and supply are equal at an equilibrium price of *OA* and an equilibrium quantity of *OB*. Assume that the demand for central heating increases – this is shown by a rightward movement of the demand curve from *D* to D_1. This immediately produces a disequilibrium situation as at the price *OA* the quantity demanded has increased to *OC* but supply remains at *OB* (illustrated by the dotted lines). There is a situation of excess demand as demand exceeds supply and price will need to rise.

The market functions of allocation and incentive indicate to the producer that more *factors of production* need to be allocated to this product and that increasing prices mean increased revenue. As the price rises some consumers will leave the market (contracting back up D_1) as the rationing function of the market rations the product to those who can afford it and supply will extend up the supply curve *S* as more central heating equipment is produced.

The price rises to a new equilibrium *OE* where demand and supply are equal at the quantity *OG*. The market has moved back into equilibrium. The effect of an increase in demand has been a rise in price and an increase in the quantity demanded and supplied.

The diagram on the right-hand side shows the *factor market*, where the demand curve for engineers is represented by the curve *D* and supply of engineers by the curve labelled *S*. The change in the demand for central heating is likely to disturb the equilibrium in the factor market as the factors of production that make and fit the product will experience an increase in demand for their services; the demand for engineers therefore is derived demand as it comes from the demand for central heating installation. The initial equilibrium for central heating engineers is at wage (price) *OW* and quantity *OQ*. The increased demand for their services shifts the demand curve to the right to D_1. This produces a disequilibrium situation as demand for engineers at the wage of *OW* has increased to OQ_2 while the supply has remained at *OQ*. This situation of

Links

If you cannot remember what is likely to cause demand to increase look back at Chapter 2.

excess demand will trigger the allocative and incentive functions. Those engineers who are perhaps retired will consider supplying their services, as wages have increased and existing engineers may be prepared to work for extra hours. School leavers will have an incentive to train as engineers as wages are rising and as a result of the incentive function factors will move where they are required. A new equilibrium wage will be achieved as the supply of engineers extends up the supply curve and demand contracts as some consumers drop out of the market, because the service is too expensive for them – the rationing function. A new equilibrium will be reached at wage OW_1 where supply and demand are equal at OQ_1.

In the diagram the supply curve of engineers has a fairly steep curve as the supply of them will take time to increase due to the time required for training. This leads to a fairly steep increase in their wage but it has not initially led to a great increase in the supply of them. Under a situation of increasing wages the incentive function of the price system is likely to lead to an increasing number of workers trying to enter the occupation.

A decrease in demand and complementary products

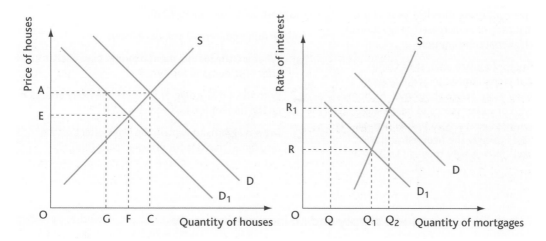

Figure 4.7 *A decrease in demand and complementary products*

The left-hand side of Fig. 4.7 shows the goods market where the demand and supply for houses is in equilibrium at price OA where the quantity demanded and supplied are OC. A fall in demand for houses causes the demand curve to shift to the left, so that at price OA only OG is demanded but OC is still supplied. A situation of excess supply exists where supply exceeds demand. The supplier has an incentive to move factors away from the production of this product and to reallocate them into an area where prices are increasing. The excess supply will cause price to fall and supply will contract down the supply curve. Some consumers will now be able to afford houses and enter the market and this will be shown as an extension down the demand curve until a new equilibrium is reached at price OE and quantity demanded and supplied of OF. The result of a decrease in demand has been a fall in the price and a fall in the quantity demanded and supplied.

An associated market to housing is the market for mortgages and a fall in the demand for houses is likely to lead to a fall in the demand for mortgages. In the diagram above right, the original equilibrium demand D and supply of mortgages S was at rate of interest (price of mortgages) OR_1 and quantity OQ_2. The fall in demand for mortgages to D_1 has led

to an excess supply where supply OQ_2 exceeds demand OQ. Firms will reallocate finance away from mortgages and into another area of loans, where customers are demanding money and a new equilibrium will emerge at the rate of interest OR where OQ_1 mortgages are demanded and supplied.

Both the fall in the demand for houses and the fall in the demand for mortgages will have an effect on the labour markets for the relevant industries.

Activity

The popularity of the Chelsea Tractor (or 4×4s by their official name) is falling.

The financial firm KPMG surveyed 150 executives from the car industry and found that sales will be hit by concern for the environment and higher fuel prices. Many feel that when purchasing a car, the major criteria for customers will be the car's fuel efficiency. Monthly sales in the UK stand 15 per cent lower than last year. Those against 4×4s say that they have increased congestion in the UK and have a high fuel consumption.

Mark Fulthrope, a motor industry analyst of CSM Worldwide, says that North American and European drivers were becoming more aware about fuel economy 'The North American consumer seems to be waking up to some consciousness with regard to fuel pricing, and those designs are typically the heaviest and least fuel efficient,' he said. 'Increasingly they are looking at

newer, lighter designs particularly from the Japanese and Korean manufacturers. We also see that in Europe as well.'

The London congestion charge will be increased for highly polluting vehicles and some councils are even looking into higher parking costs for larger cars. As of March 2007 the chancellor raised vehicle excess duty for the most polluting cars to £210.

Source: Adapted from © bbc.co.uk/news

1. What are the factors mentioned that are likely to affect the demand for 4×4s?

2. With the aid of a diagram analyse the likely effects on the market for 4×4 vehicles.

3. Draw diagrams to explain the likely effect on the associated markets for (a) small cars, (b) fuel.

Joint supply and an increase in supply

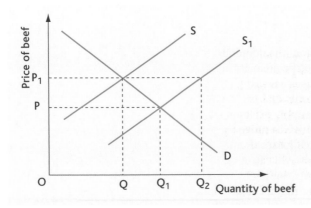
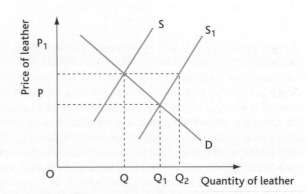

Figure 4.8 *An increase in supply*

The market under consideration in the left-hand side of Figure 4.8 is the market for beef. The demand for beef is shown by the demand curve D and the supply of beef by the supply curve S. The original equilibrium price is OP_1 where demand and supply are equal at OQ. An increase in supply of beef cattle perhaps brought about by government subsidies to farmers shifts the supply curve to the right from S to S_1. At price OP_1

supply OQ_2 exceeds demand OQ, a situation of excess supply (indicated by the dotted line). The operation of both the signalling and allocative function should ensure that the price would fall. A new equilibrium occurs at the price OP where demand and supply are equal at OQ_1. The effect of an increase in supply is a fall in price of beef and an increase in the quantity demanded and supplied.

A related market to the beef market is the market for leather as beef and leather are in joint supply. (You may like to consider what effects this might have on the market for leather shoes.) In the diagram above right the increased supply of leather from S to S_1 has led to a new equilibrium price of OP and quantity OQ_1. As the supply of beef has risen so too does the supply of leather as they are produced together. Again changes in one market area affect another.

> ### AQA Examiner's tip
>
> Try, when you examine a market, to think about the inter-relationships with other markets.

A decrease in supply

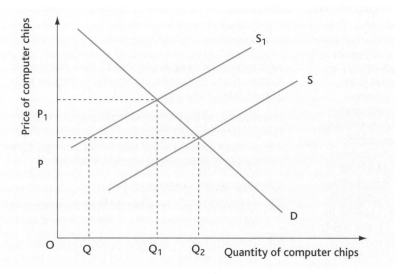

Figure 4.9 *A decrease in supply*

> ### ◼ Activity
>
> In 1995 Kobe in Japan was hit by an earthquake that among other things destroyed two factories manufacturing computer chips. The original equilibrium is shown in the diagram above left at price OP and quantity OQ_2. The reduction in the supply of 'chips' shifts the supply curve to the left from S to S_1. There is excess demand in the market at the price OP as demand has remained at OQ_2 while supply has fallen to OQ. The operation of the rationing function will mean as the price is rising so some consumers will leave the market (they will ration their demand) and the incentive and signalling functions that will lead remaining firms to increase production results in a new equilibrium at price OP_1 and quantity OQ_1.
>
> Explain with the aid of a diagram what the likely effect would be of this supply shock to the computer market.

At AS Level there are five main types of associated markets for you to consider.

◼ *Factor markets* – where an initial change in demand for one good will lead to a change in demand for the factors of production that are used to make it.

- *Joint supply* – where the increase in supply of one good increases the supply of the other as was shown in the beef and leather example.
- *Composite demand* – where increases in the demand for one good reduce the available supply of another – an example might be in building land. If more land is used to build factories and business premises it reduces the land available for residential housing. Or if more tickets to a big sporting event are given to corporate sponsors and their clients then it reduces the available supply to normal fans.
- 💡 *Complementary goods markets* – when demand for one product rises, for example housing, then demand for associated markets such as mortgages and legal services (e.g. solicitors and conveyancing) increases also.
- 💡 *Substitute markets* – where the changes to prices or availability of substitutes affect the demand for another good; for example if Tesco reduces prices then demand for services from Asda or Sainsbury's is likely to fall.

■ Activity

The 2012 Olympic Games in London provides a huge opportunity for businesses in many areas from construction to hotels to capitalise on the massive investment into east London. The development of the Olympic Park at Stratford will provide not only the main stadium but also the aquatic centre and housing for most of the athletes. There are a number of associated issues emerging with the winning of the right to host the games. The need to clear and build the Olympic Park has already had an effect on the cost of local housing in the area. There has been a flood of new investors looking for housing in that area of London and interest in the area is rising on the promise of new transport links to the City and the redevelopment as well as access to the brand new facilities.

Initial estimates of £2.5bn of the cost of staging the Games were optimistic. The VAT on building costs was not included in the initial projections and it is feared this may impact on ticket prices for the Games themselves. In addition, construction costs are rising faster than predicted, partly as the workers in the construction industry are already in high demand for house building and the development of additional office space in the City of London. It is also true that raw material costs in construction are rising as China and India's rapid growth further affects demand for construction materials such as steel, copper and glass.

The expectation is that there will be up to two million foreign visitors coming to London for the Games and it is hoped that they will spend substantial sums of money whilst visiting, which will boost the UK economy.

Using appropriate diagrams explain:

1. The likely impact on ticket prices of the omission of VAT on construction costs of the Olympic stadium.

2. The likely impact on wages of construction workers building new homes in and around the London area.

3. The prices of houses in the local area around the Olympic Park.

4. The prices of construction materials such as steel, which will be the main raw material in the new stadium.

5. Discuss the possible impact on the demand for other attractions such as the London Eye and Alton Towers in the weeks around the Olympics in 2012.

■ Price ceilings and price floors

It is sometimes the case that governments and regulatory authorities impose minimum and maximum prices on goods and services or factors of production. This may be in the form of minimum wages as we have seen in the UK, agricultural prices or ticket prices. Where this happens it is possible that a disequilibrium price may exist within a market and the market mechanism does not correct it.

Maximum prices

Fig. 4.10 illustrates the situation where a **maximum price** or price ceiling exists in the market that has been set that is below the free market

■ Key terms

Maximum price: a price ceiling above which the price of a good or service is not allowed to increase.

equilibrium price. The maximum price clearly means prices cannot rise above the price ceiling, *OPmax*, to the free market equilibrium at *OPe*. At *OPmax*, OQ_2 will be supplied but OQ_1 is demanded. There is excess demand shown by Q_2 to Q_1. Normally in these circumstances prices would rise to eliminate the excess demand and encourage an extension in supply. This cannot happen and so the excess demand remains, typically in the form of a queue or a waiting list.

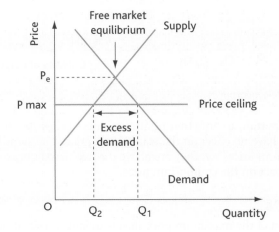

Figure 4.10 *Maximum prices*

The impact of such a maximum price may be to cause bribery and corruption of officials who regulate the queues. Individuals in effect are trying to bypass the maximum price. Alternatively, secondary markets may emerge (commonly known as black markets) where additional illegal supply is sold or supply from the primary market is resold to those prepared to pay more. A classic example of this is the secondary market for sports events sold by ticket touts around the stadium and increasingly on eBay.

If the maximum price is imposed that is above the free market equilibrium then it will have no effect.

Minimum prices or price floors

Minimum prices work in the same way as price ceilings but instead of there being a maximum price instead prices are not allowed to fall below a price floor set by law. The minimum wage is a good example – it was designed to create improved standards of living for low paid workers. Wages are not allowed to fall below the minimum set by government. In Fig. 4.11 it shows the likely effects.

At the minimum price, *OPmin*, demand is OQ_3 but supply at this price is OQ_1; as shown there is excess supply Q_3 to Q_1. As before, in normal free market conditions excess supply problems are solved through the price mechanism by falling prices causing extensions in demand (movement along the demand curve) and contractions in supply (movements along the supply curve) until a new equilibrium is reached at $OP_e OQ_2$.

Other examples seen of minimum prices are when governments intervene in agricultural markets to protect the incomes of farmers. However, it is important to recognise that intervention of this kind prevents the market from working and can distort the signals within the market, which leads to a misallocation of resources.

AQA Examiner's tip

Often this is tested in the objective test questions. It is essential to refer to the free market price and decide whether the maximum or minimum price will have any effect.

Activity

1 Identify markets where minimum or maximum prices are used.

2 Why do you think these prices are set in this way?

3 Examine the effects these prices may have on the resource allocation.

Links

We will examine the agricultural market in more detail in Chapter 6.

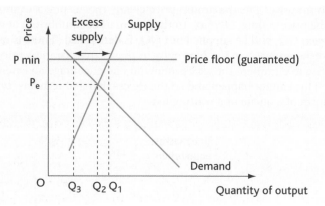

Figure 4.11 *Minimum prices*

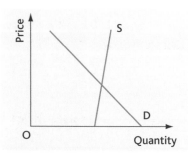

Figure 4.12 *Zero pricing*

AQA✓ Examiner's tip

Candidates at AS Level must be able to explain the mechanism by which the equilibriums shift. They must be able to use diagrams to illustrate the old and new equilibrium positions and should recognise that any shift in equilibrium means a re-allocation of resources. If the equilibrium quantity increases then this means more resources are allocated to that market and vice versa.

Activity

Stretch and challenge

1. Consider the reasons why, when conditions of excess demand or supply exist, equilibrium might not be restored.

2. What conditions are necessary for markets to function effectively?

3. Consider the effects on the revenues of firms from changes in equilibrium prices caused by a rise in demand and a fall in supply.

4. Research task: Investigate the reasons why house prices have changed in the UK so dramatically over the past decade.

5. Discuss whether there should be a maximum level of house prices set by government.

It is also important to note that minimum prices below the free market price would have no effect on the equilibrium price. The same is true with maximum prices – if they are above the free market price they will have no impact on the equilibrium price.

Zero pricing

An extension of the maximum price idea is to look at the effect of markets where goods are provided free at the point of use. This means there is a market price of zero. Examples where this may be the case is in the provision of NHS health care. Although we eventually pay for it through taxation it is free at the point of use and as such it has zero price. If demand for health care is greater than the available supply then clearly there will be excess demand and we end up with a waiting list for treatment. This means there is a position of disequilibrium.

The same is true with road use, at peak times such as rush hour, demand exceeds supply and we end up with traffic queues, otherwise called congestion. The solutions to such problems are very much under debate but clearly one solution already at play in London is the congestion charge, where a price is imposed on road use. The effect of this is to ration the demand of users of road space, causing a contraction of demand to a point at which the demand for road use is equal to the supply. If the technology can be made to work a system that charges different prices for different times of the day might be effective in rationing demand at peak times when demand exceeds supply.

☑ *After completing this chapter you should:*

■ understand the notion of market equilibrium and disequilibrium

■ recognise and be able to explain the factors that disturb equilibrium

■ be able to explain the mechanism by which equilibrium is restored

■ recognise the role the price mechanism plays in the process

■ be confident with the use of diagrams to show shifts in both demand or supply and their effect on equilibrium

■ recognise that markets are inter-related and use this in your explanations

■ understand the impact of maximum and minimum prices

■ recognise that markets sometimes have zero price, which might mean there is disequilibrium.

Examination-style questions

1   In a market economy, the market mechanism can achieve all the following except
    (a)   signalling changes in consumer tastes.
    (b)   causing supply to respond to changes in demand.
    (c)   eliminating excess supply and demand.
    (d)   ensuring a fair distribution of all types of good.   (AQA, 2006)

2   Resources are allocated through the market mechanism partly by
    (a)   the existence of external costs.
    (b)   the signalling function of prices.
    (c)   the provision of public goods.
    (d)   over-supply of merit goods.   (AQA, 2006)

3   **Coffee Prices Falling**
    World price of Coffee Beans US$
    Coffee Prices Tumbling

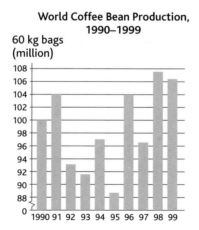

Figure 1 *Coffee beans*
Source: Financial Times, 24 February and 27 October 2000

Figure 2 *What you pay for in a £1.50 Cappuccino*
Source: adapted from Financial Times *15th January 2001*

The world price of coffee continues to fall and farmers in some of least developed countries are finding it hard to make a living. Despite the sharp frosts in southern Brazil in 2000, the world's largest producer of coffee, which had a very brief upward effect on the world price, coffee prices have been under pressure for some time due to increased global production from countries such as Kenya and Vietnam. Vietnam has jumped from being an insignificant player to becoming the world's second largest producer after Brazil. Indonesia too is a large producer and although they would like to see prices rise, so far they have taken no action to support prices. An Indonesian spokesman said that the country could not afford to take action to support prices.

Intervention has worked in the past in 1993/4 when coffee-producing countries took action together, but the introduction of new players into the market undermined those efforts. Coffee drinkers are paying a higher price for their coffee despite the falling prices of the raw coffee

Some of the bigger coffee-bar chains such as Starbucks have been increasing prices. At Costa, a leading UK chain, the price of a grande-cappuccino has risen from £1.85 to £1.99

The chain argues that coffee beans form a small part of the final price of a cup of coffee. The biggest cost, especially in large cities, is the cost of purchasing or renting prime sites for their coffee bars. There is fierce competition amongst the retailers for the prime sites, especially in London.

Coffee drinkers see smart coffee as part of their lifestyle now. They know they can sell their products practically at any price, so there is no need to pass on any reductions in raw material prices to consumers. The real casualties though are not the consumers but the farmers who cannot afford the fertilizers for their crops

(a)   Describe the relationship between changes in the prices of coffee beans and changes in world production as shown in Fig. 1.   *(4 marks)*

(b)   With the help of a demand and supply diagram, explain the changes in prices of coffee beans since the peak in 1994.   *(6 marks)*

(c)   Use the information in the extracts to analyse why changes in coffee beans have not reflected changes in the prices in coffee bars.   *(8 marks)*

(d)   Discuss the case for and against the Brazilian government intervening in the market for coffee beans to help increase incomes for farmers.

(12 marks)

(AQA, 2006)

5 Elasticity

In the previous chapter we have been developing our understanding of what happens to both price and quantity of goods and services consumed when there are changes in demand and supply. We have focused mainly on the direction of change – will the equilibrium price or quantity rise or fall. In this chapter we are going to extend this analysis to ask the really important question of how much will price or quantity change. The concept of elasticity will help us do this and it is an absolutely crucial part of the 'economists' tool kit' and can be used at both an individual market level (in microeconomics) but also at a whole economy level (in macroeconomics).

The concept of elasticity

The concept of elasticity tries to identify the impact of changes that one variable, perhaps price, has on another variable, typically quantity demanded. Economists and real-life businesses want to know what will happen if they lower their prices, for example. Our previous theory explained that if price falls we would expect demand to rise. This is quite straightforward, however the real question is how much will demand change? If a small fall in price brings about significant rises in demand then it may well be a worthwhile thing for a business to do in its marketing strategy. This idea could then be applied to any variable. If income rises what will happen to demand? Again typically we would expect demand to rise but how much? If the prices of competing goods or substitutes fell a firm might ask how much would demand for its product change? Firms need to understand these issues in order to help them make decisions and the concept of elasticity is used to help.

Similarly, we will need to consider the impact of price changes on how much firms and individuals are prepared to supply. If prices rise we expect there to be an increased incentive to supply goods and services, but again how much more will be supplied. The concept of price elasticity is therefore used to explore the extent to which either demand or supply are responsive to other variables such as price, income and the prices of other goods.

Price elasticity of demand (PeD)

Price elasticity of demand refers to how much demand changes when there is a change in price. A firm might decide to cut prices to get rid of surplus stock in the Christmas sales. The question facing the managers is how much should they reduce prices by to get rid of remaining stock whilst maximising their revenue and profit. If they knew that by cutting price by 20 per cent they would get 50 per cent more sales this would be helpful. Price elasticity of demand attempts to measure the likely effect on demand of price changes.

For example, if the price of a chocolate bar falls from 40p to 36p and demand rises as a consequence from 1,000 bars per week to 1,200 bars per week then there has been a 10 per cent fall in price but a 20 per cent increase in quantity demanded. Using the formula below, the price elasticity can be calculated.

■ Key terms

Price elasticity: the responsiveness of demand to a change in the price level. The formula is percentage change in quantity demanded divided by percentage change in price.

$$\frac{\text{Percentage change in quantity demanded} =}{\text{Percentage change in price}} \quad \frac{+20}{-10} = -2$$

Economists would describe the demand for this chocolate bar as relatively price elastic as a small percentage change in price brought about a bigger percentage change in quantity demanded. The answer to our calculation was above 1, which also tells us demand is price elastic. Answers below 1 imply relatively price inelastic demand whereby changes in price bring about proportionately smaller changes in demand.

The concept is very important to businesses. They need to know how to set their prices for their goods and services and whether to alter prices. If they knew their price elasticity of demand it would certainly help them in their business planning. Unfortunately in reality it is hard to calculate the exact effect of price changes because many other variables are changing at the same time and the effects of previous changes in price might not be a good guide to how price changes now will impact on demand.

You will note that we have used positive and negative signs in the calculation above. The price was cut by 10 per cent and so this is shown as a fall with the negative sign. The demand though rose by 20 per cent and is therefore positive. You will remember from your maths that a positive and a negative give a negative answer hence the answer −2.

■ Case study

Apple cuts price of iPhone

Figure 5.1 *An iPhone*

The long-awaited launch of the Apple iPhone appears to have been a tremendous success. In the first few days of trading it was reported that over half a million units were sold at the price of around $599. However, unusually Apple has cut the price by a third only 66 days after the launch. One estimate from industry sources suggested that approximately 9,000 units were selling per day before the price fell but the price cut increased this to 27,000 units a day helping Apple towards a target of one million phones.

Table 5.1 *Price elasticity calculation*

When the answer is:	What it is called	What it means	Effect on a firm's total revenue of a price cut
0	Perfectly inelastic	When price changes there is no effect on demand at all. Demand remains the same	When prices fall, because demand does not change at all then total revenue (or expenditure) must fall
Between 0 and –1	Price inelastic demand	When prices fall demand increases but by a smaller proportion than the fall in price. Demand is relatively unresponsive to price changes	Total revenue will fall. There are more customers but each one paying a proportionately lower price and therefore overall expenditure falls
1	Unitary price elasticity of demand	That a change in price brings about the same proportionate change in demand	Total revenue will remain the same from a price cut
Above 1	Price elastic demand	A fall in price means demand rises by proportionately more than the price cut (as in the example above)	Total revenue will rise
Infinity	Perfectly elastic demand	This means that a fall in price leads to an infinite level of demand.	A fall in price leads to huge increases in total revenue

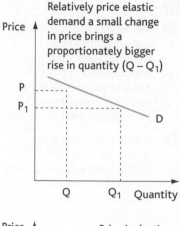

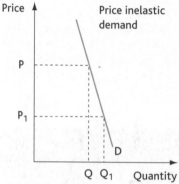

Figure 5.2 *Price elastic demand and price inelastic demand*

💡 So price elasticity of demand indicates the extent to which demand changes when price changes and also the likely effect on revenues for firms from their decisions to change prices. It also will be of interest to governments when wondering whether to impose taxes on a good or offer subsidies.

For economists new to the subject you may well hear the phrase 'price elasticity being low'. This tends to mean it is price inelastic, whereas high price elasticity means demand is elastic and responsive to changes in the price level.

■ Skills

Calculating percentage change

Often candidates will need to convert actual changes in price or quantity to a percentage change so that they can do the elasticity calculations. The way to do this is to work out the change and divide it by the original value multiplying the answer by 100.

For example, there is a rise in price from £4 to £5. The change in price is £1, the original price is £4, therefore

1   Calculate the price elasticity
    of demand for a new
    computer game if the price
    falls from £20 to £15 and
    demand responds by rising
    from 200 units per week to
    240 units per week.

2   Calculate the price elasticity
    of demand if the price rose
    from £15 per week to £20 and
    demand fell from 240 to 200
    units per week.

$$\text{Actual change} = \frac{\text{Actual change}}{\text{Original price}} \qquad \frac{1}{4} \times 100 = 25\%$$

The price change equals 25%.

Applying price elasticity to demand and supply curves

We have established that price elasticity of demand is a vital concept in explaining how firms decide on their prices and also that the impact of price changes has an effect on revenues. However, the price elasticity of demand has a big impact on the extent of price changes when there is a shift in the supply curve. In the case of a fairly elastic demand curve where the increase in supply from S_1 to S_2 brings about a relatively small change in equilibrium price from P to P_2 as you can see from the graph (Fig. 5.3) on the left. However, an inelastic demand curve for a product such as petrol as seen in the right-hand diagram below, will produce a different outcome.

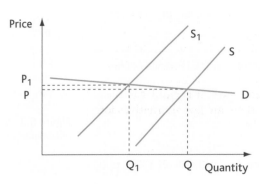
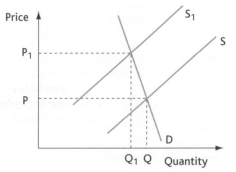

Figure 5.3 *Price elasticity*

Because demand for petrol is relatively price inelastic this means that the equilibrium price would rise quite sharply from P to P_1 but there would be a proportionately smaller fall in the quantity demanded. The impact on overall expenditure by consumers on petrol would be that expenditure would rise. This is all because there are few substitutes for petrol, especially in the short term, and so people would simply have to pay the increased price. Thus we can see that when supply changes the extent of changes in both price and quantity depends very much on the price elasticity of demand.

The factors that determine price elasticity of demand

There are a number of factors that influence the price elasticity of demand. The two key factors that often feature are the number of substitutes and time. There are other factors described here but they are not usually considered the main determinants.

a) The availability of substitutes – when there are plenty of good substitutes available that can be bought as an alternative then it is likely that the demand curve will be relatively elastic. This is because if a firm were to raise its price then consumers are likely to switch to the cheaper alternatives that are available. This assumes that consumers are not loyal to particular brands and will make the decision to purchase based on price rather than any other factor such as quality or image.

On the other hand, where there are few substitutes demand is likely to be price inelastic, this is because there are few alternatives available and so customers have little choice but to pay if prices rise. This is certainly the case for car users in the UK when the price of petrol rises. In theory they could use the train or the bus but these are not very realistic alternatives for many journeys and so car owners continue to drive despite higher prices.

b) Time – often when prices rise consumers would react by changing to an alternative product. However, when consumers need the product immediately or in the near future then they may have to accept the increase in price and so demand is unresponsive to price changes in the short term. In the longer term they may be able to switch to alternative suppliers, although this might take time and incur additional expense. In the case of oil-powered heating in people's homes, when the price of oil rises in the short term they must pay more if they want to heat their homes, they have little choice. In the longer term they may be able to switch to alternatives such as gas or solar power. In this way demand is unresponsive to price changes initially but over time if oil remains expensive people are likely to switch to other forms of domestic fuel.

c) Whether the product is a luxury or a necessity is often an influential factor on price elasticity. If the price of a luxury rises, demand is likely to fall more than if it is considered a necessity. Necessities need to be bought almost regardless of the price, so if prices rise demand falls very little. Luxuries such as days out at theme parks, though, might see their demand fall more when prices rise. This is because consumers might choose to do other things than go to the theme park. It is similar to the first point in this section because it implies there are few alternatives for necessities but many choices for luxuries.

🔲 d) Also, the proportion of income spent on a good may have an influence on price elasticity. Very low priced goods such as matches or cheap pens take up a small amount of income. If the price of these goods were to rise we might continue to buy them at the higher price because they make little difference to our standard of living. More expensive items, though, take up a bigger proportion of our disposable income and we become much more sensitive to changes in the price level as the opportunity cost of other goods foregone is greater. There is only limited evidence to support this and it would vary depending on each individual's income but some economists cite this as a factor that affects price elasticity.

Price elasticity and the incidence of tax

Quite often when market forces are not working effectively to allocate resources governments intervene either through taxes or **subsidies**. When considering the impact of indirect taxes in particular we need to consider the proportion of any tax rise that gets passed onto the customer; this is called the **incidence of tax**.

Applying price elasticity to this topic area is interesting and may give a reason why governments tend to tax some products and not others.

As you will see from Fig. 5.4(a) a tax imposed on a product is paid in the first instance by the producer or the retailer, which means the supply curve shifts to the left S_1 to S_2.

Discussing the effect of taxes can be split into four areas:

■ the effect on price
■ the effect on equilibrium quantity sold

Key terms

Subsidies: payments by government to producers to encourage production of a good or services. Often subsidies are found in farming where farmers receive funds from government per tonne or unit of output. This typically means that prices can be lower than would otherwise be the case.

Incidence of tax: the proportion of a tax that is passed onto the consumer. If most of a tax rise is added to the consumer then the incidence of tax is said to be 'high'. When demand is price inelastic then the incidence of tax tends to be high.

■ the effect on tax revenues

■ the effect on employment in that industry.

The effect on price

Firms will usually pass as much of an indirect tax onto consumers in the form of increased prices as it can. However, when price elasticity of demand is fairly elastic they struggle to do this as it would bring about significant falls in demand for the good. Therefore producers often have to absorb the taxes and reduce profits, passing only a small proportion of the tax rise onto consumers, otherwise the fall in quantity demanded would be too great. Here the tax is shown by the vertical distance between the two supply curves. However, the price increase from P_1 to P_2 is much less than the tax. In this case the incidence of tax is said to be low. In the second diagram demand is price inelastic and in this case the taxes can more easily be passed onto the consumer, hence the bigger rise in price.

The fall in quantity sold

As we have seen with price elastic demand curves the quantity demanded will fall sharply if taxes are imposed. The additional tax adds to costs and therefore prices and, as consumers are by definition in this case price sensitive the rises in price cause large changes in demand. With inelastic demand curves there is relatively little impact on sales as you can see in Fig. 5.4(b) – sales only fall from Q_1 to Q_2.

The impact on tax revenues

Increased taxes mean that although the government might collect quite high taxes per unit of sales (shown by the vertical distance between the S_1 and S_2 distance P_2 to P_3) because of the big reduction in demand caused by the increased price, in actual fact the total revenue government receive from the tax will fall quite sharply or in the cases of new taxes be much lower than a government might hope for. The total tax revenue is illustrated by the area ABP_3P_2 is much lower than if price elasticity of demand was inelastic.

If on the other hand demand for cigarettes was price inelastic then increases in taxation lead to more government revenue that can then be used to fund government spending. This tends to mean that governments are often less keen to tax products where demand is price elastic because of the effects on tax revenue and, as we shall see next, employment.

Effects of taxes on employment

Taxes on price elastic products also mean that employment in those industries is likely to fall as the quantity demanded would fall significantly. Labour is derived demand, so a fall in the demand for the product will typically mean falls in the demand for labour that produces it. The effect on employment in price inelastic markets is much less severe.

Effect of a tax on equilibrium price and quantity of output

Subsidies operate in much the same way except that they bring about a shift in the supply curve to the right and thus a subsidy on products that are demand inelastic cause relatively bigger falls in price and small increases in quantity.

Therefore we can see that price elasticity is an important concept for firms, because it influences both the level of sales and their revenues when changing prices, thus affecting profits. It also impacts on

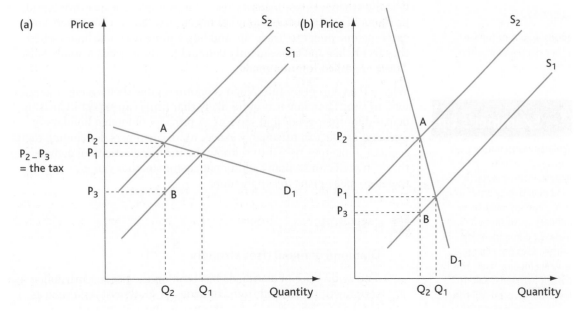

Figure 5.4 *(a) A tax on a product with relatively price elastic demand curve and (b) a tax on a product with inelastic demand*

governments through the incidence of taxes and subsidies and therefore affects households as well. Clearly if government impose taxes that have an effect on demand then it is likely there will be effects on employment in that industry as well.

Case study

Taxing alcohol and tobacco: Does it work to reduce consumption?

Alcohol and tobacco have long been areas that successive governments have sought to tax. Often the rationale given has been that these goods are not generally good for us and we should be discouraged from consuming them. Whilst this might indeed be the case (they do give us negative side effects that often affect not only ourselves but also society in general, such as passive smoking, health-related costs of alcohol and tobacco consumption and time away from work), taxing these products does very little to reduce consumption as the demand curve tends to be very inelastic, particularly in the case of smoking, which is addictive. Therefore, it is argued that taxing them is merely a way of governments raising revenue from taxes rather than trying to reduce the use of such goods.

Income elasticity of demand

Income elasticity of demand seeks to measure the responsiveness of demand to changes in income. In most cases we would expect demand for goods and services to rise when we have more income. This is broadly speaking true and we call these goods **normal goods**.

It therefore has a positive income elasticity of demand. This is not true for all goods though. Some goods and services actually suffer falls in

AQA Examiner's tip

When examining policies to reduce market failure you should attempt to consider the effect of both the incidence of taxes and subsidies and their effect on output and employment and government revenue or spending (in the case of a subsidy).

Key terms

Income elasticity of demand: the proportion to which demand changes when there is a change in income.

Normal goods: goods or services that will see an increase in demand when incomes rise.

Inferior goods: goods or services that will see demand fall when income rises.

AQA Examiner's tip

It is particularly worth noting that there is a distinction between income elastic, income inelastic demand and negative income elasticity. A common mistake by many candidates is to suggest that income inelastic demand means demand either does not change at all or falls when income rises. This is not the case. If demand is said to be income inelastic, demand will rise when income rises but simply by a lower proportion than the change in income. Negative income elasticity means demand actually falls when income rises.

Figure 5.5 *A diamond ring*

demand when people's incomes rise – for example, cheaper own brand products in supermarkets often fall into this category. Consumers with extra income prefer to 'trade up' and buy a more desirable brand when they feel richer and consequently demand for these goods actually falls. These are called **inferior goods**.

Why is the concept useful? When economies grow then average incomes tend to rise. Therefore it is quite likely that firms can expect increasing demand for their goods and services. A provider of foreign holidays or weekend breaks can reasonably expect more customers demanding their services if incomes rise. If they know the income elasticity of demand they can predict how many additional customers they can expect and therefore make plans to supply more.

■ Case study

Diamond demand rises strongly

The world price of diamonds has been on the rise recently following the growth in demand from countries in south-east Asia such as India and China. Rapid growth rates in the emerging economies has meant rising incomes and this, combined with falling stocks of diamonds has helped to push up the world price.

Incomes in India and China were said to have grown by as much as 18 per cent bringing about an overall 5 per cent increase in the world price. China and India are two of the fastest growing markets for diamonds as their economies power ahead. China's imports grew by 300 per cent, whilst those in India were up 14 per cent according to the Gem and Jewellry Promotion Council.

Source: adapted from Bloomberg, 28 August 2007

🔍 Calculating income elasticity of demand

As with price elasticity of demand it is important to use percentage changes in both income and quantity demanded.

$$\text{Income elasticity of demand} = \frac{\%\text{ change in quantity demanded}}{\%\text{ change in income}}$$

For example if a 5 per cent rise in income brought about a 7 per cent rise in demand for CDs then income elasticity would be:

$$\frac{\text{Percentage change in quantity demanded}}{\text{Percentage change in income}} \quad \frac{7}{5} = +1.4$$

As with price elasticity calculations, answers above 1 mean that demand is income elastic, positive answers also mean that the good is normal. Answers between 0 and 1 mean demand is relatively unresponsive to changes in income and described as income inelastic. As income rises, in this case by 5 per cent, demand increases by a larger percentage of 7 per cent. Answers that are negative mean demand actually falls when income rises and so these goods are called 'inferior goods'.

Income elasticity of demand is a concept that can be used very well in the applied setting. When an economy is growing then average incomes tend to be rising (assuming population is constant). So in times of rapid growth in the economy we expect demand for income elastic products, typically more luxury products such as holidays, restaurant food, clothing and jewellery, to rise at a faster rate than income. This equally means that employment in those industries is likely to grow faster than in other industries thus affecting the pattern of employment. The opposite is true in a recession; luxury producers will be hit hardest.

Activity

A market researcher working for a travel agency found that demand for holidays varied considerably depending on changes in income. He found that when local incomes rose by 5 per cent, demand for package holidays to Spain increased from 250 per week in high season to 300 per week. Holidays to destinations in the UK using holiday homes increased by 4 per cent and demand for camping holidays went from 100 per week in high season to 90 per week.

1. Distinguish between a normal and an inferior good.

2. Calculate the income elasticity of demand for the different types of holiday.

3. Predict what will happen to demand for the different types of holiday if there is a drop in incomes by 2 per cent next year.

Cross price elasticity of demand (Xped)

This concept examines the extent to which changes in the price of one good, call it good A, affect demand for another good, call this one good B. If you ran a business selling Ford cars then changes to the prices of cars of other manufacturers would affect your levels of sales. Similarly, if there were changes in prices of petrol this too might have an effect on sales of certain models of car that consume more petrol. Cross price elasticity can be used to explore the extent to which there is a close relationship between the demand for one product and the prices of other goods and services.

In the above example, if Volkswagen or Vauxhall were to cut prices of their models by 10 per cent then the demand for Fords might be expected to fall. Cross price elasticity explores how much demand might change. If demand fell by 12 per cent then the cross price elasticity of demand would be calculated as follows:

$$\text{Cross price elasticity} = \frac{\text{Percentage change in the quantity demanded of good A (Ford)}}{\text{Percentage change in price of good B (Vauxhall)}} = \frac{-12}{-10} = +1.2$$

Therefore, as the answer is above 1 (plus or minus) we can say that demand for Ford cars was relatively cross price elastic, in other words demand does respond to changes in price of other goods by a greater proportion than the change in price. The fact that the answer is positive (+1.2) shows us that these goods are competing goods or **substitutes**. Generally speaking, the higher the cross price elasticity the closer they are as substitutes.

Similarly with rises in the price of petrol we would expect falls in the demand for cars, especially those with poor fuel efficiency. This would mean that as prices of petrol rose, say, 20 per cent, demand for cars would fall perhaps 5 per cent.

The calculations based on the same formula above are:

Key terms

Substitutes: goods that can be used as alternatives to another good, for example bus and rail services or Mars Bars and Snickers. Close substitutes are good alternatives whereas weak substitutes are not very good or likely alternatives, such as gas-fired power in the UK and hydroelectric power.

$$\frac{-5}{+20} = -0.25$$

Here the answer is negative so they are *complementary goods* (they are consumed together), and as the answer is between 0 and 1 demand for cars is cross price inelastic with respect to petrol, therefore demand for cars is relatively unresponsive to changes in the price of petrol. Close complements will tend to be more cross price elastic although it is important to realise that the relative prices of the goods plays quite an important role in affecting the degree of cross price elasticity. For example, although it could be argued that sun tan cream and foreign holidays to hot destinations are complementary goods to a degree if the price of sun cream went up the demand for such holidays is unlikely to be much affected because sun cream is perhaps a tiny fraction of the cost of taking a holiday of this kind. Try to consider the closeness of the relationship between both complements and substitutes when exploring this issue.

AQA Examiner's tip

Good candidates will take care to ensure they use the correct positive and negative signs in their calculations, which are commonly tested in objective test questions, but will especially focus on using the concept to explore the closeness of the relationship between goods and services.

Activity

Gaming firm ALCo Ltd produce children's games that can be downloaded from the company site priced at £20 each and run on home PCs. The demand for home PCs has increased by 20 per cent over the past two years as computer prices have fallen 10 per cent. At the same time the demand for ALCo games has increased by 25 per cent.

1. Calculate the price elasticity of demand for home PCs.

2. What is the cross price elasticity for games with respect to the price of computers?

3. If the income elasticity of demand for games is +1.4 calculate and briefly comment on the effect of a rise in incomes from £20,000 per annum to £24,000 per annum.

Price elasticity of supply (PeS)

Price elasticity of supply refers to the responsiveness of supply to changes in the price level. In the earlier part of this chapter we looked at the impact of price changes on demand. In the same way here we will investigate the effect on supply of goods and services. From our earlier chapters we know that entrepreneurs are keen to increase output and supply more when the price level they believe they can receive is higher because they stand to increase their profits. The concept of price elasticity of supply looks at how much supply will change as prices change.

The formula for calculating Price elasticity of supply is:

$$\frac{\text{Percentage change in quantity supplied}}{\text{Percentage change in price}}$$

Just as with price elasticity the resultant answer indicates the degree to which supply is elastic. Answers below 1 are said to be price inelastic supply and answers above 1 indicate supply is more price elastic.

Price elasticity of supply is often used to explain why prices rise or fall quite dramatically when there are changes in demand. In agricultural markets, for example, the supply of tomatoes is relatively fixed in the short term; it is simply not possible to grow more by next week. Therefore if there were a sudden increase in demand, supply would be unresponsive; supply could not change in the short term and thus no matter what the price offered no more can be offered for sale.

Commodity markets in general often have the same characteristics. The supply of oil is relatively inelastic in the short term, as is the supply of petrol. Both of these supply curves are inelastic because despite increases in price levels it is difficult to increase oil production – there is a need to drill new wells and build pipelines, etc. Petrol needs refining and refineries may take years to build and come on stream and therefore if there is no spare capacity it is very hard to increase production even if the price rises sharply.

On the other hand, price elasticity of supply may be much more elastic if a firm has stock-piled raw materials and has spare capacity and therefore can respond to changes in demand relatively quickly and without substantial additional costs.

Factors affecting the price elasticity of supply

- As with price elasticity of demand, time is a key factor in determining price elasticity of supply. If a producer sees prices rising in the market they would ordinarily want to take advantage of this and sell more output. However, it may take time to produce extra output and so in the short term they cannot meet the additional demand. A rapid increase in the demand for vintage wines cannot be met until new wine has been made and allowed to mature – this could take several years. The same is true with supplies of agricultural products, increases in the price of wheat on the world market would see farmers wanting to respond, but it might take six months or a year until they can harvest a new crop.

- The supply of many raw materials is often price inelastic because mining firms need to explore and find new resources before they can increase supply. Even if they did know about reserves they might need to dig new mines or drill new wells to exploit them, all of which takes time.

- The availability of stocks or stock-piling. Firms that hold stock of finished goods are likely to have a more elastic supply curve in the short term. When prices increase they are already in a position to increase supply. This is part of the reason why firms will often keep stocks available so that they can react to unforeseen surges in demand.

- The ease of switching between alternative production – if firms can switch between production of different goods relatively easily then it may be able to expand production of one product quite quickly should its price rise. Take a textile manufacturer producing replica shirts, if one team's shirt is selling very well and a shortage has driven up the price, if the manufacturer makes a variety of different shirts for different teams they could switch production from less popular teams and increase supply of the most popular shirts quickly.

- The availability of spare capacity – firms with spare capacity have the capability to expand output relatively quickly in response to changes in the price. Firms at full capacity would find it very difficult to respond in the same way – they would be unable to respond if prices rose. This point can be applied to both a firm and an economy and may form part of your analysis in macroeconomics of aggregate supply and its shape.

- The number of firms in the market and ease with which firms can enter a market. Supply is determined by all firms in the market, if

Key terms

Commodity: a good that is traded, but usually refers to raw materials or semi-manufactured goods that are traded in bulk such as tea, iron ore, oil or wheat. Often they are unbranded goods (homogeneous) where all firms' products are very similar and undistinguishable from each other.

Figure 5.6 *An oil rig*

AQA **Examiner's tip**

This concept is important and can certainly be applied both at a macro- and a microeconomic level. It can be applied to aggregate demand and supply analysis or simply demand and supply of individual product and factor markets.

it is easy to enter a market then resources not currently involved in the supply of a particular good might enter a market if they see prices rising and an opportunity to generate profits. If there are little or no barriers to entry and exit from a market then it is likely that firms will move into a market swiftly, increasingly the supply when prices in that market rise. If there are no restrictions on foreign workers coming into the UK, rises in average wages will act as an incentive for new migrants to come to the UK, thereby increasing the supply of labour. Similarly, if overseas firms see prices rise in the UK of a particular good they may rush to enter the UK market, thus increasing supply.

■ The ability to alter production methods might also be a factor influencing price elasticity of supply. If a firm can transfer quickly to alternative methods of production, for example more capital intensive production, then the supply curve will become more elastic.

Perfectly inelastic supply curves are sometimes a feature on exam questions. In these cases supply cannot increase even when price rises (especially in the short term). Examples commonly are of the supply of road space, land for building within a city, and sports and entertainment venues that have limited numbers of seats.

Case study

Sell out crowds fill new Wembley

The fans have been happy as the National Team have been producing more convincing performance on the pitch and demand to watch England at their new home has been high. There are, however, problems for fans wanting to get tickets. The new Wembley stadium has a capacity of 90,000 seats. After all the tickets have been sold, there are no more that can be supplied and fans desperate to get into the game, particularly the bigger matches against teams like Germany and Brazil, have had to pay extremely high prices to secure tickets. Often on the second-hand market ticket touts are selling for as much as 10 times the face value of the ticket.

Case study

Gas prices in the UK

In the winter of 2006 domestic and commercial gas prices rose very substantially as the price of gas on the market rose. Many commentators expressed growing concern about the impact for both UK producers and consumers and the effect on the UK economic performance as a whole. Partly to blame for the rising prices is the dwindling supply of gas from UK operated fields in the North Sea. Many analysts believe that the UK will have to import increasing amounts of gas in the coming years. Both Norway and Russia, the two major European producers are set to become key suppliers of gas supplying up to 80 per cent of UK gas requirements in the years to come. The UK position has been made worse with only minimal facilities to store gas and until very recently there was very limited capacity to receive gas from mainland Europe because the infrastructure to pipe gas to the UK in sufficient quantities did not exist. Only in early 2007 did we open new pipeline facilities allowing a greater flow of Russian gas into the UK.

Economic recovery in the Eurozone and strong growth in the new EU member states has meant increasing demand for gas at a time when supply is stretched. If the price of gas is to fall, given predictions of demand, then new supply is required but at the moment this looks unlikely.

Activity

Stretch and challenge

Table 5.2 *Elasticity along a demand curve*

Price £	10	9	8	7	6	5	4	3	2	1
Quantity	1	2	3	4	5	6	7	8	9	10

1. Plot a demand curve using the information above.

2. Calculate the price elasticity of demand for the following price changes, in each case you will need to convert the actual price and quantity changes to percentage changes (as illustrated earlier in this chapter):

   a. a cut in price from £10 to £9
   b. a cut in price from £5 to £4
   c. a cut in price from £2 to £1.

3. Describe the pattern you observe in price elasticities.

4. Calculate the total revenue at each level of output (the formula is price × quantity demanded).

5. Is there a relationship between price elasticity of demand and changes in total revenue?

6. How might this information be used to help a firm decide on its pricing strategy?

✓ *After completing this chapter you should:*

- understand the concept of elasticity in general and price, income and cross elasticity of demand in particular

- be able to calculate and comment on elasticities of demand and supply

- recognise that elasticities can be both positive and negative and be able to apply this knowledge to explain the relationships between products

- understand and explain the factors affecting price elasticity of demand and supply

- understand how the elasticity of demand impacts on the incidence of taxes and subsidies (the impact on producers also)

- recognise the impact price changes might have on revenue for firms and governments and how this information might be used to determine pricing strategy and taxation.

AQA Examination-style questions

1   The cross elasticity of demand between two complementary products is always
  (a)   negative.
  (b)   positive.
  (c)   zero.
  (d)   greater than 1.   (AQA, 2007)

2   Price elasticity of supply for games consoles is likely to be higher
  (a)   the higher the income of consumers.
  (b)   in the long term than in the short term.
  (c)   the slower the rate of change in technological progress.
  (d)   the less firms are able to switch resources from the production of other goods into the production of games consoles

3   The cross elasticity of demand between two products measures the extent to which a change in the:
  (a)   demand for one product affects the price of the other product.
  (b)   price of one product affects the demand for the other product.
  (c)   demand for one product affects the quantity sold of the other product.
  (d)   quantity sold of one product affects the demand for the other product.
                                                               (AQA, 2004)

4   Sony slash prices of Playstation 3

    Sony announced the cut in price of its new Playstation 3 by 20% as it seeks to boost sales against rivals Nintendo and Microsoft. The fall in price announced from its Tokyo Headquarters was partly in response to crucial delays in the launch that allowed rivals to get ahead and concerns over the price from consumers. The original price of around $600 was seen as uncompetitive in the rapidly changing console market.

    Sony hope that the price fall will see sales respond strongly in the months to come and that they can win back market share from their rivals. Hopefully, Sony will be able to recover some of the lost revenue from its consoles through increases in the demand for its games. Often game users are loyal to a manufacturer of consoles and buy the upgrades because the games they have already are usually compatible with the updated console.

    Source: adapted from © bbc.co.uk/news

  (a)   Sony is expecting a fall in revenue from sales of consoles following the price reduction. What can be concluded from this about the price elasticity of demand for its consoles?   (*4 marks*)
  (b)   If the cross price elasticity of demand for Playstation games in relation to Playstation consoles is −1.2, explain the likely effect on the demand for games as a result of the price cut. Use a supply and demand diagram to support your analysis   (*6 marks*)
  (c)   Discuss the likely effect on demand for both Playstation consoles and games if there were a decline in real incomes in their major markets such as the UK, USA and Japan.   (*15 marks*)

                                                               Transport data (UK)

5   **Extract A**

In recent years, traffic congestion in the UK has become an increasing problem. Rising incomes and changes to how we live have seen more and more people driving for a range of different activities and reasons. Out of town shopping, fears over child safety, the development of 'dormitory' towns where people live but work elsewhere are just a few of the reasons for the greater number of car journeys.

The government has been considering a range of different solutions to the problems caused by the rising demand for road space. At present, drivers do not pay directly to use roads (except for a few toll roads like the M6 toll road just north of Birmingham and a few toll bridges such as that which crosses the River Severn near Bristol). Extending the use of road pricing is very much under consideration although it is likely that the technology is still some way from being ready.

Motoring groups such as the AA and RAC complain that a solution needs to be found otherwise the country's roads will become increasingly gridlocked and damage the economy. However, in recent years, a number of new road programmes have been scrapped on environmental grounds and because campaigners have successfully argued that new roads simply create more traffic.

(a)   Using the data, compare changes in the amount of traffic
        from cars and taxis to the amount of motorways   (5 marks)

(b)   Using a supply and demand diagram, explain the likely effect
        of the data in the table showing the relative costs of train,
        bus and car travel on the demand for private car use.   (6 marks)

(c)   Use the concept of cross elasticity of demand to explain the
        likely relationship between demand for cars and the demand
        for bus journeys to school   (8 marks)

(d)   The short run supply curve for road space is vertical. Explain
        why this is likely to be the case.   (6 marks)

(e)   The government would like to ease congestion on the roads
        in the UK. Using supply and demand diagrams as
        appropriate, analyse and evaluate the policies that they could
        implement to bring about such an effect.   (25 marks)

                                                                               (AQA, 2007)

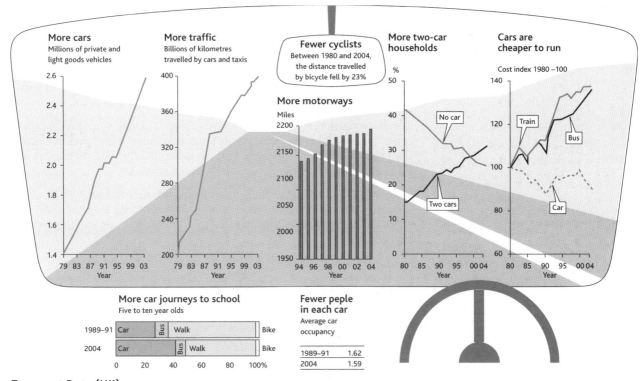

Transport Data (UK)
Source: The Times 31 January 2006

Market case studies

The main aim of this chapter is to apply the ideas seen in previous chapters to a range of real-world markets. Often exam questions focus on areas such as housing, the environment, agriculture and commodity markets in general as well as sport and leisure, transport and markets for manufactured products like televisions, cars or clothing. In this chapter we will look at some markets while providing a commentary on some of the things to look out for in examinations but also provoking you to think about how the ideas and concepts studied can be applied.

In addition you might start to consider how well markets work to solve the problems facing us in real life. You can evaluate the effectiveness of the market mechanism in allocating resources and perhaps hypothesise about the conditions necessary for a market to work effectively.

■ The housing market

The price of houses has risen quite steeply over the past ten years as supply has not been able to keep up with demand. In 2003 the Chancellor asked Kate Barker, a member of the Bank of England's Monetary Policy Committee, to look into the supply of UK housing. Among other things her report stated:

> I believe that continuing at the current rate of house building is not a realistic option, unless we are prepared to accept increasing problems of homelessness, declining affordability and social division, decline in public service delivery and increased costs of doing business in the UK – holding back our economic success.

In 2001, around 175,000 houses were built in the UK – the lowest level since the Second World War. And over the past 10 years the number of new homes built has been 12.5 per cent lower than in the previous decade (source: Kate Barker, Review of Housing Supply, *Delivering Stability: Securing our Future Housing Needs*, 2004. Available from www. barkerreview.org.uk).

The Barker report suggests that a further 70,000 houses need to be built each year over and above existing forecasts. Without additional housing the report says there is a threat to our macroeconomic stability and it will limit the ability of workers to move between regions.

It is likely that there are supply-side constraints as a market would normally be expected to respond to an increase in price by increasing supply as new suppliers are attracted into the market and existing firms expand:

■ Elasticity of supply is very low – as it takes time to build houses and therefore it is not possible simply to respond immediately to additional demand.

■ Government intervention in the market through planning controls limits the availability of building sites.

■ Antagonism from existing residents who worry about the increasing environmental cost of additional housing, pressure on the social infrastructure, especially in the south-east, where congestion is already an issue and schools and other amenities are over-subscribed.

Shortages in the factor markets as the UK has a lack of skilled building tradesmen.

Demand has tended to outstrip supply for a number of reasons:

Social and demographic trends, such as people choosing to live alone as well as people living longer.

Strong positive migration patterns as foreign workers come to the UK (this should help reduce the skilled labour constraint).

Continued economic growth in the UK has led to rising incomes and relatively low interest rates that have increased pressure on housing demand.

Houses are seen as an **investment good** that will continue to increase in price and price rises lead to increasing demand from those desperate to get onto the housing ladder.

From the points made above there are several concepts that could be considered and you would be advised to keep them in mind when considering the housing market:

The link with the demand for housing and income elasticity.

The relationship between interest rates that reflect the cost of repaying a mortgage (long-term loan) that is taken out to buy property) and the demand for houses.

That lower interest rates reflect the falling cost of a complementary product and as they are close complements we would expect the cross price elasticity of demand to be high and negative.

Renting is a substitute for buying but is often seen as an inferior good – this should suggest that demand for house ownership has high positive income elasticity of demand.

For substitute goods we would expect the cross price elasticity of demand to be positive.

The likely effects of a continuous programme of house building in already crowded areas on congestion, pressure on services and environmental degradation. In areas where green recreational land is scarce such a building programme is clearly not **sustainable**.

You might consider that there is both **market** and **government failure**. The market fails to increase supply in the short term and in the long term is unable to do so as government intervention through planning controls further restricts supply.

The rental market and government intervention

Fig. 6.2 shows the demand and supply of rented accommodation. Equilibrium occurs at a price of £300 per month where the quantity of rented accommodation demanded and supplied is 100 properties.

Assume that the government feels that the rents are too high and establishes a maximum rent (price ceiling) below the equilibrium at £120. Supply falls from 100 to 30, while demand increases from 100 to 200. There is a shortage as the demand exceeds the supply by 170 units. The maximum rent stops the price mechanism from automatically adjusting and may lead to:

1 Owners trying to evict tenants so that they can sell their properties as income from the renting market has fallen. If owners are unable to evict they may allow the properties to deteriorate in that they do not do repairs in the hope that tenants will leave.

2 Far fewer properties will be available for rent – 30 according to the diagram.

Figure 6.1 *A new housing development*

Key terms

Investment good: a product that will increase in value over time.

Sustainable: an activity carried out today that does not stop future generations maximising their welfare.

Market failure: where the market fails to produce what consumers require at the lowest possible cost.

Government failure: when government intervention to correct market failure does not improve the allocation of resources or leads to a worsening of the situation. The costs of government intervention may therefore exceed the benefits.

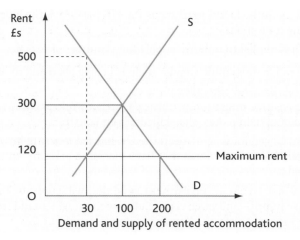

Figure 6.2 *Demand and supply of rented accommodation*

Activity

Stretch and challenge

1. To what extent is the market mechanism working with regard to allocating sufficient resources to house-building?

2. Identify policies that might prevent prices rising further and reducing affordability for new home owners.

3. With the aid of a diagram analyse whether the government should put a maximum price limit on housing to help affordability for first-time buyers.

3. A 'black market' – this is where some properties are available illegally above the minimum price. If all 30 properties were offered on the black market their rents would increase to £500. This is an example of the price system establishing equilibrium where demand and supply equate.

4. The policy is abandoned and the government give a subsidy to poor tenants who cannot afford the market rate to help them get accommodation. This will mean that more properties will be available as owners will receive the market rate. In effect this will move the supply curve to the right.

5. The government commission firms to build council or social housing so that more accommodation is available. In the diagram above this would shift the supply curve to the right so supply and demand were equal at a lower price.

Activity

1. Identify three factors that have influenced demand for housing.

2. Using a supply and demand diagram explain the likely effect of a reduction in house building on the equilibrium price of new homes.

3. The prices of houses have doubled in the past decade. Explain how we might have expected the house-builders, such as Barratt homes and George Wimpey, to react to this.

4. Explain the relationship between low interest rates and the demand for houses.

5. What conclusions can be drawn about the price elasticity of supply of new homes from the evidence given?

Agricultural markets

Agriculture has often been treated as a special case as the provision of food is a requirement for human welfare and shortages of supply lead to malnutrition and sickness. Economists have long accepted that the agricultural market is a special case as it suffers from particular problems that are not present in other markets:

In free markets agricultural prices fluctuate from year to year depending on the level of output affecting both the farmers' income and ability to make long-term plans.

Production in many parts of the world is still subject to unplanned variations due to factors beyond human control like pests, bad weather and natural disasters. In some cases this has led to the setting up of **buffer stocks** to ensure consistent supply and income to farmers. The authorities sell from the stock when harvests are poor and buy in stock when harvests are good. This prevents huge price increases in bad times and low farmers' incomes when harvests are good.

The operation of a type of buffer stock scheme can be seen in Fig. 6.3 where the supply of agricultural products for three separate years is shown as perfectly inelastic. Assuming that the authorities want to maintain the price of OP then the supply will need to be OQ. However, fluctuations in output – in a good year to OQ_1 will lead to a price fall to OP_2 and in a bad year to OQ_2 will lead to a price increase to OP_1. In a good year when OQ_1 is produced if the authorities purchase Q-Q_1 and store it, only OQ is released onto the market and the price remains at OP. In a bad year when supply falls to OQ_2 price would increase to OP_1 but if the authorities sell Q_2Q from their stock OQ will be on the market and the price will remain at OP in the market.

AQA Examiner's tip

- If you shift the demand curve the magnitude of the change in price and output will depend on the price elasticity of supply.
- If you shift the supply curve the magnitude of the change in price and output will depend on the price elasticity of demand

Key terms

Buffer stocks: an intervention system that aims to limit the fluctuations of the price of a commodity.

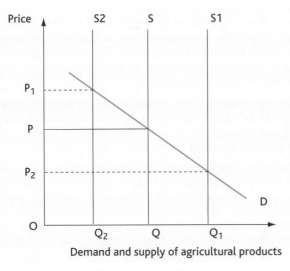

Figure 6.3 *Demand and supply of agricultural products*

While this seems a simple enough scheme there are several problems that require consideration:

- The problem of financing buffer stocks – who pays: producers, government or taxpayers.
- The difficulties involved in establishing target prices as consumers want a low price but producers will want a high price.
- The problems faced by buffer stocks as technology changes – substitutes are developed and demand patterns change, for example sugar.
- Problems of storage costs and perishability particularly if there are too many years of bumper harvests. Problems of inadequate supplies if there are too many years with a poor harvest.

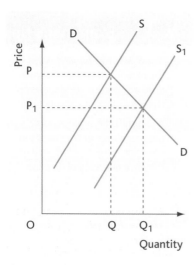

Figure 6.4

■ Activity

1. Define the term substitute and explain how an increase in the demand for bio-fuel has led to a derived demand for many agricultural commodities (read the text on agricultural commodities).

2. With the aid of a diagram show how the effect of an increase in the demand for bio-fuels will affect the price of corn.

3. Using your economic knowledge and the information from the table explain what you understand by 'income elasticity of demand has been calculated as 0.03 and price elasticity of demand at (−)1.17'.

The agricultural market displays a number of features not present in other markets:

■ There is a huge disparity in the methods of production used, ranging from subsistence agriculture in sub-Saharan Africa to huge commercial farms in the US.

■ Both the demand and the supply curve of arable agricultural products tend to be extremely inelastic and a small change in output or demand is sufficient to trigger a large change in price, possibly leading to resource misallocation. In Fig. 6.4, the small increase in supply from OQ to OQ_1 leads to a large fall in price from OP to OP_1. The resulting price signal would suggest to the farmer that resources should be reallocated and less should be planted the following year. In such a case the price system may result in resource misallocation as the relatively small change has been magnified out of all proportion by the relative elasticities of demand and supply.

■ In some parts of the world the farming community has been able to exercise influence over politicians and persuade them that the solution to the agricultural problem is subsidies that will ensure sufficient food production and reduce the potential instability of farmers' incomes. Often domestic firms are protected from foreign competition, which effectively imposes a price floor on agricultural products.

■ This has led to over-production especially in Europe where, to remove the problem of large surpluses the excess has been sold onto the world market, which depresses the price and distorts the market for those farmers in developing countries who do not benefit from tariffs and find it more difficult to compete.

■ Recently some sectors of the farming industry have benefited from the increasing demand for agricultural products that can be used to manufacture bio-fuels that can be substituted for petroleum products such as gasoline or diesel.

The long-term problem in most developed economies is that the income elasticity of demand for many agricultural products is very low. As incomes increase demand for agricultural goods rises less than proportionately and increases in productivity together with government subsidies are likely to increase supply, depressing prices and profits and resources will need to move out of agriculture. This poses problems for the authorities who do not want a depressed agricultural sector and for environmental reasons do not want agricultural land to become industrialised, or for a rural way of life to be destroyed.

■ **Agricultural commodities**

Analysts agree that demand has increased for many agricultural commodities such as corn, sugar, palm oil, rape seed oil, coconut oil and soybean oil because the need for bio-fuels as a substitute for fossil fuels has increased. Demand will get stronger from the emerging countries such as India and China with growing populations placing a strain on existing grain reserves. Furthermore, the emergence of a middle class in these countries is creating more demand for commodities associated with a higher standard of living, such as meat and dairy products. The Organisation for Economic Co-operation and Development predicts beef consumption in developing countries will increase by a third by 2015 as incomes rise because income elasticity of demand has been calculated at 0.03 and price elasticity of demand at (−)1.17.

Supply is constrained as land available for farming is decreasing worldwide, due to issues such as urbanisation and desertification. Many agricultural commodities are experiencing record low stocks. Demand for wheat, for example, has exceeded production in six of the past seven years and reserves are extremely low.

Source: adapted from Paul Farrow, 'Corn: The pick of the investment crop', *The Daily Telegraph*, 25 July 2007.

Poverty

The World Trade Organisation announced that its 147 members had approved proposals that it claims will help reduce poverty in the developing world and boost the global economy by an estimated $500bn.

If future meetings are successful, this would potentially spell the end for the £1.8bn worth of annual subsidies handed out to European Union farmers and change the face of Western agriculture.

Supachai Panitchpakdi of the WTO said: 'For the first time, member governments have agreed to abolish all forms of agricultural export subsidies. They have agreed to substantial reductions in trade-distorting domestic support in agriculture.'

India, one of the dissenting nations at Cancun, welcomed yesterday's decision. Its trade minister, Kamal Nath, said: 'Developed countries have recognised that agricultural trade with a heavy subsidy component is not free trade.'

The UK National Farmers' Union welcomed the decision. But France and Switzerland, whose agriculture sectors are heavily subsidised, warned that their economies could be damaged by these reforms.

The oil market

The oil market is an international market where some of the suppliers are organised in a cartel that is known by the acronym OPEC – the Organisation of the Petroleum Exporting Countries. The principal aim of the organisation is 'to coordinate and unify the petroleum policies of member countries and ensure the stabilization of oil markets in order to secure an efficient, economic and regular supply of petroleum to consumers, a steady income to producers and a fair return on capital to those investing in the petroleum industry'. OPEC nations account for two-thirds of the world's oil reserves and 41.7 per cent of the world's oil production, affording them considerable control over the global market.

OPEC, by reducing the supply of oil, can cause the price of crude oil to increase and this leads to an increase in the price of petrol diesel and domestic fuels. Increases in the price of oil increase the **inflationary pressure** in the economy as firms try to pass increased costs and prices onto consumers. Increased growth in India and China has increased the demand for oil and demand in the developed world remains strong. The UK government imposes extremely heavy taxation on both petrol and diesel.

Activity

1. Define the term subsidy (read the text on poverty).

2. With the aid of a diagram explain how a subsidy will affect the price and how this is dependent on the price elasticity of demand for the product.

3. Explain what the writer means by 'trade-distorting domestic support in agriculture'.

4. Using diagrams to illustrate your answer explain why France and Switzerland are concerned that abandonment of subsidies will damage their economies while the UK National Farmers Union has welcomed the decision.

Key terms

Inflationary pressure: occurrences that are likely to lead to increased prices.

Activity

Crude oil

In 1998, the price of crude oil fell dramatically, reaching a low of $10 a barrel in 1999. The low price caused OPEC to intervene in the market in order to stabilise the price of oil at a higher price. To achieve this, OPEC members agreed to reduce production. Their target price range was between $20 and $30 a barrel. However, because of changing demand and supply conditions, and because of OPEC's reduced market share, OPEC's intervention became less successful in the first decade of the 21st century.

The factors that changed the conditions of demand included speculation, and the effect of China's rapid industrialisation and economic growth. On the supply side, virtually all OPEC members except Saudi Arabia were already producing close to full capacity. In the past, Saudi Arabia had successfully stabilised oil prices by maintaining a large buffer of spare production capacity. This meant the Saudis could quickly increase supply to cool the price of oil whenever there was a sudden surge in demand. However, years of under-investment in new drilling rigs and oil refining capacity have almost wiped out this buffer. Now, in 2005, it is much more difficult to increase supply to meet a sudden increase in demand. Although Saudi Arabia might once again wish to stabilise the price of oil, for example between $55 and $65 a barrel, the changed conditions of demand and supply may make this impossible.

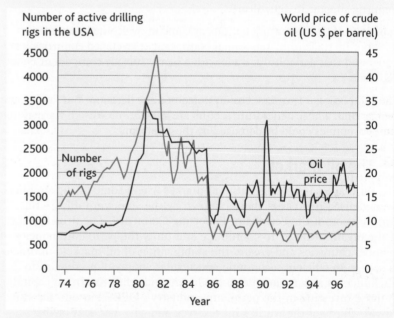

Figure 6.5 *Number of rigs digging for oil*

1. Using the information given above, compare the price of crude oil and the number of active drilling rigs in the USA over the period from 1974 to 1997.

2. Using at least one demand and supply diagram and the information above, explain how Saudi Arabia might try to stabilise the world price of oil between $55 and $65 a barrel.

3. Do you agree that the price of oil should be determined by free market forces rather than through the intervention of governments or organisations such as OPEC? Justify your answer.

Adapted from AQA June 2006 ECN 1/2

The leisure market

One of the interesting features of the leisure market is that a number of popular leisure activities, for example football matches, concerts, plays and films, are held in venues where the number of seats is limited. In Fig. 6.6 this is shown with a perfectly inelastic supply curve at, say, 20,000 seats. The demand for the event shows an equilibrium price of £50 a ticket. Should the organisers feel, as they may in the case of a football match that this is too expensive for their core, genuine supporters they may reduce the price to £30 a ticket. This effectively imposes a price ceiling at which the club is prepared to sell the tickets. In terms of the diagram, demand has now increased to 24,000 tickets and outstrips the available supply by 4,000 tickets. A number of outcomes may result from this action:

- First come, first served – if the match is popular there are likely to be long queues of fans outside the grounds hoping to get a ticket before they are all sold out. The price system is unable to perform its rationing function as the price is unable to equate supply and demand.

- Rationing – the club may *ration* the available tickets to its genuine supporters. This may be difficult as for this type of rationing to work the club will need some technique to identify 'genuine supporters'.

- A 'black market' in tickets where 'touts' have managed to obtain tickets, possibly by queuing or buying them from 'genuine supporters', and are selling them above the price fixed by the club. It is an example of the price system re-establishing an equilibrium where demand and supply are again equal.

The computer games market

The computer games market is made up of a few firms that manufacture the hardware (consoles), and firms that manufacture the software, the games manufacturers. Information from the Department of Trade and Industry shows that over an eight-year period over 25 million dedicated gaming devices were sold in the UK. There are three major games console manufacturers – Nintendo, Sony and Microsoft – who fight for market share. As the software tends to be dedicated to a particular console, buyers are likely to become brand loyal once a console is purchased.

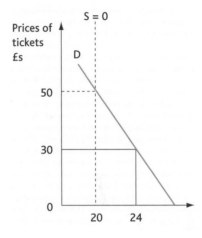

AQA Examiner's tip

Always remember that most places – buildings, pitches, stadiums and even beaches – have an inelastic supply curve. Note that the question requires you to interpret graphical data – this is a skill that you need to practise.

Figure 6.6 *Demand and supply of tickets (000's)*

Activity

Extract A

Video-game consoles will be scarce and lines could be long upon next week's North American launch of Microsoft Corp.'s Xbox 360 – with some retailers warning that they won't even have enough at first to fill all the orders placed by customers months ago.

Among gaming enthusiasts, the situation has fuelled a conspiracy theory: Is Microsoft purposefully holding back on shipments, trying to create an artificial appearance of extraordinary demand? A spokesman from Microsoft told analysts that the worldwide Xbox 360 supply should catch up to demand sometime in the first half of next year.

Sid Shuman, producer for GamePro a video-game site, said he is inclined to believe Microsoft when it says it isn't purposefully creating shortages. The buzz factor aside, the company risks losing sales if it's not able to meet demand for an extended period of time.

Source: from Todd Bishop, 'Questions surround Xbox 360 shortage', *Seattle Post*, 18 November 2005.

Extract B

Forget video game violence, Sony Corp.'s new PlayStation 3 delivered a dose of real-world insanity yesterday as it hit retail shelves across the country – and sold out moments later. Low supply led to long lines and short tempers outside retail outlets.

Sony delivered 400,000 units of the PS3 to the United States for the launch and said it would ship 2 million units worldwide this year.

The low supply, caused by a component shortage, has sparked a demand so high that the $500 and $600 devices were selling for thousands of dollars on the online sites and the ability to make a quick $2,000 or more by selling PlayStations on the Internet caused profiteers to join gaming enthusiasts in the long lines and tent cities that popped up outside stores this week.

Source: adapted from Mike Musgrove, 'Video game consoles debut sparks violence', Washington Post, 18 November 2006.

1 With the aid of a diagram explain the effect on the market of Microsoft and Sony holding back shipments of video games consoles.

2 'Profiteers are depriving genuine gamers of a chance of obtaining consoles and this amounts to resource misallocation.' How far do you agree with this statement?

3 Analyse why the companies might take this approach and the possible results of this strategy.

■ Key terms

Negative externalities: costs imposed on a third party not involved with the consumption or production of the good.

In some markets the authorities intervene in order to restrict the consumption of the products to people over a certain age, for example, alcohol and tobacco. These products have what are called **negative externalities** in that consumption of them may impose a cost on society. For example, people who drink too much may become violent and smokers may contract lung cancer and their treatment is paid for by society. Apart from attempting to stop consumption by young people, who are not considered sufficiently mature to control their actions or realise the potential dangers to their health, government heavily tax the products to dissuade even mature consumers. While both video games and films are rated and juveniles can be prevented from cinema entry, control over watching or playing is less secure when games are purchased and films are released as DVDs. The problem is illustrated in the extracts below:

■ Activity

Extract A

The growth of electronic games has not been without controversy, however, and the subset of games that feature violence, gore, and antisocial behaviour has raised concern among parents, educators, child advocates, medical professionals, and policy makers.

Children picking up games meant for older audiences are not the fault of the game makers nor the stores that sell these games, but rather the responsibility of the parents who don't monitor their children's playing habits.

Source: adapted from David Walsh, 'Video game violence and public policy', http://culturalpolicy.uchicago.edu/conf2001/papes/walsh.html.

Extract B

Cartoonish and fantasy violence is often perceived (incorrectly) by parents and public policy makers as safe even for children. However, experimental studies with college students have consistently found increased aggression after exposure to clearly unrealistic and fantasy violent video games. Indeed, at least one recent study found significant increases in aggression by college students after playing E-rated (suitable for everyone) violent video games.

Source: Craig A. Anderson, 'Violent video games: Myths, facts, and unanswered questions', Psychological Science Agenda: Science Briefs, 16(5), pp1–3.

1 With the aid of a diagram examine the effect of an increase in the level of tax imposed on video game manufacturers.

2 Explain why an economist might argue that violent video games create negative externalities.

Market failure: the economics of the environment

The environment is an example of market failure as external costs have been created by the actions of both individuals and firms, which have created pollution and threaten to damage the planet.

Governments have used a number of techniques to reduce market failure:

- Taxes that decrease the supply and increase the price to take into account the negative externality created. In practice, the external cost is difficult to measure and it is doubtful whether the government would get the right level of tax. Also, the price elasticity of demand will affect the change in quantity and price.

- Regulations – governments have imposed regulations through direct controls, for example catalytic converters to ensure that emissions of pollutants are less than certain specified amounts. The problem with direct controls is that they are inefficient as they treat all situations in the same way, bureaucratic in that they are slow to change and expensive in that they have to be policed.

- Subsidies – may be granted to activities that reduce pollution and environmental damage. This would ensure a higher level of consumption than through the free market.

- Tradable permits – this allows an industry a certain level of maximum emissions. The firms in the industry are sold permits to pollute by the authorities but are informed that the total number of permits issued to the industry and therefore the allowed levels of pollution will be reduced each year. This is a market-based solution in that firms are allowed to trade permits and provided the authorities do not over-issue permits this approach may be successful. Opponents of tradable permits argue that by providing permits, rather than outlawing pollution above some amount, the government is condoning pollution.

- Property rights – these concern those who own property, and are poorly defined in terms of environmental resources – air, land, rivers, sea. If property rights were defined then those who imposed external costs would have to pay compensation. If compensation could be claimed the externality would be internalised.

French 'guzzler tax' under fire

France is coming under intense pressure from overseas car makers hoping to block government plans to introduce a 'sin tax' of up to £2,300 on gas-guzzling SUV 4×4s (Sports Utility Vehicle four-wheel drive) and big luxury cars from January 2005.

AQA **Examiner's tip**

Governments often impose taxes on harmful activities, i.e. those with negative externalities, while subsidising beneficial activities, i.e. those with positive externalities.

Prime Minister Jean-Pierre Raffarin is due to set out details on Thursday of the pioneering anti-pollution scheme that has been cheered by many in France as a blow against drivers who barge their way through urban traffic on board two-tonne off-road vehicles. Under the plan, buyers of low-polluting cars will benefit from a £550 purchase tax reduction. Buyers of the dirtiest vehicles, big 4×4s and the largest saloons, will finance the reductions with the penalty tax, reducing the affordability of 4×4s, while leaving no cost to the state. Half of all vehicles, in the middle polluting range, will not be affected and the measure will apply only to new vehicles.

The scheme, which has run into opposition from motoring organisations, comes after a warning from Paris city council earlier this month that it wants to ban big 4×4s from the capital as a menace to safety and the environment. Denis Baupin, a deputy mayor and Green Party official, said that the big vehicles, which emit up to four times the carbon dioxide and particles of average cars, should have no rights to use the city's streets.

The French government's approach to 4×4s was endorsed last weekend by Professor David Begg, the British government's most senior adviser on transport. He suggested higher car tax and congestion charges for drivers of what he described as irresponsible and dangerous vehicles with high social costs.

The French plan has prompted quiet satisfaction from Renault and Peugeot-Citroen, France's two big manufacturers. The reason, industry sources say, is that they make no models that would qualify for the highest penalty, and only a few people-carriers that would incur a £1,030 tax.

The big 4×4s and saloons account for 17.3 per cent of the French car market, and there has been a 16 per cent increase in sales since last year. Taking Britain and France together, they account for 6 per cent of new private vehicle sales. As well as being more polluting, they are up to three times more likely than small cars to kill pedestrians because of their extra bulk and weight. They are mainly made by American, British, Japanese and German manufacturers. The foreign makers are likely to claim that the proposed law breaches EU rules on free trade by being discriminatory. France lost a similar legal challenge brought by foreign brewers two years ago after it tried to tax high-alcohol beer. No French brewers produced such beer.

Source: adapted from an article by Charles Bremner, *The Times*, 29 June 2004.

Activity

Read the extract 'French "guzzler tax" under fire' and look at the SUV sales figures.

1. Define the term 'social costs'.

2. Use the concept of elasticity of demand to explain why the 'affordability' of 4×4s is likely to be an important influence on the sales figures shown in Fig. 6.5.

3. Paris city council is planning to ban 4×4s whilst the French government is planning to tax them more heavily. Explain the likely economic effects of the two policies.

4. Should governments leave car prices to market forces, or actively intervene to influence the demand for and supply of cars that may be damaging the environment? Justify your answer.

Adapted from ECN 3 Question 2, January 2006

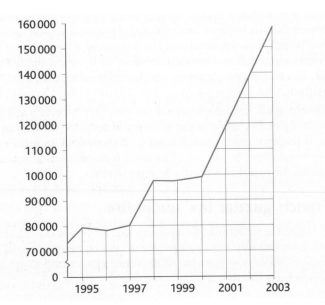

Figure 6.7 *SUV sales figures, UK*

7 Production and efficiency

Key terms

Specialisation: the production of a limited range of goods by an individual factor of production or firm or country.

Division of labour: breaking the production process down into a sequence of tasks, with workers assigned to particular tasks.

This chapter contains some principles that were first established over two hundred years ago but which are keenly relevant today. You will discover why, in a modern economy, it is preferable to have production based on the specialisation of individuals and firms rather than each attempting to be a 'jack-of-all-trades'. Whilst many small firms continue to be successful, there are a number of cost-reducing benefits to firms of increasing their scale of production, which may help to explain why many markets seem to be dominated by large, powerful, often multinational firms.

Specialisation, the division of labour and exchange

Specialisation involves an individual person, firm or country, producing a limited range of goods or services. These may then be exchanged for the output of other individuals, firms or countries. When specialisation occurs between nations, a country like China, for example, can produce textiles and trade those for computer software developed in the USA. Specialisation also occurs within economies. In the UK, the 'square mile' of the City of London specialises in financial services.

Specialisation at the level of the individual is known as the **division of labour**. Adam Smith, in his famous book *The Wealth of Nations* (1776), describes the division of labour between workers in a pin factory:

> One man draws out the wire, another straightens it, a third cuts it, a fourth points, a fifth grinds it at the top for receiving the head; to make the head requires two or three distinct operations; to put it on is a peculiar business, to whiten the pins is another; it is even a trade by itself to put them into the paper.

He asserted that one worker might be able to make 20 pins per day if he were to complete all the processes alone, whilst ten workers specialising in the various tasks could hope to make 48,000 pins!

Benefits of the division of labour

- *Increased aptitude* Repetition of tasks leads to them being done more expertly, for example as with typing.
- *Time saving* There is likely to be less time spent switching between different tasks. Less time may also need to be devoted to training.
- *Working to one's natural strengths* Division of labour allows people to do what they are relatively best at, for example some people are physically strong whilst others have strong communication skills. Division of labour allows people to focus upon those activities they are best suited to.
- *Use of capital equipment* As tasks are subdivided, it becomes worthwhile to use machinery, saving further effort. In fruit juice production, for example, if production only amounts to a few hundred cartons, then specialist bottling equipment may not be justified; but if a firm is producing many thousands of cartons, then it becomes worthwhile to use specialist machines for this.

Figure 7.1 *Adam Smith*

Specialisation has enabled people to enjoy a standard of living that would be impossible to achieve through self-sufficiency. Specialisation, however, requires exchange. Workers can only specialise in financial services, for instance, if they know they will be able to exchange their services for other goods and services such as food and housing.

Exchange for most of history has relied upon a system of barter, that is, exchanging goods and services for other goods or services. But barter has many disadvantages, which would limit the development of a modern, sophisticated economy. It was the development of money that enabled trade and specialisation to transform economies into what we are used to today.

■ Production, productivity and productive efficiency

Production

Production converts inputs, or the services of factors of production such as capital and labour, into final output. Production refers to the total output of goods and services produced within a market. Production is also the means by which consumer wants are satisfied.

Productivity

When economists talk about productivity they are usually referring to how productive labour is. But productivity is also about other inputs into production. So, for example, a company could increase productivity by investing in new capital machinery that embodies the latest technological progress, and that reduces the number of workers required to produce the same amount of output. The government aims to improve labour and capital productivity in the UK economy.

Measuring productivity

Labour productivity measures output per worker, or output per hour worked.

$$\text{Labour productivity} = \frac{\text{Total output per time period}}{\text{Number of units of labour}}$$

Capital productivity measures the output per unit of capital. Total factor productivity is the average productivity of all factors of production (i.e. the physical factors of production – capital equipment, land and labour), and is measured by dividing total output by the total amount of inputs used.

The advantages of higher productivity

Higher productivity can provide the economy with a number of advantages over time.

- *Lower average costs* Improvements in labour and capital productivity allow businesses to produce output at a lower average cost. These cost savings might be passed onto consumers in the form of lower prices, encouraging an expansion of demand, higher output and possibly an increase in employment.

- *Improved competitiveness in international markets* Productivity growth and lower unit costs are key determinants of how competitive UK firms are in domestic and overseas markets. From improved productivity, businesses can develop a competitive advantage in markets where there is strong price competition from overseas suppliers.

- *Higher profits* Efficiency gains leading to increased productivity are a source of greater profits for firms, which might be re-invested to support further growth of the business.

- *Higher real wages* Over time there is a positive relationship between improvements in labour productivity and the real wages paid to labour as a factor of production. Firms are better able, and arguably more willing, to afford higher wages when their labour force increases its efficiency.

- *Growth of the economy* The capacity of our economy to produce goods and services depends on the stock of factors of production available (i.e. the active labour supply, the stock of capital inputs and natural resources) plus the productivity of those factors. If we can raise the rate of growth of productivity this will lead to an outward shift of the PPB. However, rising productivity will lead to unemployment if the rate of growth of total demand in the economy is less than the rate of productivity growth.

Industries with the most up-to-date capital machinery, together with well-honed managerial skills and highly qualified and trained workforces tend to achieve much higher levels of productivity. Studies have revealed that the availability of large production plants and good industrial relations are also crucial in achieving improvements in output per person employed.

The strength of demand also affects productivity. When demand is high and production plants are running close to full capacity, then output per worker employed is likely to be rising because factors of production including labour and capital are being used to their full extent. Conversely, during a recession or a slowdown in demand, the utilisation of labour and capital falls. Productivity growth often slows down during a period of weak demand and falling output.

■ Case study

Latest productivity research – 'It's not just what you do, it's how you do it'

A new report 'Catching up with the Continent', an extensive study comparing productivity in manufacturing across France, Germany and the UK, published today by the Engineering Employers' Federation (EEF), the manufacturers' organisation, provides further substantial evidence that investing across the board in new technology, skills and innovation holds the key to improving company performance.

Based on a survey of 600 senior manufacturing managers in the three countries, the report shows that the companies in all three countries that invested strongly in all two areas achieved substantially higher rates of growth in productivity, which led to higher profitability.

However, the survey also showed that, in the UK, the difference in performance between our best performing companies and the rest of the sample was smaller than in the other two countries. This suggests that other factors, including the need to make more effective use of modern working practices such as lean manufacturing and high-performance working also need to be addressed if the UK is to succeed in closing the productivity gap with its competitors.

Commenting on the report, EEF Chief Economist Stephen Radley said: 'The survey proves that investing across the board in capital equipment, skills and innovation holds the key to success. However, even this may not be enough if companies are not making the best use of modern working practices.'

Source: adapted from www.eef.org.uk, 21 June 2004

Case study

Comparing UK and international productivity

UK productivity has traditionally lagged behind other major industrial countries. However, there is recent evidence that the UK is tentatively narrowing the gap to many of these other countries, as highlighted in Fig. 7.2.

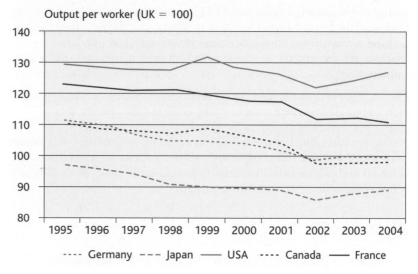

Figure 7.2 *International comparisons of productivity*

Source: **HM Treasury**

Based on the measure of output per worker, productivity in the UK since 1995 appears to have narrowed the gap between France, Germany and Japan, though French output per worker remains 11 per cent greater than in the UK and the USA seems to be widening the gap in recent times, to over 25 per cent. Strong relative productivity is likely to lead to improved competitiveness and stronger economic growth in those countries that have higher levels of productivity than the UK.

Productive efficiency

Productive efficiency is achieved when a firm's output is produced at minimum average total cost (ATC), that is, when a firm is exploiting the available economies of scale (see below). Productive efficiency exists when producers minimise the wastage of resources in their production processes. For the firm shown in Fig. 7.3, Q_1 is the output at which average total cost of production is minimised, and is therefore the point of maximum productive efficiency.

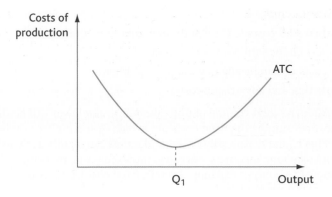

Figure 7.3 *Illustrating productive efficiency*

Efficiency and the production possibility boundary

Productive efficiency can also be illustrated using a model introduced earlier – the production possibility boundary (PPB), as shown in Fig. 7.4. Assuming a simple, two-product economy, point *X* implies there are unused resources. Increasing employment of all factors of production leads to point *Y*, at which it is not possible to produce more, given the current stock of factors of production. Thus point *Y*, or indeed any point on the PPB, is where productive efficiency is maximised.

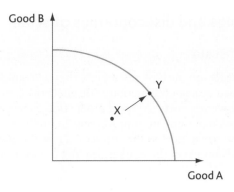

Figure 7.4 *A PPB to illustrate productive efficiency*

■ Costs of production

When entrepreneurs combine the factors of production to produce output there will inevitably be costs involved. Here we will consider the private costs to firms.

Costs are those expenses faced by a business when producing a good or service for a market. Every business faces costs – these must be recouped if a business is to make a profit from its activities. A firm will have fixed and variable costs of production. A firm's total costs are made up of these **fixed costs** and **variable costs.**

Fixed costs

These costs relate to the fixed factors of production and do not vary directly with the level of output. Examples of fixed costs include:

■ rent on buildings and business rates

■ the depreciation in the value of capital equipment due to age

■ Activity

1 Explain the difference between production and productivity.

2 With the aid of a suitable diagram, explain what is meant by productive efficiency.

3 Explain the effect that increased productivity will have on the UK economy, analysed with a PPB diagram.

4 To what extent will increased division of labour boost productivity?

■ Links

Costs to other members of society that firms do not consider when producing their output, such as pollution, are examined in greater detail in Chapter 8.

■ Key terms

Fixed costs: costs of production that do not vary as output changes.

Variable costs: costs of production that vary with output.

- insurance charges
- salaried staff costs (e.g. for staff on permanent contracts)
- interest charges on borrowed money
- the costs of purchasing new capital equipment
- marketing and advertising costs.

The greater the total volume of units produced, the lower will be the fixed cost per unit as the fixed costs are spread over a higher number of units. This is one reason why mass production can significantly reduce the unit costs for consumers – because the fixed costs are being reduced continuously as output expands. Average fixed cost (AFC) is the fixed cost per unit of output produced.

Variable costs

Variable costs vary directly with output; that is, as production rises, a firm will face higher total variable costs because it needs to purchase extra resources to achieve an expansion of supply. Examples of variable costs for a business include the costs of raw materials, labour costs and consumables. Average variable cost (AVC) is the variable cost per unit of output produced.

Total costs

Total cost (TC), logically equals fixed cost (FC) plus variable cost (VC). Average total cost (ATC) is the cost per unit of output produced.

💡 Economies and diseconomies of scale

Economies of scale

Economies of scale are the cost advantages that a business can exploit by expanding their scale of production. The effect of economies of scale is to reduce the average costs (ATC) of production as output increases. These lower costs represent an improvement in productive efficiency and may be passed to consumers in lower prices. They also give a business a competitive advantage in the market, leading to lower prices and/or higher profits.

There are many different types of economy of scale. Depending on the particular characteristics of an industry or market, some are more important than others. They rarely come from one single source. Why, for example, are the prices of consumer electronics such as high-performance personal computers, digital cameras and MP3 players falling all the time? The answer is that economies of scale have been exploited bringing down unit costs of production and eventually feeding through to lower prices for consumers.

Internal economies of scale

Internal economies of scale arise from the growth of the firm itself. Examples include:

1 *Technical economies of scale*
- Large-scale businesses can afford to invest in expensive, specialist capital machinery. For example, a national newspaper can invest in large-scale printing presses that increase productivity and reduce unit costs. It would not, however, be viable or cost-efficient for the producers of a church newsletter to buy this technology.

- Specialisation of the workforce in larger firms occurs by splitting complex production processes into separate tasks to boost productivity, for example the division of labour in mass production of cars.

- The law of increased dimensions. This is linked to the cubic law where doubling the height and width of a tanker or building leads to a more than proportionate increase in the cubic capacity. This is an important economy of scale in distribution and transport industries as well as in travel and leisure.

2 *Marketing economies of scale* A large firm can spread its advertising and marketing budget over a large output.

3 *Managerial economies of scale* This is a form of division of labour. For example, large law firms can justify having specialist senior managers in particular disciplines such as company law and intellectual property. Better management and investment in human resources raises productivity and reduces unit costs.

4 *Financial economies of scale* Larger firms are usually rated by banks to be more 'credit worthy' and are given access to credit facilities with more favourable rates of borrowing. Conversely, smaller firms often face higher rates of interest on their overdrafts and loans, being judged more 'risky'. Businesses quoted on the stock market can normally raise extra financial capital more cheaply through the issue of shares. In addition, if the firm has strong buying power, it can purchase its raw materials in bulk at negotiated discounted prices – for example the ability of the electricity generators to secure lower prices when negotiating coal and gas supply contracts. Major supermarkets also have significant power when purchasing supplies from farmers and wine growers.

5 *Network economies of scale* Some networks and services have huge potential for economies of scale. As they are more widely used, or adopted, they become more valuable to the business that provides them. Good examples are the expansion of a common language and a common currency. Network economies of scale can be found in areas such as online auctions and air transport networks. Network economies can be explained by saying that the extra cost of adding one more user to the network is close to zero, but the resulting benefits may be huge because each new user to the network can then interact and trade with all of the existing members or parts of the network. The rapid expansion of e-commerce is a very good example of the exploitation of network economies of scale.

External economies of scale

External economies of scale occur outside of a firm, but within an industry. Thus, when an industry's scope of operations expand due to, for example, the creation of a better transportation network that might lead to cost reductions for a company working within that industry, external economies of scale are achieved. The development of research and development facilities in universities that several local businesses can benefit from lead to external economies of scale. The relocation of component suppliers and other support businesses close to the main centre of manufacturing can also lead to an external cost saving.

Diseconomies of scale

A firm may eventually experience a rise in average costs caused by **diseconomies of scale**. Potential diseconomies of scale may arise from:

■ **Key terms**

Diseconomies of scale: where an increase in the scale of production leads to increases in average total costs for firms.

1 *Control* Monitoring the productivity and the quality of output from thousands of employees in big corporations is difficult and costly.

2 *Coordination* It can be difficult to coordinate complicated production processes across several plants in different locations and different countries. Achieving efficient flows of information in large businesses is expensive, as is the cost of managing supply contracts with hundreds of different suppliers at different points in an industry's supply chain.

3 *Cooperation* Workers in large firms may feel a sense of alienation and subsequent loss of motivation. If they do not consider themselves to be an integral part of the business, their productivity may fall leading to wastage of factor inputs and higher costs.

Avoiding diseconomies of scale

■ Developments in human resource management (HRM) are an attempt to avoid diseconomies of scale. HRM describes improvements to recruitment procedures, training, promotion, retention and support of staff. This is especially important to a business when the skilled workers it needs are in short supply. Recruitment and retention of the most productive and effective employees makes a sizeable difference to a firm's performance.

■ Similarly, performance-related pay schemes can provide incentives for the workforce, leading to an improvement in motivation.

■ Companies are increasingly out-sourcing their manufacturing and distribution operations as they seek to supply growing markets. Out-sourcing to specialist firms may overcome problems of control and coordination.

Illustrating economies and diseconomies of scale – the average cost curve

Fig. 7.5 shows what might happen to the average costs of production as a business expands from one scale of production to another. As we move from Q_1 to Q_2 to Q_3, so the scale of production is increasing. From Q_1 to Q_2, the firm is clearly benefiting from one or more economies of scale and Q_2 is where average costs are minimised, that is, the output at which the firm is productively efficient. From Q_2 to Q_3, average costs are rising, that is, the firm is suffering diseconomies of scale.

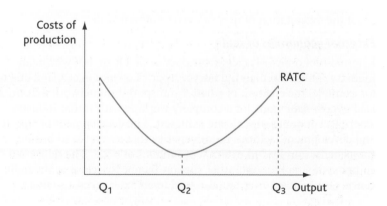

Figure 7.5 *Economies and diseconomies of scale*

■ Activity

Table 7.1

Units of labour	Units of capital	Quantity produced	Cost per unit of output (£)?
5	7	10	
6	8	18	
7	9	25	
8	10	32	
9	11	35	
10	12	37	

The table above shows the output of a firm given different levels of factor inputs. Assuming labour costs are £100 per unit and capital costs are £1,000 per unit:

1 Complete the final column of the table.

2 Over what output range does the firm begin to experience diseconomies of scale?

3 Assume the data relate to a manufacturer of home computers. Explain two possible economies of scale that might be available to the firm.

4 Discuss the view that diseconomies of scale are unavoidable as firms continue to expand their output.

■ Competition and monopoly

Economists generally accept that a high level of **competition** is necessary for markets to function well. An extremely competitive market situation is referred to as 'perfect competition'. Some of the key arguments in favour of competitive markets are as follows.

1 A high level of competition will lead to productive efficiency, that is, with goods and services produced at the minimum possible cost per unit. Any firm that cannot achieve this will find its market share competed away by other firms with lower costs, thus able to charge lower prices for an identical product.

2 A high level of competition will be more likely to ensure that firms produce precisely what consumers want, that is, there will be consumer sovereignty. Indeed, any firm that does not produce what consumers want will not survive for long, since there will be many other firms producing the goods and services valued most highly by consumers.

Whilst it may be argued that, through the development of the internet, some markets in modern economies have moved closer to 'perfect competition' as consumers and firms alike are more able to compare prices and shop around, many markets do not have a high level of competition, which causes markets to fail. There are some reasons why we might expect certain markets not to be highly competitive.

■ Economies of scale mean that as a firm expands its output, the cost of producing a unit of output falls. Indeed, there are considerable economies of scale to exploit in several industries, meaning firms have to be large to reap the full benefits. Furthermore, in some

■ Key terms

Competition: a market situation in which there are a large number of buyers and sellers.

Key terms

Monopoly: a market structure dominated by a single seller of a good.

Activity

Stretch and challenge

Evaluate the view that a high level of competition in a market is always in the best interests of the consumer.

industries this may mean that there is only room for a small number of firms or even just one firm (known as a **monopoly**) to exist.

■ The existence of the profit motive provides an incentive for firms to compete away other firms in the market, legally or otherwise. Furthermore, profits generated from being able to exploit economies of scale could be invested in research and development which may allow a dominant firm to provide new goods and services that consumers prefer over those of rival firms, further eliminating competition.

☑ *After completing this chapter you should:*

■ be able to define, and explain the benefits of, specialisation and division of labour

■ be able to define and explain production and productivity

■ be able to define, explain and illustrate productive efficiency

■ be able to define and give examples of economies and diseconomies of scale and assess their implications for the growth of firms and the structure of markets.

 Examination-style questions

1   To benefit from specialisation it is necessary
     (a)   to have an effective means of exchanging goods and services
     (b)   for labour productivity to be high
     (c)   for the production possibility boundary of the economy to be moving outwards over time
     (d)   for significant economies of scale to be gained in all industries.
                                                                        (AQA, 2006)

2   One reason why specialisation raises labour productivity is because
     (a)   specialisation shifts the production possibility boundary to the left
     (b)   labour replaces capital to produce goods and services
     (c)   specialisation allows an economy to produce on its production possibility boundary
     (d)   the division of labour makes it cost-effective to provide workers with specialist equipment.

3   Which of the following is a measure of productivity?
     (a)   the amount produced
     (b)   the quantity of capital employed divided by its price
     (c)   output divided by employment
     (d)   the percentage increase in production.
                                                                        (AQA, 2005)

8   Market failures

Markets often function very well, particularly in the provision of most private goods. However, there are some situations in which the free market fails to allocate resources efficiently or equitably. For an optimum allocation of resources, prices must reflect the full costs and benefits associated with market transactions, and not be open to the undue influence of firms. In addition, there may be some occasions when the characteristics of products themselves lead to market failure.

The meaning of market failure

Market failure occurs when the free market, left alone, fails to deliver an efficient allocation of resources. The result is a loss of economic and social welfare.

Markets can fail because of:

1 Negative externalities (e.g. the effects of environmental pollution) causing the social cost of production to exceed the private cost.
2 Positive externalities (e.g. the provision of education) causing the social benefit of consumption to exceed the private benefit.
3 Imperfect information meaning merit goods are under-produced while demerit goods are over-produced or over-consumed.
4 The private sector in free markets being unable to supply important pure **public goods** and **quasi-public goods** profitably to consumers.
5 Market dominance by monopolies can lead to under-production and higher prices than would exist under conditions of competition.
6 Immobility of factors of production causes unemployment and therefore productive inefficiency.
7 Equity (fairness) issues. Markets can generate an 'unacceptable' distribution of income and subsequent social exclusion that the government may wish to correct.

We can also say that market failure occurs when one or more of the three functions of prices break down. For example, as we shall see, in the case of externalities, the signalling function of prices has broken down since the full costs and benefits of market transactions are not taken into account. The high prices arguably charged by monopoly firms should create an incentive for other firms to enter the market. However, there are significant barriers to entry that prohibit the entry of firms into such markets. Relatively high prices of some fossil fuels should lead to a considerable rationing effect and reduced consumption. However, this does not appear to be the case.

Market failure and economic efficiency

Market failure results in productive inefficiency. Businesses are not maximising output from given factor inputs. This is a problem because the lost output from inefficient production could have been used to satisfy more wants and needs. Furthermore, resources are misallocated and producing goods and services not wanted by consumers. This is a problem because resources can be put to a better use making products that consumers value more highly.

Key terms

Externalities: costs or benefits that spill over to third parties external to a market transaction.

Marginal private cost: the cost to an individual or firm of an economic transaction.

Marginal external cost: the spillover cost to third parties of an economic transaction.

Marginal social cost: the full cost to society of an economic transaction, including private and external costs.

Marginal private benefit: the benefit to an individual or firm of an economic transaction.

Marginal external benefit: the spillover benefit to third parties of an economic transaction.

Positive externality: a positive spillover effect to third parties of a market transaction.

Marginal social benefit: the full benefit to society of an economic transaction, including private and external benefits.

AQA Examiner's tip

Do not confuse external costs with social costs. External costs are merely the additional spillover cost of a transaction. Together with private costs these make up social costs.

AQA Examiner's tip

Do not confuse external benefits with social benefits. External benefits are merely the additional spillover benefit of a transaction. Together with private benefits these make up social benefits.

Externalities

Externalities are third-party effects arising from production and consumption of goods and services for which no appropriate compensation is paid. Externalities cause market failure if the price mechanism does not take account of the wider costs and benefits to society of production and consumption. Externalities occur outside of the market, that is, they affect individuals not directly involved in the production and/or consumption of a particular good or service. For example, the noise from a rock concert held in a city park may be heard by local residents, who may also suffer increased road congestion in their neighbourhood.

Negative externalities: social costs exceed private costs

The existence of externalities in production and consumption creates a divergence between private and social costs of production and also the private and social benefits of consumption. The **private costs** of any action are those suffered by the individual decision maker. The **social costs** of a particular action are *all* the conceivable costs associated with that action.

When negative externalities exist, **social costs** exceed **private costs**. This leads to the private optimum level of output being greater than the social optimum level of production. The individual consumer or producer does not take the effects of externalities into their calculations. For example, if you decide to make a car journey, you only consider the costs of petrol and any toll or congestion charge you may have to pay. You are unlikely to seriously consider the additional costs you may be imposing upon others, such as congestion, pollution and other environmental damage. Much microeconomic theory uses the concept of 'the margin' to be able to pinpoint specific points of equilibrium. The marginal cost or benefit is the additional cost or benefit derived from producing or consuming one more unit of something. For an economist, therefore, it is more precise to consider marginal costs and benefits to private individuals, firms and society. So:

Marginal social cost = Marginal private cost + Marginal external cost

Positive externalities: social benefits exceed private benefits

Positive externalities arise when third parties benefit from the spillover effects of production and consumption. If you 'consume' education through several years of schooling, and thus improve your skills and productivity, you will have the private benefit of tending to be more attractive to employers and hence having a relatively high earning potential. At the same time, other members of society will benefit, albeit in a small way, from your contribution to the increased living standards of the nation.

Marginal social benefit = Marginal private benefit + Marginal external benefit

Externalities as market failure

The problem created by externalities is that they result in the 'wrong' amount (i.e. too much, or too little) of a good or service being produced. The free market fails to produce an efficient allocation of resources.

Industrial examples are frequently used to illustrate negative externalities. So, if we consider a firm operating an incinerator for domestic and industrial waste, the private costs of waste incineration would include the costs of building and powering the facility, wages, heating and lighting. These costs are paid for by the firm (or local authority). However, there are likely to be other costs involved as well, which might include atmospheric pollution, along with associated environmental clean-up and health costs, and the eyesore created by the incinerator itself, along with lorries carrying waste to the location. These are external costs which, in a free market, will not be taken into account by the firm or local authority when setting the price of its activities. The firm will only take into account the private costs of incineration. This will mean that the price will be lower than if the full costs to society were accounted for. Thus the level of production along with the quantity demanded will be higher than if the full social costs had been considered. This is illustrated in Fig. 8.1. If there are negative externalities, we must add the external costs to the firm's supply curve to find the social cost curve. If the market fails to include these external costs, then the equilibrium output will be Q_1 and the price P_1. From a social welfare viewpoint, we want less output from production activities that create an 'economic bad' such as pollution. A socially efficient output would be Q_2 with a higher price P_2. At this price level, the external costs have been taken into account. We have not eliminated the pollution (we cannot do this), but at least the market has recognised them and included them in the price of the product.

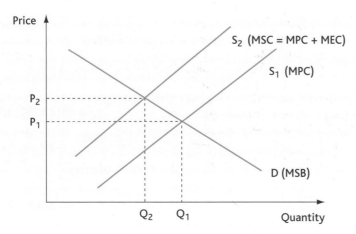

Figure 8.1 *Over-production leading to a negative externality*

AQA Examiner's tip

Learn how to draw externality diagrams accurately – they are often called for in exams and students often make errors with labelling, or shifting curves wrongly.

■ Activity

US pollution may damage UK health

Pollution created by consumers and producers in one country can often cause external costs in other countries. The classic example of this is the effects of the nuclear fall-out from the Chernobyl disaster in 1986. Recent news reports have claimed that polluted air from America could be damaging the health of people in Britain. A study from the Intercontinental Transport of Ozone and Precursors programme has found that airborne chemicals from 8,000 km away are being dumped in the UK and Western Europe and may be to blame for a rise in lung disease. They claim that 'It is highly likely that air leaving the States contains a cocktail of nitrogen oxides and hydrocarbons, which are emitted from vehicle exhausts and power stations.' The US consumes 25 per cent of the world's fossil fuels – mostly oil – and it is predominantly the consumption of fossil fuels that creates pollution.

Source: Tutor2u, adapted from news reports, June 2004

1. What is meant by the term 'external cost'?
2. Why are externalities considered to be an example of market failure?
3. Use a diagram to show how over-production of chemical pollution leads to a divergence of private and social costs.

In the case of positive externalities, the problem is that 'too little' of a good or service is produced. If someone asks their doctor for a 'flu injection, the individual concerned may well only consider their private benefits of not getting ill, ignoring the wider benefits to society. This is illustrated in Fig. 8.3. This time, the problem occurs on the demand-side. D_1 (MPB) represents the private benefits which, equated with supply, leads to a free market equilibrium price of P_1 and quantity Q_1. However, if the full benefits to society were taken into account, demand would be greater, at D_2, leading to a socially optimal price of P_2 and quantity Q_2. In this case we can say that, in a free market, there would be under-production and consumption of 'flu injections of $Q_2 - Q_1$.

Figure 8.2 *A case of negative externalities?*

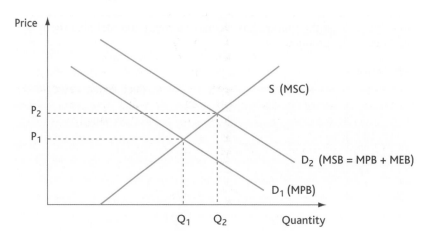

Figure 8.3 *Under-production leading to a positive externality*

Figure 8.4 *Vaccination can create positive externalities*

The problems of identifying and valuing externalities

Valuing external costs and benefits is difficult and controversial. Two methods are possible:

Key terms

Ex ante: a term that refers to future events.

Ex post: a term that refers to after the event.

1. **Ex-ante** (before the fact) valuations estimate the amount of money consumers are prepared to pay to avoid an externality, e.g. the price people might be willing to pay for insurance against an event occurring.

2. **Ex-post** (after the fact) valuations estimate the cost of putting right the externality, e.g. the costs of cleaning up a beach following an oil spill, or the costs of a road accident. Economists seek to place a monetary value on the spillover effect. In practice, estimating the value of time savings, injury, loss of life, environmental damage, lost countryside or loss of a species is very difficult. How should we estimate the harmful impact of passive smoking on non-smokers or value the loss of natural habitat resulting from an oil spillage?

The table below shows benefits and costs of a new motorway.

Private benefits	£130 million	Private costs	£110 million
External benefits	£20 million	External costs	£30 million

From the table it can be concluded that:

a the social costs are £80 million

b the social costs are less than the private costs

c the private costs are less than the social costs

d social benefits are £20 million

The importance of property rights

External costs and benefits are around us every day. The key point is that the free market may fail to take them into account when pricing goods and services. Often this is because of the absence of clearly defined property rights. For example, who owns the air we breathe, or the natural resources available for extraction from seas and oceans around the world? Property rights confer legal control or ownership of a good. For markets to operate efficiently, property rights must be clearly defined and protected, perhaps through government legislation and regulation. If an asset is un-owned no one has an economic incentive to protect it from abuse. This can lead to what is known as the 'tragedy of the commons', that is, the over-use of common land, fish stocks, etc. that leads to long-term permanent damage to the stock of natural resources. Pollution creates negative externalities but the free market may not take them into account.

Case study

Cheap food – at a huge price

Why do the British shop in supermarkets? Easy. Price, convenience, quality and choice: the mantra of the market economy. But is perception matched by reality?

Supermarkets are very cheap for some goods, but what you save on the loss-leading swings, you lose on the marked-up roundabouts. Take fruit and vegetables. Last summer we compared prices between supermarkets and street markets of the old-fashioned endangered variety. Like for like, the markets won on almost every count. Even getting to the store by car may be far from convenient. Over the past 20 years, the number of shopping trips has increased by a third, and driver shopping mileage has more than doubled. Given Britain's congestion, more journeys of increasing length doesn't sound very convenient. Nor is it: in the 1960s, according to Professor Jonathan Gershuny of Essex University, consumers spent on average 41 minutes per day shopping and in related travel. In the 1980s this had risen to 70 minutes with studies showing that food shopping accounted for more than three-quarters of total shopping time. According to Professor Gershuny, 'the increase in shopping time reflects the growth of "self-servicing" and the growth in size of supermarkets...the larger the supermarket, the more walking for the shopper and the greater the average distance from the shopper's home...The retail industry in effect externalises a large part of its costs.'

On quality and choice, supermarket products may be varied and consistent – but is what you see what you really get, and are you paying the real costs? Supermarkets' huge buying power and demand for absolute consistency means that fruit and vegetable production are now industrialised processes. Multiples have 60 per cent of the market and suppliers who cannot supply 52 weeks a year need not supply. Your Brussels sprouts may be perfectly formed, but at what costs to the countryside? Biodiversity on the shelf is increasingly at the cost of biodiversity in the field.

While it has long been recognised that the perceived benefits of the supermarkets are not evenly spread between social groups (the chief executive of the supermarkets' own research organisation acknowledges that old and poor people will have serious problems over where to buy food because of the growth of superstores and the lack of town centre stores), our research leads us to believe that, even for the better-off and mobile, the advantages of supermarkets are beginning to be outweighed by the drawbacks. The decline of the town centre is well documented and attributable, at least in part, to the development of out-of-town shopping centres. The big retailers' claims to efficiency in transport are bogus. Much freight transport is unnecessary – produce could be sold locally. More than a third of the increase in freight transport since the late 1970s has been food, drink and tobacco – which together account for less than one-tenth of the economy. Next time you use a motorway, count the supermarket trucks. No wonder the big retailers are such lavish supporters of the British Road Federation. It's the same story with packaging. According to the government, 'the stocking policies of supermarkets...largely contributed to non-returnable [packaging] attaining [its] present share of the market'.

Source: adapted from Hugh Raven and Tim Lang, 'Cheap food – at a huge price', *The Independent,* 10 January 1995

■ Information failure: merit goods and demerit goods

Merit goods

Merit goods are those goods and services that the government feels that people will under-consume, and which ought to be subsidised or provided free at the point of use so that consumption does not depend primarily on the ability to pay for the good or service. Both the public and private sector provide merit goods and services. For example, we have an independent education system and people can buy private health care insurance. Consumption of merit goods is believed to generate positive externalities where the social benefit from consumption exceeds the private benefit. A merit good is a product that society values and judges that everyone should have regardless of whether an individual wants them. The government believes that individuals may not act in their own best interest in part because of imperfect information about the long-term benefits that can be derived. Thus we say that merit goods are linked to a **failure of information** to a consumer. Good examples of merit goods include health services, education, public libraries, and inoculations for children and students. Merit goods are a good example of **partial market failure**, i.e. where the free market will lead to the provision of a product, but in the wrong quantity, leading to a misallocation of resources.

Activity

Read the case-study 'Cheap food – at a huge price' and answer the following questions:

1   Outline the private and external costs and benefits arising from the existence of supermarkets.

2   Who are the main winners and losers outlined in the article?

3   Firms that create external costs can be subjected to government controls such as fines, taxes or regulations. Should supermarkets be subjected to controls?

■ Key terms

Merit good: a good that would be under-consumed in a free market, as individuals do not fully perceive the benefits obtained from consumption.

Failure of information (or information failure): where economic agents do not properly perceive the benefits or disadvantages of a transaction.

Partial market failure: where the free market provides a product but with a misallocation of resources.

Case study

Education as a merit good

Education is provided by both the state and the private sector. The argument concerning imperfect information is an important one. Parents with relatively poor educational qualifications may be unaware of the full longer-term benefits that their children might derive from a proper education. Because the knowledge of these private benefits is an ongoing learning process, children themselves will tend to underestimate the long-term gains from a proper education. Education is a long-term investment decision. The private costs must be paid now but the private benefits (including higher earnings potential over one's working life) take time to emerge. Education should provide a number of external benefits that might not be taken into account by the free market. These include rising incomes and productivity for current and future generations; an increase in the occupational mobility of the labour force that should help to reduce unemployment and therefore reduce welfare spending. Increased spending on education should also provide a stimulus for higher-level research that can add to the long-run trend rate of growth. Other external benefits might include the encouragement of a more enlightened and cultured society, less prone to political instabilities and one that manages to achieve a greater degree of social cohesion. Providing that the education system provides a sufficiently good education across all regions and sections of society, increased education and training spending should also open up a higher level of equality of opportunity. The reality is of course that there are very deep and wide variations in educational performance and opportunities across the country.

Demerit goods

Demerit goods are those goods considered 'bad' for you. Examples include alcohol, cigarettes and drugs or the social effects of gambling addiction. The consumption of demerit goods can lead to negative externalities, which consumers may be unaware of, since they have imperfect information about potential long-term damage to their own health. Again, demerit goods are linked to a failure of information. Thus the government seeks to reduce consumption of demerit goods.

The problems caused by merit and demerit goods

Merit goods tend to be under-produced and under-consumed in a free market, since a lack of information about the benefits derived from consumption, will result in 'too little' of the product being demanded. Because the benefits occur over time in many cases, e.g. education, consumers may not be able to accurately appreciate the benefits which may arise, nor be able to afford it. This under-consumption is illustrated in Fig. 8.5. If we assume that consumers can correctly perceive the actual private benefits, demand would be given by D_2. This would lead to an equilibrium price of P_1 and quantity Q_1. However, because the consumer effectively undervalues the product, the level of actual demand remains less, at D_1, leading to a free market price of P_2 and quantity Q_2.

In the case of a demerit good, the social optimum level of demand, as shown in Fig. 8.7, is given by D_1, leading to an equilibrium price of P_1 and quantity produced and consumed of Q_1. Consumers overestimate the

■ Key terms

Demerit good: a good that would be over-consumed in a free market, as it brings less overall benefit to consumers than they realise.

AQA Examiner's tip

In the exam, you may be required to make a judgement about whether a product is either a merit good or a demerit good.

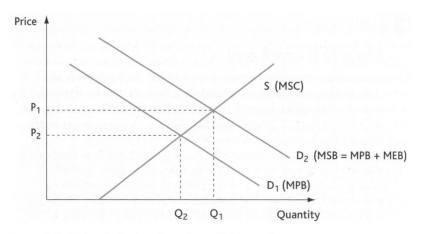

Figure 8.5 *Under-production of a merit good by the market*

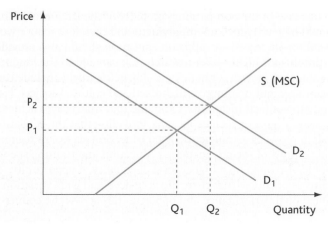

Figure 8.7 *Over-production of a demerit good by the market*

benefits arising from the product, and so demand is at D_2 instead. This leads to a free market price of P_2 and quantity Q_2. Again, the consumer is unable to properly value the relative costs and benefits arising from their consumption of the product.

■ Public goods

Another type of good that may lead to market failure is referred to as a **public good**. Here it is not a matter of whether too much or too little of a good or service will be provided by the free market, but whether the product will be provided at all. A public good may be defined by the two key characteristics it must possess to be so-called:

1 *Non-excludability* The benefits derived from the provision of pure public goods cannot be confined to only those who have actually paid for it. In this sense, those that do not pay can enjoy the benefits of consumption for no financial cost. This is known as the **free-rider problem**.

2 *Non-rivalry in consumption* Consumption of a public good by one person does not reduce the availability of a good to others, therefore we all consume the same amount of public goods even though our valuation of the benefit we derive from them might differ.

Examples of public goods include flood control systems, street lighting, lighthouse protection and also national defence services.

Quasi-public goods

Some goods and services do not fully possess the two characteristics of non-rivalry and non-excludability. These are known as **quasi-public goods**, quasi meaning near or almost. It is difficult, in practice, to categorise all goods and services as either 'public' or 'private' (with **private goods** being the opposite of public goods, i.e. they are both rival and excludable in consumption). Indeed, several products lie somewhere in between these two extremes. A good example might be a national park such as the Lake District. This national park is open to all, and thus appears non-excludable, but it is possible to exclude consumers by reducing access rights and charging for entry, as seen in some US national parks. Equally, the national park is non-rival up to a point. If you are the first to sit down at a picnic site, your enjoyment will not be spoiled too much by a few other families doing the same. There comes a point, however, that this ceases to be the case. As space becomes increasingly limited, enjoyment will be significantly diminished. Thus the national park has some of the characteristics of non-rivalry, but not all, and is arguably a quasi-public good.

Public goods and market failure

Pure public goods are not normally provided at all by the private sector because they would be unable to supply them for a profit. Thus the free market may fail totally to provide important pure public goods and under-provide quasi-public goods. This would be termed **complete market failure**. It is therefore up to the Government to decide what output of public goods is appropriate for society. To do this, it must estimate the social benefit from the consumption of public goods. Putting a monetary value on the benefit derived from street lighting and defence systems is problematic. The electoral system provides an opportunity to see the public choices of voters but elections are rarely won and lost purely on the grounds of government spending plans and the turnout at elections continues to fall.

The essence of the problem is known as the 'free-rider problem'. Consumers behaving rationally will naturally attempt to gain a 'free ride' from other consumers who purchase a good or service. As stated above, one of the key characteristics of a public good is that it is non-excludable. Therefore, once one consumer has purchased the product all other consumers cannot be prevented from benefitting. In the case of national defence, if those who feel more vulnerable to invasion fund the armed forces, then it is difficult not to defend those who have not paid.

Case study

The airwaves – a public good or a quasi-public good?

The airwaves used by mobile phone companies, radio stations and television companies are essentially owned by the government of a particular country. Normally we would say that they are a pure public good, since one person's use of the airwaves rarely reduces the extent to which other people can benefit from utilising them. However, when demand for mobile phone services is high at peak times – try sending a text message on New Year's Eve – the airwaves become crowded and access to the networks can become slow. In this sense the airwaves can be considered a quasi-public good.

Key terms

Quasi-public good: a good that has some of the qualities of a public good but does not fully possess the two required characteristics of non-rivalry and non-excludability.

Private good: a good that is both excludable and rival in consumption.

Complete market failure: where the free market fails to provide a product at all, i.e. the case of public goods.

💡 Monopoly as a market failure

As outlined in the previous chapter, it is generally accepted that for markets to function well, there needs to be a high level of competition. However, there is often concentration of power among a small number of firms in numerous markets, which may lead to market failure. A 'pure' monopoly exists where only one firm supplies the market.

The main case against a monopoly is that firms can earn higher profits in spite of not producing goods and services that consumers value most. Since firms have a high level of control over the market, there may be no incentive to produce the goods and services valued most by consumers. Consumers are unable to switch to an alternative and thus resources are not allocated according to consumer wants, leading to allocative inefficiency. The market has therefore failed. Conversely, in a highly competitive market, firms will be obliged to produce the goods and services that consumers want in order to survive. However, under conditions of monopoly, the goods and services made available are determined by the firm rather than the consumer. Therefore, we might say that under conditions of monopoly, consumer sovereignty has been partially replaced by producer sovereignty.

In addition, monopolistic firms are not obliged to produce goods and services at the minimum possible cost. Indeed, the monopolist restricts output in order to raise its price, as shown in Fig. 8.8. When competition is tough, businesses must keep firm control of their costs because otherwise they risk losing market share. There is no incentive to cut costs as there are no competitors forcing them to do so. Thus monopoly firms are unlikely to be productively efficient – again a market failure. Some economists go further and say that monopolists may be even less efficient because, if they believe that they have a protected market, they may be less inclined to spend money on research and improved management. These inefficiencies can lead to a waste of scarce resources.

Figure 8.8 *The monopolist restricts output (Q₁ to Q₂) to raise the price of its product (P₁ to P₂)*

Activity

Which one of the following, A, B, C or D, distinguishes merit goods from public goods?

	Merit goods	Public goods
a	Provided by governments	Provided by companies
b	Provided at a cost	Provided at no cost
c	Limited in supply	Have an infinite supply
d	Consumption reduces availability	Consumption does not reduce availability

---

The potential benefits of monopoly

We must also consider the possible economic benefits of monopoly power, implying that the government and the competition authorities should be careful about intervening directly in markets to try to break up a monopoly. Market power can bring advantages both to the firms themselves and also to consumers. These should be included in any evaluation of a particular market or industry.

1 *Research and development (R&D) spending* Large corporations enjoying high profit levels are in a position to allocate some of their profits to fund capital investment spending and research and

development projects. The positive spillover effects of research include a faster pace of innovation and the development of improved products for consumers. This is particularly the case in industries such as telecommunications and pharmaceuticals. Indeed, there are several markets dominated by a small number of major global manufacturers that are nevertheless highly competitive, e.g. for DVD recorders. Manufacturers are engaged in a constant battle for market share to meet consumers' ever-changing needs and wants and are thus willing to invest significant portions of their profits into R&D.

2 *Exploitation of economies of scale* Because monopoly producers often supply goods and services on a large scale, they may achieve economies of scale, leading to a fall in average costs of production. Lower costs might well lead to an increase in profits but the gains in productive efficiency may potentially be passed onto consumers through lower prices. Some economists argue that in some industries there might well be a case for allowing a single firm to dominate due to the possibility of significant economies of scale. This is the so-called 'natural monopoly' situation. Large, possibly even continuous, economies of scale, as shown in ATC_2 in Fig. 8.9 would present a strong argument for allowing the dominance of a large firm. Even if economies of scale are not continuous, the potential for economies of scale might be an argument for allowing large firms to control a market, though diseconomies of scale may eventually take effect, as shown by ATC_1.

3 *Monopolies and international competitiveness* One argument in support of businesses with monopoly power is that the UK economy needs multinational companies operating on a scale large enough to compete in global markets. A firm may enjoy domestic monopoly power, but still face competition in overseas markets. A good examples is Corus, the UK/Dutch-owned steel manufacturer.

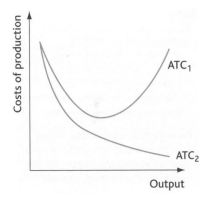

Figure 8.9 *Monopoly and economies and diseconomies of scale*

■ Case study

Monopoly – benefits for society

Monopoly power can be good for innovation, according to research by Professor Federico Etro, published in the April 2004 edition of the *Economic Journal*. Despite the fact that the market leadership of firms like Microsoft is often criticised, their investments in research and development can be beneficial to society because they expand the technological frontier and open new ways to prosperity. Many technological innovations are developed by firms with patents on leading-edge technologies. These firms perpetuate their leadership and market power through innovation.

Source: Tutor2u, adapted from press releases from the Royal Economics Society

Many markets have firms with monopoly power but they seem to work perfectly well from the point of view of the consumer. Although there is agreement among many economists that competition is a force for good in the long run, we should be careful not to simply assume that monopoly power is bad and competition is good. There are persuasive arguments on both sides. In recent years many markets have become more competitive with the entry of new suppliers and much greater choice for consumers. Many factors have contributed to this including:

- *Technological change* such as the rise of e-commerce and the internet.
- *Globalisation* – fresh low-cost competition from emerging market economies such as China and India.
- *Deliberate government policies* to open up markets and give new businesses the right to compete (e.g. in the markets for postal services, car retailing and telecommunications).

■ Immobility of factors of production (labour)

While we have so far largely focused on failures of product markets, it is also possible for factor markets to suffer from a lack of efficiency or equity.

The labour market is a key factor market and, for it to function properly, labour must be perfectly (i.e. completely) mobile. However, in practice, workers may not, for example, be able to move easily from one type of employment to another. This is known as **occupational immobility** of labour. As employment patterns change, through changes in the structure of the economy, a Cornish tin miner for example, may not easily be able to secure a job as a financial adviser. The redundant tin miner is unlikely to have the relevant skills to become a financial adviser, and would require considerable retraining. As industries naturally decline, due to changes in the pattern of demand and the advent of new technologies, workers must move occupations in order to maintain employment, but may not possess the skills to do so, and thus be unable to get a new job. This type of unemployment is known as 'structural unemployment'. This is a market failure, as labour is not being fully utilised.

In addition, labour may not easily be able to move from a job in one place of employment to another, either at local, regional or national level. Reasons for this may include family ties to a particular region (e.g. dependent relatives, friends, or schooling), or lack of knowledge about where the job opportunities are. Significant differences in house prices can also make it difficult for someone to move from a relatively low-cost to a high-cost region. This **geographical immobility** of labour may mean that when employment opportunities diminish in one part of the country and expand in another, workers are unable to move to the flourishing region. Unemployment may again be created, leading to a further market failure.

■ Key terms

Occupational immobility: as patterns of demand and employment change, many workers may find it difficult to easily secure new jobs, since they may lack the necessary skills.

Geographical immobility: where workers find it difficult to move to where employment opportunities may be, due to family ties and differences in housing costs.

■ Case study

Rover: structural unemployment and immobility of labour

Almost one in four of the workers at the collapsed carmaker MG Rover are still without a job nearly two years after Rover went into administration with the loss of over 6,000 jobs, while many of the rest have been forced to take lower-paid employment. The survey, conducted by the trade union Amicus found that 23 per cent of Rover workers were still unemployed or on training courses, while one in five of those in work were earning the equivalent of the minimum wage, compared with the average MG Rover salary of £22,000.

Source: adapted from Mark Milner, 'A quarter of Rover workers still unemployed', *Guardian*, 5 February 2007

Unequal distribution of income and wealth

In a free market economy, an individual's ability to consume goods and services depends upon his or her **income** or **wealth**. Note that these two concepts are linked but are not the same thing. Income is a flow of earnings over a period of time, perhaps a wage or salary in return for labour, while wealth is a stock of owned assets, such as property or a portfolio of shares. In a free market, someone who possesses a particular sporting talent, for example the endurance of a racing cyclist or reactions of a top F1 racing driver, could command a high income. The main source of wealth in the UK is still through inheritance. An unequal distribution of income and wealth may result in an unsatisfactory allocation of resources, which may be judged as unfair or inequitable. The relatively poor do not have access to the range of goods and service consumed by 'average' citizens. High inequality may also lead to alienation and encourage crime with wider negative consequences for society. A lack of fairness or equity in the distribution of income and wealth can be seen as a failure of the free market.

Key terms

Income: a flow of earnings to a factor of production over a period of time, e.g. wages or salaries.

Wealth: a stock of owned assets, e.g. housing property or a portfolio of shares.

Case study

Top of the income ladder

'The richest have continued to get richer. The richest one per cent of the population has increased their share of income from around six per cent in 1980 to 13 per cent in 1999. Inequality in disposable income (after taxes and benefits) appears to have slightly increased since 1997 after significant increases in the 1980s.'

'The poorest continue to be more likely to suffer from crime. Around 4.8% of people earning less than £5,000 a year were burgled last year, compared with 2.7% of those earning over £30,000.'

Source: adapted from 'The State of the Nation', Will Paxton and Mike Dixon, London: Institute for Public Policy Research (ippr), August 2004

When we are discussing inequality and poverty, we cannot escape having to make value judgements, or normative statements. Ultimately, what constitutes an 'unacceptable' distribution of income and what if anything the government should do about this is a value judgement and is a political issue beyond the scope of economics. That said, there is plenty of evidence that high and rising levels of inequality of income and wealth can lead to negative social consequences, i.e. external costs that affect the whole of society.

☑ *After completing this chapter you should:*

■ be able to define what is meant by market failure and give examples

■ be able to explain, with examples, the difference between complete market failure and partial market failure

■ be able to define, explain and give examples of externalities, public goods, merit goods and demerit goods

■ understand the potential advantages and disadvantages of monopoly

■ be able to explain why immobility of factors of production, of labour in particular, leads to market failure

■ recognise the equity issues relating to an unequal distribution of income and wealth.

AQA Examination-style questions

1   Which one of the following is an example of market failure?
   (a)   Prices do not reflect the full social costs of production.
   (b)   Prices rise so that consumers cannot afford to buy all the
            goods that they used to purchase.
   (c)   Demand falls so that firms have to make workers redundant.
   (d)   A firm goes out of business because it cannot find a market for its products.

                                                                              (AQA, 2006)

2   The National Grid is a system that distributes electricity throughout Britain. It is currently a
   monopoly. A possible advantage of this monopoly position to electricity customers is that:
   (a)   a lack of competition in the electricity distribution industry encourages lower prices
   (b)   the monopolist is able to offer lower prices to customers
            because it can exploit economies of scale
   (c)   by charging high prices, the monopolist is able to ensure an
            efficient allocation of resources
   (d)   there will be no need for innovation and invention in the
            electricity distribution industry and so customers can enjoy lower prices

                                                                              (AQA, 2006)

3   The end of the video cassette?
   Study Extracts A, B and C, and then answer all parts of the question that follows.

   Extract A: Sales of pre-recorded video cassettes and DVDs in the UK, 1998–2002

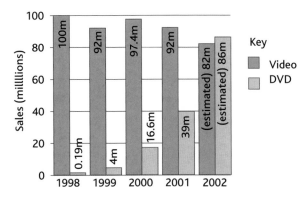

   Extract B: DVD kills the video
   We are living in a period in which digital versatile disc (DVD) technology is replacing video
   cassette technology. Prices of DVD players have recently fallen below £100. Video cassette
   recorders (VCRs) and video cassettes currently have two advantages, though these are soon likely
   to disappear. First, there is a much larger back-catalogue of films to buy or rent on video cassette
   than on DVD. Second, VCRs can record TV programmes as well as play prerecorded films. By
   contrast, only pre-recorded discs can be used with DVD players available at a similar price to
   VCRs. In 2001, Philips manufactured and sold a DVD recorder that enabled the user to record
   TV programmes as well as to play pre-recorded DVDs. Since then, rival manufacturers, such as
   Sony, have marketed their own recorders. Prices of DVD *recorders* are still much higher than
   prices of DVD *players*, but a price war is developing, and prices are likely to fall rapidly over the
   next few years.

Source: adapted from the *Daily Mirror*, 12 August 2002

Extract C: Winning technologies

Over twenty years ago, when VCRs first hit the market, three different and incompatible technologies fought for market dominance. During this struggle, sales of VCRs were held back because consumers did not know which type of machine would win the battle for market dominance. JVC's VHS format eventually emerged the winner. Now, virtually every VCR incorporates the technology originally developed and controlled by JVC. In the consumer market, rival technologies developed by Sony and Philips disappeared without trace. In a similar battle involving computer software, Microsoft's Windows PC operating system beat off the challenge of Apple's operating system. History may be repeating itself with DVD recorders. Currently, DVD recorders developed by different manufacturers use different technologies. Remembering the earlier battle over twenty years ago, consumers may keep their old VCRs for a few more years rather than spend hundreds of pounds on the wrong DVD recorder technology.

(a)   Using Extract A, compare the changes in sales of pre-recorded video cassettes with the changes in sales of digital versatile discs (DVDs) for the period 1998 to 2002. *(5 marks)*

(b)   Define the term economies of scale and outline two possible scale economies available to a consumer electronics manufacturer. *(8 marks)*

(c)   Extract B (lines 11–12) states that the prices of DVD recorders are likely to fall rapidly over the next few years. With the help of a supply and demand diagram, explain how this may affect the market for video cassette recorders. *(12 marks)*

(d)   Extract C describes how markets for electronic goods and software are sometimes dominated by a single type of product, which incorporates the technology developed and controlled by one of the firms in the market. Do you agree that this reduces competition and is bad for consumers and producers? Justify your answer. *(25 marks)*

(AQA, 2004)

Government intervention in markets

A failure of the free market and the price mechanism to deliver an optimum allocation of scarce resources is normally regarded as justification for some form of government intervention in the economy. This intervention is designed to correct instances of market failure and achieve an improvement in economic and social welfare. But what if intervention leads to further inefficiencies? What if government policies prove to be costly to implement but ineffective in achieving their desired outcomes? What happens if intervention distorts markets still further?

Reasons for government intervention in markets

In a free market, scarce resources are allocated through the price mechanism where the preferences and spending decisions of consumers and the supply decisions of businesses come together to determine equilibrium prices. The free market works through price signals. When demand is high, the potential profit from supplying to a market rises, leading to an expansion in supply to meet rising demand from consumers. In general, the free market mechanism is a very powerful device for determining how resources are allocated among competing uses. The government may choose to intervene in the price mechanism largely on the grounds of wanting to change the allocation of resources and achieve what they perceive to be an improvement in economic and social welfare.

The main reasons for policy intervention are:

1 To correct for instances of market failure.
2 To achieve a more equitable distribution of income and wealth.
3 To improve the performance of the UK economy both domestically and on the international front.

Forms of government intervention

There are many methods of government intervention.

Government legislation and regulation

Parliament can pass laws, for example prohibiting the sale of cigarettes to under-18s, or ban smoking in public places. The laws of competition policy act against examples of price-fixing or other forms of anti-competitive behaviour by firms within markets. Employment laws may offer some legal protection for workers by setting maximum working hours or through the setting of a minimum wage. The economy operates with a huge and growing amount of regulation. There are government appointed regulators who can impose price controls in most of the main utilities such as telecommunications, electricity, gas and rail transport. Free market economists criticise the scale of regulation in the economy arguing that it creates an unnecessary burden of costs for businesses, with a huge amount of so-called 'red tape' damaging the competitiveness of businesses. Regulation may be used to introduce fresh competition into a market, for example breaking up the existing monopoly power of a service provider. A good example of this so-called market liberalisation is the attempt to introduce more competition for British Telecom.

Direct provision of goods and services

Because of privatisation, the state-owned sector of the economy is much smaller than it was before 1980. The main state-owned businesses in the UK are the Royal Mail and Network Rail. State funding can also be used to provide merit goods and services and public goods directly to the population. For example, the government pays private sector firms to operate prisons and maintain our road network.

💡 Financial intervention

Financial intervention can be used to alter the level of demand for different products and also the pattern of demand within the economy.

1 **Indirect taxes** can be used to raise the price of demerit goods and products that generate negative externalities in order to reduce the quantity demanded towards a socially optimal level. An indirect tax is imposed on producers, i.e. suppliers, by the government. Examples include excise duties on cigarettes, alcohol and fuel and also VAT. Taxes are levied by the government for a number of reasons, among them as part of a strategy to curb pollution and improve the environment. The opposite of an indirect tax is a tax levied directly on income, known as a direct tax.

2 A *subsidy* to consumers will lower the price of merit goods, for example EMA allowances to students in further education to reduce the private costs of education and subsidies to companies employing workers on the New Deal programme. They are designed to boost consumption and output of products with positive externalities.

3 *Tax relief* The government may offer financial assistance such as tax credits for business investment in research and development. Alternatively, a reduction in corporation tax (a tax on company profits) could be granted, to promote new capital investment and extra employment.

4 *Changes to taxation and welfare payments* can be used to influence the overall distribution of income and wealth, for example higher direct tax rates on rich households or an increase in the value of welfare benefits for the poor.

Key terms

Indirect tax: a tax on spending.

Case study

The economic arguments surrounding a 'fat tax'

A study in the *Journal of Epidemiology and Community Health* argues that more than 3,000 fatal heart attacks and strokes per year would be prevented by adding VAT to 'unhealthy' foods that are high in salt, sugar and/or fat. Such foods might be termed demerit goods. Researchers who produced the study suggest that a 17.5 per cent increase in the price of such foods would lead to a 15 per cent reduction in consumption and that the time is right to open up a debate into setting a so-called 'fat tax'. Some commentators have argued that increasing the price of such foods will penalise low-income families and simply result in increased consumption of cheaper, even less nutritious foods. Subsidising healthier alternatives might be a better approach.

■ Activity

Read the case study 'The economic arguments surrounding a "fat tax"' and answer the following questions:

1. Define what is meant by the term demerit good.

2. Using the information in the case study, calculate the price elasticity of demand of 'unhealthy' foods.

3. Using a supply and demand diagram, analyse the impact of an indirect tax on unhealthy foods.

4. Evaluate the effectiveness of using an indirect tax to correct market failure in this case.

■ Case study

The UK coal industry

There has been a huge decline in the scale of coal production in the UK over the last three decades. Much of our demand for coal now comes from cheaper imports from countries such as South Africa and demand has also been affected by the switch towards gas partly on grounds of the environmental effects of using sulphur-rich coal. Is there a case for continued subsidy of what remains of our coal industry? Thousands of jobs still depend directly or indirectly on keeping the few remaining pits open even if, on economic grounds, there is little justification in maintaining production. On equity grounds, the government may decide that further financial assistance is required to prevent structural unemployment and poverty in areas where coal mining is still an important source of employment. There may also be a strategic motivation behind subsidies, i.e. to give the UK an alternative fuel supply if gas and oil are cut off.

Source: adapted from Tutor2u

Intervention designed to close the information gap

Often market failure results from consumers suffering from a lack of information about the costs and benefits of the products available in the market place. Government action can have a role in improving information to help consumers and producers value the 'true' cost and/or benefit of a good or service. Examples might include:

1. Compulsory labelling on cigarette packages with health warnings to reduce smoking.

2. Improved nutritional information on foods to counter the risks of growing obesity.

3. Anti-speeding television advertising to reduce road accidents and advertising campaigns to raise awareness of the risks of drink-driving.

4. Advertising health screening programmes/information campaigns on the dangers of addiction.

■ The effects of government intervention on markets

One important point to bear in mind is that the effects of different forms of government intervention in markets are never neutral. Financial support given by the government to one set of producers rather than another will always create 'winners and losers'. Taxing one product more than another will similarly have different effects on different groups of consumers.

Public goods

As we saw in the previous chapter, public goods, such as policing, need to be financed by the government, but need not be produced by the government. The government will decide upon the appropriate level of spending on policing and finance it through taxation. One issue facing the government is deciding upon the fairest or most equitable method of raising this tax revenue. The government could tax citizens based on their ability to pay tax. This means that those who have the highest incomes or largest wealth will pay most tax. Indeed, this is the system adopted in most countries and is referred to as a progressive tax system.

Another way a government can tax individuals is on the basis of the benefits they receive from public goods. In practice, however, it may be difficult to accurately place a value on the benefit each citizen receives from a public good.

Externalities

Regulation

Governments may use regulation to correct for externalities. A factory producing chemicals, which also pollutes the surrounding rivers, might be subjected to government intervention which sets limits that restrict the amount of polluting chemicals that can be legally deposited. The government would subsequently establish a system to regulate and inspect the factory to ensure it wasn't exceeding the set limits. If the factory was found to exceed the limit, large fines could be levied.

Pollution permits

One method of controlling the total amount of pollution firms produce is through the use of **pollution permits**, which is essentially using the market to address the problem, rather than through regulation. Here, the government issues or sells permits to firms, allowing them to pollute up to a certain limit. These permits can be traded, creating an incentive for firms to be relatively 'clean' so that if they do not use up their full allocation of permits they can sell any remaining allocation to other, less 'clean' firms. The incentives of this system are a key advantage. Firms with relatively inefficient production methods will face higher overall costs and should be encouraged to generate less pollution. The system also allows governments to control the total amount of pollution generated, since this will be determined by the number of permits granted. However, the system still needs to be enforced, which may still require teams of factory inspectors as well as careful thought about what level of fines is sufficient to penalise firms and deter further pollution beyond the permitted level.

Financial intervention: taxes

The government could levy a tax upon any individual or firm causing a negative externality. This allows the external costs to be 'internalised', i.e. accounted for by the price mechanism. In Fig 9.2, the free market equilibrium price and quantity are P_1 and Q_1, where S_1, given by MPC (marginal private cost), equals demand D_1, which is given by MSB (marginal social benefit). However, if we wish to include external costs

> ### Key terms
>
> **Pollution permit:** a permit sold to firms by the government, allowing them to pollute up to a certain limit.

Figure 9.1 *Could a system of pollution permits help?*

then the supply curve shifts leftwards to S_2, or MSC (marginal social cost). Note that the vertical distance between these two is the marginal external cost, MEC. The government could therefore intervene in this market to impose a tax equal to the marginal external cost, the effect of which is to shift the supply curve left from S_1 to S_2. This would correct the market failure, leading to a socially optimal level of output at Q_2.

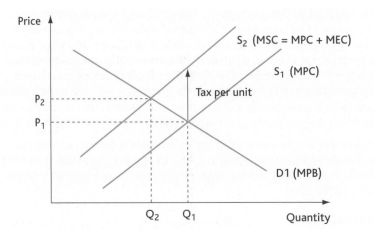

Figure 9.2 *Using an indirect tax to correct negative externalities*

Financial intervention to address market failure caused by external benefits or positive externalities will be in the form of a subsidy. This is illustrated in Fig.9.3. The free market equilibrium occurs where $D_1 = S_1$ or where $MPC = MPB$ at price OP_1 and quantity OQ_1. As there are external benefits society requires consumption to increase to OQ_2. This will only occur if the price to the consumder is lower at OP_3 and the price to the supplier is increased to OP_2. If the government subsidises production of this product, then the supply shifts right to S_2, which equals MPC minus the subsidy. The optimum quantity is Q_2 at price P_3.

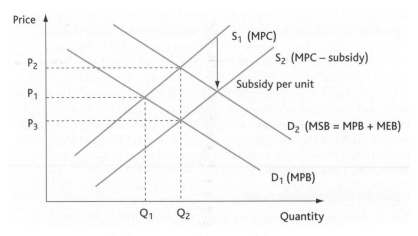

Figure 9.3 *Using a subsidy to correct positive externalities*

Activity

1. Government intervention in a market economy can lead to an increase in economic welfare if

   a the market mechanism fails to allow for externalities

   b it leads to an increase in the consumption of demerit goods

   c the price elasticity of supply of private goods is high

   d the demand for inferior goods rises as incomes increase

2. 'Increasing carbon dioxide emissions from aviation are a potentially significant contributor to climate change and the cause of increasing concern about the growing environmental impact of air travel.'

   The environmental damage caused by air travel, referred to in the above passage, would be reduced if

   a airlines charged passengers for the negative externalities cause by air travel

   b air travel created positive as well as negative externalities

   c government policy increased competition in the airline industry

   d air travel was a merit good

3. Governments often place taxes on certain goods because these goods

   a are price elastic in supply

   b impose costs on non-users

   c might be under-provided by the market

   d include external benefits in their prices

4. One reason why governments provide health care is because

   a the private benefit from health care is less than the social benefit

   b health care cannot be provided by the free market

   c all health care is both a merit good and a public good

   d this ensures the provision of health care is maximised

Correcting information failures

Shops and other suppliers are legally obliged to provide the consumer with information about the price and composition of the product being offered for sale. Similarly, consumers are legally protected from being sold faulty products or with misleading information. In many circumstances, however, complete information about a product is not available, or existing information is too complicated to be properly interpreted by a consumer.

Programmes such as compulsory labelling on packs of cigarettes and nutritional labelling of food and drink are really designed to change the 'perceived' costs and benefits of consumption for the consumer. They don't have any direct effect on market prices, but they seek to influence 'demand' and therefore output and consumption in the long run. Of course it is difficult to accurately identify the effects of any single government information campaign, whether we consider road safety campaigns or encouraging people to give up smoking. Increasingly adverts are becoming more hard-hitting in a bid to have an effect on consumers.

Price intervention

Maximum prices

The government can set a legally imposed maximum price, or price ceiling in a market, that suppliers cannot exceed, in an attempt to prevent the market price from rising above a certain level. To be effective a maximum price has to be set below the free market price. One example of a maximum price might be when shortage of essential foodstuffs threatens large rises in the free market price. Other examples include rent controls on properties, for example the system of rent controls still in place in Manhattan in the USA. A maximum price seeks to control the price but also involves a normative judgement on behalf of the government about what that price should be. An example of a maximum price is shown in Fig. 9.4.

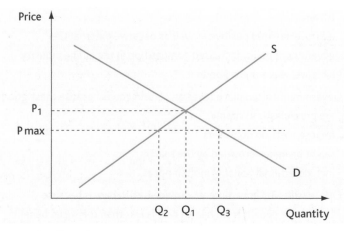

Figure 9.4 *The effect of imposing a maximum price*

The normal free market equilibrium price is shown at P_1 – but the government decides to introduce a maximum price of *Pmax*. This price ceiling creates excess demand for the product equal to quantity $Q_3 - Q_2$ because the price has been held below the normal equilibrium. It is worth noting that a price ceiling set above the free market equilibrium price would have no effect whatsoever on the market – because for a price ceiling to be effective, it must be set below the normal market clearing price.

Minimum prices

A minimum price is a legally imposed price floor, below which the normal market price cannot fall. To be effective the minimum price has to be set above the normal equilibrium price. The National Minimum wage was introduced into the UK in 1999. It is an intervention in the labour market designed to increase the pay of lower-paid workers and thereby influence the distribution of income in society. The minimum wage is a price floor, i.e. employers cannot legally undercut the current minimum wage rate per hour. This applies both to full-time and part-time workers. Fig. 9.5 can be used to show the effects. The market equilibrium wage for this particular labour market is at P_1, where demand = supply. If the minimum wage is set at *Pmin*, there will be an excess supply of labour equal to $Q_3 - Q_2$ because the supply of labour will expand (more workers will be willing and able to offer themselves for work at the higher wage than before) but there is a risk that firms' demand for workers will contract if the minimum wage is introduced.

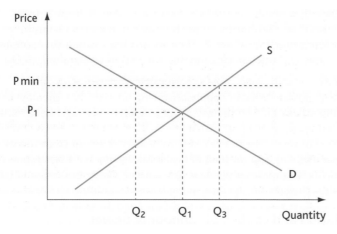

Figure 9.5 *The effect of imposing a minimum price*

Buffer stocks

Governments may intervene where markets suffer considerable volatility in the free market price. They will try to manipulate the free market price through the use of buffer stock schemes. Agricultural and commodity markets are notorious for huge price instability due to the largely unpredictable weather and relatively inelastic demand and supply curves.

This price instability can lead to unpredictable incomes for farmers and their families and devastation of markets, especially in less developed countries. Because of this governments have often tried to stabilise these prices over time. The essential ingredients of a price stabilisation policy are illustrated in Fig. 9.7. The first step is to select a target price to keep stable, in this case P_1, which corresponds to the average long-term equilibrium price, and then to use a buffer stock system to avoid the price effects of fluctuating supply.

Following a supply shock resulting in an increase in supply from S_1 to S_2, such as a very good coffee harvest, this would lead to a fall in the equilibrium price level to a point below P_1. The government should thus buy up the excess supply $(Q_3 - Q_1)$ and put this into its buffer stock.

Figure 9.6 *Coffee farming in Brazil*

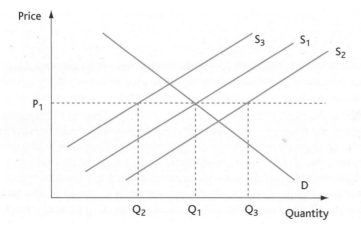

Figure 9.7 *How a buffer stock system works*

If, on the other hand, there was a decrease in supply from S_1 to S_3, following a frost that harms crops, this would lead to a rise in the equilibrium price level above P_1. The government would therefore need to sell off some its buffer stock to match the excess demand $(Q_1 - Q_2)$.

If the target stabilisation price is correctly estimated, with 'shock' increases and decreases in supply offsetting one another, then over time the buffer stocks held by the government will, on average, be zero. Buffers built up during times of excess supply will be run down again during bad harvests. However, practice is likely to be very different from theory and there are likely to be a number of problems arising with price stabilisation policies, such as in deciding what the 'correct' target price should be along with the substantial bureaucratic costs of administering the system.

Regulation and control of monopoly power

There are three main strands of policy open to governments to control monopoly power. They can block the merger of companies that would potentially lead to one large firm otherwise likely to dominate the market. They can also impose regulations on the firms that dominate the industry and finally the government can look to remove any artificial barriers that allow firms to dominate a market.

Figure 9.8

Any merger seen as likely to lead to firms securing a dominant position in a market can be referred to the Competition Commission, or CC (formerly the Monopolies and Mergers Commission). This government body is responsible for ensuring any merger is not against the public interest – that is, that the consumer will not be exploited through high prices and reduced output. The dominant firm may seek to charge prices that are considerably higher than the cost of production, knowing that there are no competitors consumers can turn to for lower prices. Furthermore, a monopolist is also likely to restrict output below the point at which average total costs are minimised, leading to productive inefficiency. In this case, the government may impose price controls upon the firm to ensure prices do not rise above an acceptable level. This type of approach is common in the case of companies supplying utilities, such as gas, electricity and water. A monopoly could also exploit the consumer by offering a poor quality product. A rail company that frequently delivers late running or cancelled train services could have its franchise withdrawn or be made to pay fines.

So-called 'natural' monopolies, where significant economies of scale are present, and where it can therefore be considered uneconomic for more than one firm to supply the market, could be placed into government ownership. This would ensure that competitive prices, equal to the cost of production are charged. Public utilities and railways that were previously nationalised, i.e. government-run, have been privatised in recent decades, however, as it was felt that they may be more efficiently run when faced with the profit motive.

One final method of controlling the power of monopolies is to make the markets they dominate more contestable. This involves the removal of barriers preventing the entry of competitors. The justification is that if other firms could enter the market with relative ease, dominant firms will have more incentive to set keener prices and provide high quality products. For example, before 1986, the National Bus Company was the only company allowed by law to supply the majority of local bus services. Upon removal of this legal barrier, private companies were allowed to contest the market, though this may have led to reduced services to less profitable, remote destinations.

Redistribution of income

The methodology used to create an equitable, i.e. 'fair', distribution of income is likely to differ from those used to correct other forms of market failure. What constitutes an equitable distribution of resources is largely the field of normative rather than positive economics and different governments, with different sets of politics and views on 'social justice' are likely to have different views on the matter. Different governments will certainly have different views on what scale of income inequality is acceptable.

If the government decides to intervene, it may choose to increase the amount of 'means-tested' or 'in-kind' benefits to lower income groups and/or increase the levels of tax paid by higher earners. Means-tested benefits are those dependent upon personal circumstances, in particular household income, as opposed to universal benefits paid regardless of income. In-kind benefits are goods or services provided by the government free of charge at the point of consumption, for example prescriptions or dental treatment to low-income groups, children and full-time students.

Unsurprisingly, the provision of benefits requires considerable expenditure by the government that will be raised from tax revenue. For the purposes of income redistribution from higher income groups to lower income groups the government will wish to take a larger percentage of income from the former and a lower percentage from the latter.

💡 The possibility of government failure

Even with good intentions governments rarely get their policy application right. They can tax, control and regulate but the eventual outcome may be a deepening of the market failure or even worse a new failure may arise. Government failure may range from the trivial, when intervention is merely ineffective, but where harm is restricted to the cost of resources used up and wasted by the intervention, to cases where intervention produces new and more serious problems that did not exist before. The consequences of this can take many years to reverse.

Causes of government failure

Government intervention can prove to be ineffective, inequitable and misplaced.

Political self-interest

The pursuit of self-interest amongst politicians and civil servants can often lead to a misallocation of resources. Decisions about where to build new roads, schools and hospitals may be decided with election aspirations in mind. Additional influence exerted by special interest groups can create an environment in which inappropriate spending and tax decisions are made, for example boosting welfare spending in the run-up to an election, or bringing forward major items of capital spending without the projects being subjected to a full and proper cost-benefit analysis to determine the likely social costs and benefits. Critics of current government policy towards tobacco taxation and advertising argue that government departments are too sensitive to political lobbying from major corporations.

Policy myopia

Critics of government intervention in the economy argue that politicians have a tendency to look for short-term solutions or 'quick fixes' to

AQA Examiner's tip

Try to identify examples of government intervention and failure in newspapers etc. This will sharpen your thinking for the exam.

AQA Examiner's tip

Do not confuse government failure with market failure.

Figure 9.10 *Lobbying local government. Could this lead to government failure?*

difficult economic problems – for example, the view that building more roads and widening existing roads and motorways is the most effective strategy to combat the worsening problem of traffic congestion. A decision to build more roads and bypasses might simply add to the problems of traffic congestion in the long run by encouraging an increase in the total number of cars on the roads. Critics of government subsidies to particular industries also claim that they distort the proper functioning of markets and lead to inefficiencies in the economy. For example, short-term financial support to coal producers to keep open loss-making coal pits might prove to be a waste of scarce resources if the industry has little realistic prospect of achieving a viable economic rate of return in the long run given the strength of global competition.

Regulatory capture

This is when the industries under the control of a regulatory body appear to operate in favour of the vested interest of producers rather than consumers. Some economists argue that regulators can prevent the market from operating freely. Examples may arise in agriculture, telecommunications and the main household utilities. Critics of the system of agricultural support known as the Common Agricultural Policy (CAP) argue that it has operated too much in the interests of farmers and the farming industry in general, working against the long-term interest of consumers, the environment and developing countries. The latter claim that they are being unfairly treated in world markets by the effects of import tariffs on food and export subsidies to loss-making European farmers.

Case study

The Common Agricultural Policy (CAP)

In the EU, a system of intervention is in place to protect the farming sector, known as the Common Agricultural Policy (CAP). The objectives of the CAP are:

- The stabilisation of agricultural markets
- The guarantee of regular supplies
- An increase in agricultural productivity and efficiency
- Maintaining reasonable consumer prices
- Maintaining a reasonable standard of living for the farming community.

The main method of intervention under the CAP is a system of price support, in effect a buffer stock system as outlined earlier, which in practice has meant that European consumers pay prices determined by the least efficient European producers rather than world market conditions.

Activity

Read the case study on the Common Agricultural Policy (CAP) and answer the following questions:

1 Using an appropriate diagram, outline how the CAP system of price support might be expected to work.

2 Discuss whether the market for agricultural products in the EU should be left to the free market.

Disincentive effects

Free market economists argue that attempts to reduce income and wealth inequalities can worsen incentives and productivity. They would argue against the National Minimum Wage because they believe that it artificially raises wages above their true free market level and can lead to real-wage unemployment. They would also argue against raising the higher rates of income tax because it is deemed to have a negative effect on the incentives of wealth-creators in the economy and generally acts as a disincentive to work longer hours or take a better paid job.

Policy decisions based on imperfect information

How does the government establish what citizens want it to do? It is very difficult to accurately discover the true revealed preferences of the total population. The current electoral system is certainly not an ideal way to discover this, since turnout in every type of election is falling and there seems to be a general lack of interest in the political process. Furthermore, people rarely vote purely out of their own self-interest or on the basis of a well-informed and rational assessment of the costs and benefits of different government policies. Free market economists argue that the market mechanism is, in the long run, the best way of finding out what consumer preferences are and aggregating these preferences based on the number of people that are willing and able to pay for particular goods and services.

The law of unintended consequences

This law lies at the heart of many of the possible causes of government failure in markets. The law of unintended consequences is that actions of consumers and producers, and especially of government, always have effects that are unanticipated or unintended. People do not always act in the way that the economics textbooks would predict, since we do not live our lives in laboratories where all of the conditions can be controlled. The **law of unintended consequences** is often used to criticise the effects of government legislation, taxation and regulation. People find ways to circumvent laws, shadow markets develop to undermine an official policy, and people act in unexpected ways because of ignorance and/or error. Unintended consequences can add hugely to the financial costs of some government programmes so that they make them extremely expensive when set against their original goals and objectives. A decision by the government to raise taxes on demerit goods such as cigarettes might lead to an increase in attempted tax avoidance, tax evasion, smuggling and the development of 'grey markets' where trade takes place between consumers and suppliers without paying tax.

Costs of administration and enforcement

Government intervention can prove costly to administer and enforce. The estimated social benefits of a particular policy might be considerably outweighed by the administrative costs of introducing it.

Conflicting objectives

At a macroeconomic level, it is possible that the policy objectives of government may not be compatible. For example, a government wishing to reduce unemployment by stimulating total demand in the economy may generate **inflation** if the supply capacity of the nation is limited.

> ### ■ Key terms
>
> **Law of unintended consequences:** when the actions of consumers, producers and governments have effects that are unanticipated.
>
> **Inflation:** a persistent increase in the level of prices.

■ Case study

Government failure: the landfill tax

The government introduced a landfill tax in the mid-1990s designed to raise the price to individuals, or cost to firms, of using landfill sites to dump household and industrial waste and subsequently encourage a switch to recycling and incineration, which is thought to be friendlier to the environment in the long term. The effects have been more costly than anticipated. Very little progress has been made in reducing the volume of waste recycled and thousands of people opted to fly-tip their waste on open land rather than pay the higher cost at a landfill site.

Source: adapted from Tutor2u

 Activity

Ofgem (Office for Gas and Electricity Markets) has issued a warning to the UK's main gas suppliers that they should not deliberately delay passing on the recent reductions in wholesale gas prices to their customers. This is in response to criticisms from Energy Watch, which acts as a watchdog for consumers. Cheaper gas from Norway and from the Netherlands has led to sharp falls in the wholesale price of gas with forward gas prices for the first three months of 2007 now just touching 40p a therm. But gas prices for the final consumers remain very high, indeed some service providers that had guaranteed prices during 2006 will, in the New Year, lift their tariffs. The average household is now paying £1,000 for their gas, over 50 per cent higher than two years ago. Demand for gas is inelastic and the suppliers know that consumers have little choice but to pay. Energy Watch preaches the value of consumers searching for the best deals and switching their supplier whenever possible but, realistically, there are limits to how many people are willing or able to do this. In January 2007, the European Commission will publish a long-awaited report on the deficiencies in competition in the market for gas supplies across the European Union. Regulators often have the reputation for suffering from regulatory capture, from acting in the interests of businesses rather than consumers. Perhaps Ofgem will bare its teeth and use some of the powers vested in it by the 2002 Competition Act?

1. How can Ofgem ensure energy suppliers act in the public's best interest?

2. How might government failure worsen the allocation of resources in energy markets?

After completing this chapter you should:

- be able to outline the reasons for government intervention in markets
- be able to outline, analyse and evaluate the various forms of government intervention in markets
- be able to define government failure
- be able to explain the reasons why government intervention in markets may fail to improve the allocation of resources.

AQA Examination-style questions

1   Study **Extracts A and B**, and then answer **all** parts of the question which follows.

Extract A: The predicted effects on car ownership and car use of toll charges for road use and a higher fuel tax

Type of pricing	Effect on car ownership (%)	Effect on car use (%)
Toll charge of 6.2 euros (£4.36) a kilometer	-9.4	-19.6
50% increase in fuel tax	-0.8	-5.9

Source: adapted from J Boot, P Boot and E Verhoef, *The long road towards the implementation of road pricing: the Dutch experience*, 1999

Extract B: The price is not right

In July 2005, the Government announced that it intended to introduce a national road user charge to replace the current forms of taxation that are paid by private car and lorry users. This radical system will not operate for almost 10 years, however. This apparently radical proposal surprised few economists who had for many years been advocating road pricing as a method of dealing with the market failures associated with increasing road congestion in the UK. Many economists would argue that currently the price is not right, i.e. some users pay far less than they should, whilst others pay more. The proposed national road user charge is designed to correct this situation.

The highest charge is estimated at £1.30 per mile, to apply where vehicles are used during peak periods in heavily congested towns and cities. An estimated 0.5 per cent of road users would pay this on a regular basis. The lowest charge will be as little as 2p per mile for vehicles used on most rural roads. By varying the charge, this is arguably a relatively precise way of bringing the price paid by road users into line with social costs, and is likely to be more precise than London's £8 per day congestion charge. If we are reluctant to take steps to correct this market failure, we may be faced with Los Angeles style gridlock. Levels of traffic continue to rise at around 2% per annum despite attempts to introduce more sustainable transport policies. The choice facing motorists is simple: queue or pay for scarce road space. Other methods of attempting to reduce road congestion include measures to make public transport or car-sharing more attractive, cycle-to-work schemes, city-centre pedestrianisation and tolls.

(a)   Using Extract A, compare the predicted effects of toll charges
and higher fuel taxation on car ownership and car use.   *(5 marks)*

(b)   Extract B states that 'The choice facing motorists is simple:
queue or pay for scarce road space'. Using a supply and
demand diagram, explain how road pricing may ration scarce
road space.   *(12 marks)*

(c)   Using the data and your economic knowledge, evaluate the
advantages and **disadvantages** of alternative policies for
reducing road congestion.   *(25 marks)*

(AQA, 2006)

Market failure and government failure case studies

In this chapter you will learn:

- to recognise instances of market failure and/or government failure in the context of a case study

- to apply the skills learned in the course so far in identifying, explaining, analysing and evaluating the issues presented in a case study

- that many moral and ethical issues need to be considered that make the 'real-life' work of governments and economists difficult.

In the Unit 1 examination, you will be expected to recognise situations of market failure and possible government failure in the context of a case study. This chapter has been designed to reflect the types of case study scenario that might appear in your exam and therefore should be considered an essential part of your exam preparation.

Buffer stock intervention

The price of nickel

During 2003, the price of nickel rose from under $8,000 to over $14,000 a tonne. Two-thirds of the world output of nickel goes into the production of stainless steel, used for products such as cutlery and kitchen sinks. The factors that influenced the price of nickel included:

- A strike by workers at a large nickel mine in Canada. The mine normally produces 9 per cent of the world output of nickel; 9,000 tonnes of nickel production was lost each month for several months.

- Early in 2003, Russian producers sold 36,000 tonnes of nickel from their stockpile, which was the largest in the world. In June 2003, the Russians sold a further 24,000 tonnes to offset supply concerns caused by the strike in Canada.

- Output of manufactured goods grew throughout the world in 2003. In China, surging output of stainless steel affected the nickel market.

- Speculative demand also affected the market. When speculators believe prices are going to rise, they buy the commodity in order to make a profit by selling at a higher price in the future. In the nickel market, changing demand conditions and running down of stocks led to speculative activity in 2003. Stocks had been the only buffer in the market stabilising the price of nickel.

Market traders expect the price of nickel to grow in 2004, as the world economy continues to grow and production falls due to the lack of new mines and dwindling supply from existing ones. In the 1990s, mining companies bet on new technology lowering the cost of extracting nickel ores found in tropical soils. But innovation failed to live up to expectations and the new mines in developing countries are not expected to start production for at least another two years, leaving the market short of nickel in 2004 and 2005. Steel makers are also seeking alternatives to nickel in an effort to deal with rising prices and undersupply.

Source: adapted from Kevin Morrison, *Financial Times*, 14 June, 23 August and 18 December 2003

February	74.5
April	69.3
June	71.9
August	76.9
October	82.9
December	91.3

Figure 10.1 *Index of metal prices, 2003 (1995 = 100)*

Activity

1. With the help of a supply and demand diagram, and the information in the extract, explain two factors that caused the price of nickel to rise in 2003.

2 It is often argued that buffer stock schemes should be used to control the prices of industrial raw material such as nickel and tin. Assess the possible advantages and disadvantages of using a buffer stock scheme to control the price of an industrial raw material.

Government provision of free health care

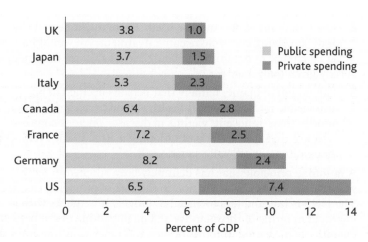

Figure 10.2 *Public and total health care expenditure as a percentage of national output (GDP), 1997*
Source: adapted from *Pressures in UK Health Care: Challenges for the NHS*, published by the Institute of Fiscal Studies, May 2000

Government intervention in healthcare

The original principles of the National Health Service (NHS) included the aim that everyone 'irrespective of means, age, sex or occupation shall have equal opportunity to benefit from the best and most up-to-date medical services available'. Supporters of the NHS believe that government intervention in the provision of health care is fairer than market provision and the charging of prices.

Market provision of health care may also be inefficient. An efficiency argument used to justify government provision of health care stems from the fact that there may be external, as well as private benefits when an individual becomes healthier. With individuals acting on the basis of their private benefits, the social benefits will not be fully achieved unless the government intervenes in some way.

Imperfect information provides another efficiency argument. When a person is very unwell, or if the need for treatment is urgent, he or she will not be able to shop around to compare advice or prices. Also, the information required to make a rational choice is often highly technical and emotionally charged.

Source: adapted from Pressures in UK Health Care: Challenges for the NHS, published by the Institute of Fiscal Studies, May 2000

1　Compare UK expenditure on health care in 1997 with that of the other countries shown in Fig. 10.2.

2　Explain

a　why supporters of the NHS believe that 'government intervention in the provision of health care is fairer than market provision and the charging of prices'.

b　with the use of examples, the difference between the private and social benefits of health care.

3　The demand for health care is increasing year by year. Using the data and your economic knowledge, discuss the advantages and disadvantages of alternative ways of rationing health care services.

Rationing and the NHS

Rationing by quantity (rather than price) is fundamental to the NHS. The guiding principle has been 'first come, first served', together with considerations of the urgency of individual cases. Those at the back of the queue are usually the most recent, least urgent cases.

Besides price and 'first come, first served', other methods of rationing are also possible:

1　Those who put in the most to the financing of the NHS could be entitled to draw out the most. This would favour the old rather than the young.

2　The lottery principle could be used. There might be a 'lucky draw' involving everyone needing treatment. All would have an equal chance of obtaining, or being excluded from, treatment in any given budgetary period.

3　The notion of blame, namely that persons deemed to be responsible for their own ill-health should be accorded lower priority than 'innocent' victims of disease. There is some evidence that this method of rationing is used in the NHS, even though it is not officially sanctioned.

A rationing principle that has definitely been adopted in recent years values outcomes in relation to the cost of providing treatment. The NHS is less and less prepared to provide treatments with a low yield in terms of the quantity and quality of life of the patient. Quantity is measured in terms of life expectancy resulting from the treatment, while quality is measured on an index from 0 (dead) to 1 (perfect health).

Source: adapted from David K. Whynes, *'UK Healthcare: Reorganisation and Rationing', in Developments in Economics, Volume 16, Causeway Press,* 2000

■ Government taxing and regulation of tobacco

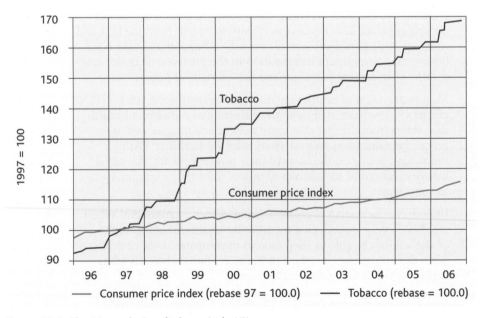

Figure 10.3 *The rising real price of tobacco in the UK*

A last gasp of defiance

'The basic point of the evening' said Neil Hulker, landlord of the Edinburgh Cellars pub, on Saturday night 'is for everyone to smoke themselves to death for one last time'. To help his regulars get to their graves that bit quicker, he had organised Smokefest, an evening of fume-filled fun at his north London bar.

A late licence had been arranged, allowing the venue to stay open until 6am, the time the smoking ban in England was due to come into force. Posters outside the pub inviting people to the free party read: *'Your last chance to legally smoke in this bar!'*

Smoking in public places creates externalities. By 10pm, the air inside was thick with the kind of smoke that takes two shampoos to wash out. Robert Logue, a 28-year-old demolition expert was already well into his first pack but vowing to become a non-smoker when last orders were called. 'Smoking is a filthy, horrible habit that stains your teeth and makes your clothes smell. I've been doing it since I was 13 and it's about time I gave up', he said. Mr Logue seemed confident that the ban would be the impetus he and the 27 per cent of English adults who smoke needed to quit.

As the ban came into force, heralding what campaigners call the biggest boost to public health since the creation of the NHS, experts disagreed about the effect on businesses. A survey from the Campaign for Real Ale said that 840,000 people who never go to a pub said they would do so after the ban. But market researchers Neilsen estimated that beer sales at pubs, bars and clubs could drop by 200 million pints a year. The volume of all drinks sold by licensed premises in Scotland is down 5 per cent following the ban in 2006.

Health secretary Alan Johnson said the government would raise the minimum age for buying tobacco from 16 to 18 from 1 October 2007.

Source: adapted from Helen Pidd, 'A last gasp of defiance – and now the ban', *Guardian*, 2 July 2007

Activity

1. Using Fig. 10.3, compare the general level of prices with the price of tobacco from 1995 to 2006.

2. Explain how smoking in public places creates negative externalities.

3. With the help of a supply and demand diagram, explain the statement that the effectiveness of higher taxes on tobacco depends on its price elasticity of demand.

4. Evaluate the view that raising the legal smoking age to 18 will be more effective than other methods for reducing the harmful effects of smoking.

Government provision of national defence and policing

Public goods in the 21st century

Most economists define public goods in terms of 'non-excludability' and 'non-rivalrous' competition.

But the crucial question for policy makers in the 21st century is this: how common are genuine public goods? For years it was assumed they were common enough. The favourite illustration of a public good was a lighthouse. Others include roads and TV broadcasts. However, the introduction of congestion charges and satellite broadcasting has thrown doubt on this assumption. Many economists now reject the view that governments must provide public goods.

Policing – a public good?

To what extent is our current system of policing an example of a public good? Some (but not all) aspects of policing might qualify as public goods. The general protection that the police services provide in deterring crime and investigating criminal acts serves as a public good. But resources used up in providing specific police services mean that fewer resources are available elsewhere. For example, the use of police at sporting events or demonstrations and protests means that police resources have to be diverted from other policing duties. The police services must make important decisions about how best to allocate their manpower in order to provide the most effective policing service for the whole community. Private protection services (including private security guards, privately bought security systems and detectives) are private goods because the service is excludable, rejectable and rival in consumption and people and businesses are often prepared to pay a high price for exclusive services. A good recent example of this has been the use of private security firms in post-war Iraq where up to 15,000 workers are said to have been working for private businesses protecting installations, coalition buildings and convoy protection.

National defence

There are a few goods that do fall into the category of pure public goods, and in this sense there is no chance that the market system will provide these goods. For instance, a nuclear deterrent and the armed forces of the UK are an extremely expensive system of national defence. It is impossible to prevent anyone from obtaining the same level of defence as the next person, and one person's protection by the system does little, if anything, to prevent another from enjoying the same protection. The market does not provide it because a firm will find it difficult to charge people for the service. You cannot provide a service and then charge people who did not want the service in the first place. The debate over the UK's involvement in the 'war on terrorism' emphasises the fiercely held views across the whole population on how we should react as a nation. It is also possible that some people may not pay because, though they are willing to be defended, they are willing to risk the fact that someone else will want defending more and will pay for them both. This is the essence of the 'free-rider' problem.

■ The operation of a market in emissions trading

Carbon trading and government failure

Coal production is on the increase in the UK and around Europe. But this is the sort of thing that isn't supposed to be happening! Even with the potential for clean coal technology, it is widely regarded as a dirty source of energy and a major contributor to CO_2 emissions. Why are the power stations turning back to coal? Because the price of carbon emissions is low and coal has become price competitive against oil and gas.

The carbon trading scheme started in January 2005 with carbon allowances being bought and sold. The largest CO_2 emitters were brought into the 'cap and trade' system. The cap places a limit on the total pot of emissions that can be released by industry – the aim is to progressively reduce this cap over time and therefore mitigate climate change. The original caps set by the EU are now seen as being set way too high and some people believe that this was not an accident; companies and businesses may have deliberately requested higher allowances than they needed, creating surplus permits that could be profitably sold on to other businesses.

Carbon Trade Watch believe that the EU has been captured by strong corporate lobbying who themselves knowingly over-estimated

Activity

1. Define the term 'public good'.

2. To what extent do you consider policing to be a pure public good?

3. Using the data and your economic knowledge, evaluate the case for a government rather than markets providing public goods.

their 'business as usual' CO_2 emissions when they submitted them to national governments ahead of the launch of the carbon trading scheme.

The surplus of CO_2 emission allowances has meant that scarcity in the market has disappeared, leading to a collapse in the price of carbon – prices are now between 20 and 30 Euro cents. Effectively, the price of polluting is close to zero. The market thus provides little incentive for businesses to invest money in reducing their emissions.

As coal production expands, so CO_2 emissions are rising, and the power stations have to buy extra emissions credits, but the price of credits is low so the consequences for the power generators are not significant. Emissions from coal-fired power stations in the UK in 2006 alone increased by 8 per cent! Consumers are paying the price of higher energy bills but they are not getting the environmental pay-off in terms of reducing carbon production as a contribution to controlling climate change.

Source: Tutor2u, 6 June 2007

Doffing the cap – tradable emissions are a popular, but inferior, way to tackle global warming

The pressure for action on climate change has never looked stronger. Even George Bush has now joined the leaders of other rich countries in their quest to negotiate a successor regime to the Kyoto protocol, the treaty on curbing greenhouse gases that expires in 2012.

Too bad, then, that politicians seem set on a second-best route to a greener world. That is the path of 'cap and trade', where the quantity of emissions is limited (the cap) and the right to emit is distributed through a system of tradable permits. The main market-based alternative – a carbon tax – has virtually no political support. A pity, because most economists agree that carbon taxes are a better way to reduce greenhouse gases than cap and trade schemes.

Misjudging the number of permits could send permit prices either skywards or through the floor. Worse, a fixed allotment of permits makes no adjustment for the business cycle (firms produce and pollute less during a recession).

Cap and trade schemes cause unnecessary economic damage because the price of permits can be volatile. America has had tradable permits for sulphur dioxide since the mid-1990s. Their price has varied, on average, by more than 40 per cent a year. Given carbon's importance in the economy, similar fluctuations could significantly affect everything from inflation to consumer spending. Extreme price volatility might also deter people from investing in green technology.

Even without the volatility, some economists reckon that a cap and trade system produces fewer incentives than a carbon tax for climate-friendly innovation. A tax provides a clear price floor for carbon and hence a minimum return for any innovation. Under a cap and trade system, in contrast, an invention that reduced the cost of cutting carbon emissions could itself push down the price of permits, reducing investors' returns.

Activity

1. Explain what is meant by the term 'government failure'.

2. Outline two ways, mentioned in the text, in which government intervention has failed to improve the allocation of resources.

3. Using a supply and demand diagram, outline how the carbon-trading scheme is supposed to reduce the level of industrial emissions.

4. Evaluate the relative advantages and disadvantages of a system of tradable pollution permits with the introduction of a carbon tax.

A third advantage of carbon taxes is that they raise revenue. Governments can use this cash to compensate those, such as the poor, who are hit disproportionately hard by higher fuel costs.

Source: adapted from © The Economist Newspaper Limited, London (16 June 2007)

After completing this chapter you should:

■ recognise instances of market failure and/or government failure in the context of a case study

■ be able to apply the skills learned in the course so far in identifying, explaining, analysing and evaluating the issues presented in a case study.

The national economy

Introduction

This unit will introduce you to macroeconomics where you consider the economy as a whole rather than look at different markets. In Chapter 11 we will begin by looking at what we mean by macroeconomic performance, how we can measure it and what indicators we might consider to see if our performance is improving our level of welfare. You will be made aware of the various types of statistical and other data that are commonly used by economists as indicators of our economic performance. You will also discover that economies do not proceed on an even pattern but are subject to fluctuations over time.

In Chapter 12 we will take one of our macromodels, the circular flow of income, and start with a very simple economy based on a desert island. During the chapter the model will be developed to allow you to appreciate how a real economy operates. The model will allow you to explain what is likely to happen to an economy if there are changes in flows into and out of the economy. The model will allow you to increase your understanding of how the economy works as it progresses.

Chapter 13 will use a model known as aggregate demand aggregate supply (AD/AS) analysis, which will allow you to look graphically at the effect of changes on the macroeconomy and predict what outcomes are likely when economic variables change. Whereas Chapter 12 explained how the macroeconomy works this chapter will allow you to show diagrammatically the effects of changes and thus increases your analytical skills. It is important that you master the AD/AS diagrams as they are an important part of your toolkit and we will build on them at A2.

In Chapter 14 we look at what are known as the macroeconomic objectives – what governments would like the economy to achieve and the objectives of their economic policy. You will also discover that governments face restrictions in their ambitions for the economy as not all of their objectives can be achieved at once and sometimes they clash with each other. Hopefully, you will find this a fascinating aspect of economics. It is an area where you will be able to exercise the important skills of analysis in showing how policy conflicts can take place and evaluation in suggesting what governments might be able to do to navigate out of their dilemma.

The next three chapters will look at the macroeconomic objectives in more detail, starting with economic growth in Chapter 15. We will consider economic growth in terms of what it is and the difference between actual and trend growth and its impact on the economy and other objectives. In order to understand the difference between trend and actual you will use a different diagram from those experienced so far, which will be referenced to AD/AS analysis. In this chapter growth will also be shown by using the production possibility boundary studied in Chapter 1.

We study the causes of inflation, deflation, employment and unemployment in Chapter 16 and their impact on the macroeconomy. We will also use AD/AS analysis to show how changes in any of these variables are likely to affect the economy and how they might interact with each other.

As the UK is a major trading country we will consider its trading position with the rest of the world when we look at the balance of payments in Chapter 17. In this chapter we will look at exports and imports and the UK's trade in goods and services and how it is changing. You need to be aware that the performance of the UK economy is influenced by its membership of the European Union (EU) and external events in the international economy.

The next three chapters (18, 19 and 20) look at government policies – monetary, fiscal and supply-side and explain what is entailed in each of them and how they assist the government in reaching their macroeconomic objectives. You will also appreciate how their operation is likely to affect the AD/AS model.

To conclude, we look at the examination and how it is set, marked and what skills you require to perform well. We explain what these skills entail and how you might achieve them.

Macroeconomics, like most other aspects of the subject, is one where knowledge of the real world gained through quality newspapers and magazines will enhance your knowledge, skills and final examination result. As a student the specification expects you to have a good knowledge of developments in the UK economy and government policies over the past ten years.

11 The measurement of macroeconomic performance

Key terms

Aggregate demand: total demand in the economy made up of consumption, investment, government expenditure and net exports. Known by the identity $C + I + G + (X - M)$.

Aggregate supply: the total value of goods and services supplied in the economy.

Links

The diagrammatic explanation of aggregate demand and aggregate supply will be considered in Chapter 13.

AQA Examiner's tip

■ Make sure you can define terms concisely and correctly as examination mark schemes always reward good definitions.

■ You should be aware that the term 'macroeconomic performance' often appears in data response questions and defining or interpreting the key concepts will improve your answer.

■ You should remember that examination questions asking about the likely effects on an economy of a particular action will require some discussion and knowledge of the macroeconomic objectives.

In this part of the course we look at the operation of the economy from a macroeconomic perspective rather than using the microeconomic approach of looking at separate parts of the economy. In this chapter we will look at how we try to measure economic performance to see if our economic welfare has improved or perhaps to compare our performance with previous years or to another economy. We will also consider statistical measures that indicate to us whether the economy has improved and whether or not our living standards have increased.

The meaning of macroeconomic performance

Microeconomics is concerned with individual markets such as agricultural, housing, oil and labour. At a micro-level we analyse the operation of these individual markets to see how they work when the conditions of demand or supply change. Macroeconomics considers the economy as a whole – the total quantities of goods and services produced by all firms in the economy. We are no longer looking at individual or household demand or the supply of an individual firm or industry but total demand and supply in the economy. We refer to total demand as **aggregate demand** and total supply as **aggregate supply**.

The interaction of these two forces will produce a macroeconomic equilibrium just as the interaction of demand and supply produced microeconomic equilibrium.

This chapter is just an introduction to the topic of macroeconomics and you will consider these areas in greater detail both at AS and A2 Level. The aim here is to assist you to understand that these are areas that will allow us to judge how well the economy is performing and that is why they are of importance to us as economists. The four areas studied, plus the questions that would be relevant to us as economists in order to assess the performance of the macroeconomy, are outlined below:

■ Economic growth – is our capacity to produce goods and services growing over time?

■ Full employment – is our economy efficient or do we have resources lying idle?

■ Stable prices – are we able to control prices so that we are competitive with other economies or are prices out of control?

■ Are we living within our means – are we buying more from other countries than we are selling to them?

The policy of any government is to improve the well-being of its citizens and this implies attempting to put in place macroeconomic policies that will ensure that they achieve a suitable outcome in the four areas mentioned. Some governments may put more emphasis on one objective rather than another as they believe that it will lead to greater economic welfare overall. Apart from measuring improvements in their economic performance over time – for example, is the economy creating more jobs than it did ten years ago – countries also compare their macroeconomic performance with other countries. For example, is our economy growing at a faster rate than that of France and are we or they the fifth richest country in the world?

◻ The measures of macroeconomic performance

Growth

One important measure of an economy's performance is whether it can deliver more goods and services to its members over time. This is known as **economic growth** and is measured by looking at the change in the level of output.

Economists have realised for years that growth is not a steady linear process but proceeds in fits and starts, usually referred to as the economic cycle. Diagrammatically it appears as Fig. 11.1.

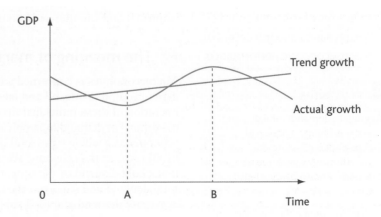

Figure 11.1 *Growth*

The *y*-axis shows the letters GDP – this is **gross domestic product** and is a standard way of measuring output. It is measured as a percentage so the expected increase in the output of goods and services over a year in the UK is 2.5–2.75 per cent.

The actual growth rate shows the performance of an economy at a particular point in time while the trend growth rate is the average performance of the economy over time. The actual growth rate represents the cyclical activity of the economy and is sometimes below trend and at other times above trend. The trend growth rate for the UK economy is thought to be about 2.5–2.75 per cent per annum. We can judge the economy as to whether it is performing above or below its trend value and how its growth rate compares to other economies. In Fig. 11.1 at OA the actual growth is below trend, which is likely to mean lower than expected levels of output and higher levels of unemployment. This is known as a **negative output gap**. In terms of the economic cycle when actual growth is below trend journalists often talk about the economy going into a recession or if the situation was extremely bad with large numbers unemployed, a slump. This is a situation where the macro economy is underperforming and the government may take action to increase aggregate demand in order to try to increase economic activity.

At *OB* actual growth is above trend, which means that the economy is growing more rapidly than is usual and incomes will be increasing. This is likely to imply that most unemployed factors have been taken up and if aggregate demand exceeds aggregate supply, prices will be rising and the economy will experience inflationary pressure. This is known as a **positive output gap.** When growth is above trend the economy is often referred to as being in a recovery or if actual growth is largely in excess of trend growth, a boom. The economy is performing above its trend or potential output and as this will lead to inflation the government is likely to try and reduce aggregate demand.

This leads to another key point in the understanding of macroeconomics that there are often conflicts between macroeconomic policy objectives. For instance, increasing levels of growth may conflict with the aim of price stability if aggregate demand outpaces aggregate supply. In a positive output gap unemployment will be low and wage levels are likely to be rising, leading to cost increases that are likely to be passed on by producers to customers. As well as adding to domestic inflationary pressure such price increases will reduce the UK's international competitiveness. The pursuit of one objective may mean an opportunity cost in terms of the other. This is often referred to in economics as a **trade-off** where an increase in one area is traded off for a decrease in the other. Thus at *OB* **imports** are likely to increase and **exports** fall as UK goods become less price competitive and people spend their extra income on imported goods.

Employment and unemployment

Both **employment** and **unemployment** are affected by the economic cycle and the levels of employment (and unemployment) are another important indicator of how an economy performs as it shows whether or not the economy is capable of producing jobs for its labour force. In Fig. 11.1, unemployment occurs in the area where actual growth is below trend growth – a negative output gap. As actual output is below potential or trend output some workers will be unable to find jobs or are likely to have been laid off. Unemployment has a huge opportunity cost in that it represents a waste of scarce resources as output lost can never be recovered. It has negative effects on the unemployed themselves, their families, the locality and the wider economy as a whole:

■ Unemployment has adverse effects on the individuals who are likely to suffer a fall in their confidence levels as well as their income, which is magnified by the length of time for which they are unemployed. Studies have shown that the unemployed are more likely to suffer from depression, alcoholism, domestic violence and family breakdown than those with jobs. The economic consequences of this may be increased government expenditure on social services with its attendant opportunity cost.

■ The situation for the family of those unemployed is also pretty dire, as their standard of living is likely to fall and purchases that were once taken for granted are now unaffordable.

■ Areas suffering from high levels of unemployment are likely to be run down with shops shutting down and crime rates rising. These adverse effects create negative externalities that impose a burden on society.

■ Government income from tax will be falling while benefit expenditure will be increasing and tax on the employed may need to rise to cover benefits to the unemployed.

Low unemployment as at present in UK is an indicator of good national economic performance and the UK economy is importing labour as jobs are increasing at a faster rate than available labour. In terms of Fig. 11.1 actual growth is above trend as aggregate demand is exceeding aggregate supply. Immigrant labour will reduce supply constraints and the 'tightness' of the labour market by ensuring that firms requiring labour can obtain it. Employment is linked with growth as rapid growth leads

■ Activity

1. Construct a trade cycle diagram showing actual and trend output.

2. Explain what you understand by the term 'output gaps'.

3. Explain why the authorities would try to reduce demand when the economy is in a positive output gap.

4. Construct a production possibility diagram and indicate the position of the economy when it is in a negative output gap.

Figure 11.2

Links

For more information on negative externalities, see Chapter 8.

Links

For more information on production possibility boundaries see Chapter 1.

AQA Examiner's tip

Be aware that some aspects of both growth and unemployment can be illustrated by using a production possibility boundary.

Activity

Using a production possibility diagram explain the statement 'reducing unemployment has no opportunity cost'.

Links

For more information on inflation see Chapter 16.

to low unemployment, as more workers are required to produce goods and services. However, as technology increases some workers are made unemployed and some with outdated or unwanted skills will be unable to find jobs. But the overall effect of growth is that it seems to create more jobs than it destroys.

Case study

How much growth can the economy take?

The economy grew at 3.0 per cent in the year to the first quarter, which is above the trend rate of growth; excluding oil and gas, output rose by 3.2 per cent. Investment is booming – capital spending jumped by 8.9 per cent over the same period – and consumers are still spending.

Business surveys suggest that the economy is operating at close to capacity, and that companies are primed to push up prices. Rapid growth in money and credit may also presage inflationary trouble. Much depends upon whether pay pressures are building up in the labour market. On the one hand, the average-earnings index grew by 4.0 per cent in the three months to April compared with the same period last year. This rate is comfortably below the level of 4.5–4.75 per cent that is consistent in the long term with the 2 per cent inflation target.

Inflation

Inflation defined as a persistent increase in the level of prices occurs over time. For example, in 1974 a pair of jeans were priced at £3.50 but similar quality jeans are presently selling for around £30.00. Rapid inflation has adverse effects on an economy, as it breeds further inflation as consumers, workers and firms react in ways that lead to increased prices. In Fig. 11.1 there is inflationary pressure when the economy is in a positive output gap and actual growth is above trend growth. When actual growth exceeds the trend labour will be scarce and in a position to push for wage increases. As aggregate demand is increasing firms will be able to pass on their increased labour costs in the form of increased prices. Eventually, actual growth will slow as rising prices are likely to lead to falling demand for firms' products from both domestic and foreign markets. As a result, unemployment is likely to rise and aggregate demand will fall and actual growth will fall below trend as the economic cycle continues. This is compounded by the effect on the demand for UK exports and imports as price increases in the UK, if they are faster than price increases elsewhere, will reduce the demand for our exports.

The government has laid down a target for inflation and it is the responsibility of the Bank of England to ensure that the target is met. As too high a level of aggregate demand during a positive output gap will increase inflation the Bank will want to reduce aggregate demand. During a negative output gap a low level of aggregate demand is likely to reduce inflationary pressure but lead to higher than desired unemployment and as a result the Bank is likely to try to increase aggregate demand. Manipulation of aggregate demand by the Bank is aimed at creating price stability. Inflation is an important measure of performance as it indicates

Figure 11.3 *Inflation cartoon (Dr Seuss)*

whether the UK is price competitive internationally and whether government policies to control price rises are successful.

International competitiveness

Most economies are involved in trading with other countries and are involved in **exporting** and **importing**. An economy needs to be able to sell goods or services abroad to earn the income that it requires to buy foreign goods and services. It needs to be competitive in order that overseas customers will purchase its goods rather than those of other economies. We have seen previously that inflation will make our goods too expensive in overseas markets and less competitive with those of our trading competitors. If our factories are inefficient and producing less per hour than other economies our products will be too expensive and not sell. This will affect our other macroeconomic objectives as falling sales mean less demand for labour and increasing unemployment. It is quite likely that our national assets will determine the goods and services that we trade internationally. Over the past two decades the UK has been selling North Sea oil to the rest of the world, while its share of basic manufactured goods has fallen because it is not able to compete with low-wage emerging economies. However, with a relatively well-educated population as one of its national assets the UK is well placed to sell sophisticated financial services and higher valued manufactured goods. In terms of Fig. 11.1 increased sales abroad will boost demand for UK

> **Key terms**
>
> **Exporting:** the sale of goods or services to a foreign country – generates income for the home country.
>
> **Importing:** the purchase of goods and services from abroad – leads to expenditure for the home country.

products and benefit the economy when it is in a negative output gap at *OA*. However, when the economy is experiencing a positive output gap, increased sales abroad would widen the gap between actual and trend growth.

One of the problems that governments face with macroeconomic objectives is that when income grows or the prices of domestic goods increase there is a surge in the number of goods and services imported. Reducing the number of goods and services purchased from overseas usually requires reducing spending in the economy to reduce the level of imports. This will lead to rising unemployment and reduced rates of economic growth. This is a further example of the possible clash and the need for a trade-off between policy objectives.

The economic cycle: gaps and trade-offs

At the beginning of this chapter we referred to the term 'trade-offs', which is the opportunity cost of one macroeconomic objective in terms of another. The fluctuations of the economic cycle produces both positive and negative output gaps. As governments do not want price instability, unemployed factors of production or an excess of imports over exports they try to exercise some influence over aggregate demand over the period of the cycle. In a negative output gap actual growth is below trend growth and the economy is underperforming its potential and as a result the increase in the economy's welfare and standard of living is lower than would be reasonably expected. And even though exports are likely to increase because demand in the domestic economy is low there is also likely to be unemployed labour in the economy. Imports will be low as consumers' purchasing power will be reduced. Governments have to take a view as to which objective they consider the most likely to increase the population's economic welfare. They also want to be re-elected and will not want the economy performing below its optimum.

In a positive output gap growth will be above trend as the economy is performing above its potential and growing faster than expected. This will reduce unemployment but there is a danger that the labour market will become 'tight' and firms will not be able to employ the workers that they require. Workers will be in a position to push for wage increases and firms will increase wages to stop labour going elsewhere. The increased costs to firms will increase inflationary pressure as firms pass on increased costs in the form of higher prices. Both increased inflationary pressure and increased wages are likely to lead to increased imports, as they will appear relatively cheaper and increased incomes in the UK leads to increased expenditure on imports. Exports may be reduced due to inflation and domestic firms targeting the expanding home market. The authorities have to decide what objective is most important to them. Governments have taken the view that control of inflation is vital to achieve their other macroeconomic objectives and to increase the welfare of the population.

Key terms

Economic indicators: economic statistics that provide information about the expansions and contractions of business cycles.

■ Indicators of macroeconomic performance

In order to decide how the economy is performing over time or how it compares with other economies the government uses '**economic indicators**', which are items of data that show different aspects of the economy's performance. They are variables that provide information about the current state of the economy and its likely future direction.

Like most items of data they are capable of interpretation in different ways according to the perceptions of the reader.

⚡ The gross domestic product (GDP)

Gross domestic product (GDP) is used to measure the value of all goods and services produced in the economy by the three wealth creating sectors – manufacturing, agriculture and the service industries.

The value of the GDP is usually stated in monetary terms though sometimes you may read that it has increased by say 2 per cent. At present the UK's GDP is around £1bn, which is a **nominal** figure, stated in terms of current prices where the effects of inflation have not been taken into account. A nominal figure does not give a true measure of the actual increased output of the economy as part of the increased output could be made up of price increases. So if next year the GDP has increased by £200m we cannot be sure how much of that figure represents an increase in **real output** or whether real output has only grown by £50m and the extra £150m represents price increases.

To remove this problem the figures need to be adjusted for inflation to obtain a measure known as **real GDP**. Using the previous example, if inflation was 3 per cent then the real increase in GDP would be £200m − 0.3% = £199.7m. This figure tells us by how much the real output of the economy increased. A change in real GDP is the indicator used to measure the change of economic growth that has taken place in the economy over a particular period of time. Real GDP can be referred to as a constant price measure.

You may also see a figure for gross national product (GNP). This figure includes income that UK residents may receive from abroad minus the amount that is paid out of our economy to people overseas. Overseas income may be generated from either working abroad or owning shares in foreign firms.

While either the GDP or GNP may give an idea as to the size of the economy compared to others it does not provide information about the amount that each person in the economy has to spend, i.e. the spending power of the average person. In order to calculate spending power of the individual, GDP is divided by the population to obtain GDP per head or **GDP per capita**, the amount available to the average person to spend. Increases in GDP per capita are an indicator of increasing living standards as they show by how much the income of the average person has risen over time. GDP per capita is a much better indicator of the population's standard of living than total GDP as there is no guarantee that increases in GDP will be distributed among the population. Some dictatorial regimes have kept the increased income for themselves or distributed it among their cronies leading to no improvement of the standard of living of the average member of the population.

Key terms

Nominal GDP/nominal national income/nominal output: GDP/income/output figures not adjusted for inflation.

Real GDP/real national income/real output: GDP/income/output figures adjusted for inflation.

GDP per capita: GDP divided by the population – a measure of living standards.

Index numbers: a weighted average of a group of items compared to a given base value of 100.

AQA Examiner's tip

You should avoid confusing a 'measure of economic performance' with an 'indicator of economic performance'.

AQA Examiner's tip

- Make sure that you can distinguish between nominal and real as data may be presented in either form.
- Remember that an increase in real GDP will shift the production possibility (boundary, frontier, curve etc.) outwards.

Activity

	France	Britain	Germany	Italy
Population (millions)	60.9	60.3	82.6	58.1
Nominal GDP (US$bn)	2,252	2,374	2,899.4	1,854
Real GDP growth	1.7	2.5	0.6	0.7
Current account balance	−0.3	−2.1	3.6	−1.4
Inflation	1.9	1.7	1.3	2.3

Using the data above

1 Calculate the GDP per capita for the four countries.

2 Which country would you expect to have the highest GDP per capita in the future? Explain your reasoning.

3 In which country is the value of money falling most rapidly?

Skills

The questions in the activity above require you to develop a skill that is vital to you as an economist. It is very important to be able to interpret and manipulate statistical data. Using fairly basic mathematics you as an economist can compare the economies in the question and reach a conclusion regarding their performance.

In addition to changes in the level of GDP, changes in the level of inflation need to be measured and this is done by using **index numbers**. Index numbers are designed to measure the magnitude of economic changes over time. Because they work in a similar way to percentages, they make such changes easier to compare. To use index numbers a base year is chosen and the index number 100 is given to the price of goods and services chosen. Table 11.1 shows how index numbers may be used to illustrate price changes of two goods.

Table 11.1 *Table for activity*

	Year 1	Index	Year 2	Index
Commodity	Price		Price	
A	5p	100	10p	200
B	£1.00	100	80p	80
		100		280
				140

Commodity A's year 1 price is 5p and is given the index of 100. By year 2 its price has doubled to 10p and as a result the index also doubles to 200. Commodity B falls in price from £1.00 to 80p and the index is revised downward from 100 to 80. Adding the year 2 indexes gives a figure of 280. A simple average of the percentage changes in price indicates that prices in year 2 are 40 per cent higher than they were in year 1 (140 −

100). Prices in following years would be expressed as percentages of those in year 1 and averaged in a similar manner.

The index numbers given above may not be particularly useful if they do not reflect the goods and services that consumers buy and the percentage of income spent by them on the product. Commodity A may be a product that consumers buy all the time, whereas B is an infrequent purchase. This problem can be overcome by using a system of **weighting** so that each commodity is given a weight proportional to its importance in the general pattern of consumer spending.

■ Key terms

Weighting: where a commodity is given a weighting proportional to its importance in the general pattern of consumer spending.

■ Case study

The housing market

After the slump of the early 1990s, the housing market improved and since 1996 the average house price has risen by 240 per cent, according to the Nationwide index; in real terms it has increased by 155 per cent. In contrast, the big upturn in the 1980s lasted for seven years, and real house prices rose by 80 per cent.

Two years ago the long boom seemed to be petering out. House prices rose by only 2 per cent in 12 months. But following an interest-rate reduction the market revived. House prices are now rising by 10 per cent a year, close to the average growth of 12 per cent in the past decade. In London and Scotland they have surged by around 15 per cent since early 2006.

■ The Retail Prices index

This is the main domestic measure of inflation in the UK. It measures the average change from month to month in the prices of goods and services consumed by most households. It is a weighted price index, which is calculated by the Office of National Statistics (ONS) and used to measure the rate of inflation, usually over a year. As well as providing headline figures it gives detailed breakdowns for particular products and services including food, catering, alcoholic drink, leisure services and holidays.

The ONS carries out about 120,000 price measurements monthly of a selection of more than 600 separate goods and services in 146 areas throughout the country. The final basket of goods contains about 650 items that are relevant to UK consumers.

Keeping the index up to date is important as the entry of new goods and services replaces older products and reflects the changes in our consumption patterns.

■ Case study

Brussels sprouts left on the shelf in UK's revised 'shopping basket'

Schoolchildren across the land can rejoice: Brussels sprouts are officially out of favour. For the first time since 1947 the unloved vegetables have dropped out of the nation's 'shopping basket' that is used to calculate inflation.

In their place, bean-counters at the Office for National Statistics

Figure 11.4

Table 11.2 *Changes in the CPI*

Month	Year	Index
January	2007	103.2
February	2007	103.7
March	2007	104.2
April	2007	104.5
May	2007	104.8
Base year 2005		

Source: ONS

AQA Examiner's tip

You should practise interpreting statistical data. Go to www. nationalstatistics.co.uk or look at quality newspapers or publications such as *The Economist* and try to follow the graphs and tables.

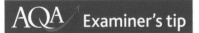

(ONS) have brought in broccoli and courgettes, in a sign of the nation's changing shopping habits.

The shopping basket is a representative sample of about 650 goods and services, whose prices are monitored each month by the ONS to calculate the inflation rate. Once a year the ONS revises the basket, adding goods that have become popular, dropping those that are no longer widely bought.

From this year food prices will be calculated with the help of olive oil, not vegetable oil, and with a list that includes a 'pro-biotic yoghurt-style drink'.

The latest shopping basket paints a picture of how new technology has transformed our homes. Flat-panel televisions have replaced portable conventional televisions in the list, and digital radios have supplanted radio CD cassette players. DVDs have taken over from videos, with blank VHS cassettes falling from the list, to be replaced with a pack of recordable DVDs. The ONS will collect statistics on the cost of processing digital prints, rather than the development of mail-order camera film, and the ubiquitous sat-nav makes it into the list.

The RPI and a number of its derivatives were used to measure changes in prices, the government's inflation target, until December 2003. In that year the Chancellor changed to a new base: the Consumer Price Index (CPI) that is used to assess price stability in the euro area. By using the CPI the government can now compare its inflation directly with that of the European Union countries.

While the change from RPI to CPI has gone smoothly, the CPI does not include changes in house prices and related areas, all of which are of extreme importance to a large percentage of the UK population. As a result consumers have felt that inflationary increases have affected them more than the CPI has revealed. At present the RPI is probably a better guide to how price increases are affecting average members of the population but no single measure of inflation can meet all users' needs. The ONS publishes data for both the RPI and the CPI.

Changes in the CPI are used today to indicate changes in the levels of prices and can be seen in Table 11.2.

During the period January to May 2007 the price index increased from 103.2 to 104.8, an increase of 1.6 per cent. However, assuming wages have not increased during the period the value of money has fallen by 1.6 per cent, as an increase in the price level will reduce real wages. Data collection by the ONS means that the authorities can track changes in the cost of living due to inflation and take appropriate action if it needs to be reduced. Price indices, by showing both inflation rates and reductions in the real value of money, enable individuals to work out whether they are better or worse off over the period of a year and what is happening to the value of their savings.

Activity

Table 11.3 *Weighting of tobacco and leisure services (parts per 1,000)*

Year	Tobacco & alcohol weight	Tobacco weight	Foreign holidays weight
1952	168	90	n/a
2003	98	30	34
2004	97	29	31
2005	96	29	32
2006	96	29	30
2007	95	29	34

Source: © Crown Copyright. National Statistics

1. Explain why the various goods and services are weighted by the Office of National Statistics.

2. What is the trend in tobacco and alcohol consumption?

3. Explain possible reasons for this change.

4. Foreign holidays do not appear in the index until 2003 – why is this?

Skills

The skills mentioned below are relevant to the exam style questions.

As an AS and later an A2 economist you will be presented with what we can call examination terminology. Two words are in constant use – analyse and evaluate.

Analyse basically means explain and interpret something – in economics there are three main ways of doing this:

- Textually, using words as I am doing at present.
- Mathematically, e.g. percentages that could be used in explaining elasticity.
- Diagrammatically, as in Fig. 11.1 above – the use of the diagram is a very important skill for economists as it enables us to portray visually what otherwise would require a vast amount of prose.

Evaluation is to draw conclusions from your analysis and can be any one of the following:

- Explaining why some points or arguments are more important than others.
- Weighing up alternative and competing theories.
- Effects of a policy and the likely knock-on effects elsewhere in the economy.
- The costs weighed up against the benefits.
- The case for versus the case against.
- The fact that one thing may depend crucially on another.

Activity

Stretch and challenge

1 a Construct a diagram showing both actual and trend output.

  b Explain what is meant by a positive output gap and a negative output gap.

  c Explain what trade-offs are likely to occur during a boom period.

2 a What are the macroeconomic objectives?

  b Explain what you understand by the term 'economic indicators'.

  c Explain how both of these terms are related.

3 a Explain what you understand by the terms 'imports' and 'exports'.

  b What does the table below suggest about the level of the UK's international competitiveness and does it give any indication about output gaps in the UK economy?

  c What factors are likely to make UK goods internationally competitive?

Year	1997	1998	1999	2000	2001	2002	2003	2004	2005	2006
£'s exports minus imports	–840	–3,195	–21,717	–24,833	–21,884	–16,513	–14,921	–19,328	–19,328	–47,781

After completing this chapter you should:

- understand the relationship between trend growth and actual growth and why actual growth fluctuates causing economic cycles

- understand how changing levels of employment and unemployment affect the economic cycle

- understand how the economy controls inflation and why

- understand why we need to maintain or improve our international competitiveness

- understand the meaning of GDP and be able to distinguish between nominal and real

- understand that an increase in real GDP is the measure of economic growth

- understand how and why an increase in real GDP per head is an indicator of increased living standards

- understand how and why economists use index numbers such as the RPI and the CPI.

AQA Examination-style questions

1 **Extract A**

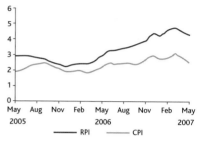

Inflation is caused by demand exceeding supply of services and goods and always leads to a fall in the real value of money. But external factors, such as a sharp rise in the price of oil, can also lead to sustained inflation by cost push unless the Bank of England curbs credit. The labour market is crucial in both. Supply shortages most often show up in tightness in the labour market. Employers bid up pay to recruit people with scarce skills. Wage bargaining can then transmit these rises across the workforce. Such pressures lead to a positive output gap.

Figure A
Annual inflation rates

The Bank's latest survey found that people on average expect inflation to be 2.7 per cent, which is above the Bank's stipulated target of 2% and is likely to lead to a trade-off in terms of employment levels. The general consensus of opinion was that without further action the economy would move into the boom period of the cycle.

(a) Using Figure A compare the two measures of inflation over the period. *(4 marks)*

(b) Using extract A explain what is meant by a fall in 'the real value of money'. *(5 marks)*

(c) With the aid of a diagram explain the phase of the cycle that corresponds to paragraph one. *(8 marks)*

(d) Using Extract A and your own knowledge, evaluate the view that 'trade-offs will be required over the period of the cycle'. *(15 marks)*

2 **Extract B**

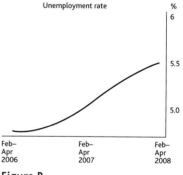

Unemployment rate

Figure B
Unemployment rate

The trend in the unemployment rate is rising at a diminishing rate and there has been a further increase in the number of people claiming Jobseeker's Allowance benefit, which has become worth more in real terms. Unemployment is still increasing, but will fall with the fluctuation of the trade cycle. While the rate of increase is diminishing, unemployment still represents a huge personal cost to individuals and families. Structural unemployment has led to run-down areas in some parts of the country. Our trading position with both the Chinese and Indian economies is that imports are far in excess of our exports and competition from these industries is hurting UK manufacturing.

The role of the authorities is quite clear; while economists worry about inflation, growth and international competitiveness, the view of the man in the street is that creating full employment should be the government's most important macroeconomic objective.

(a) Explain what you understand by the term unemployment and using Figure B, identify two features of the rate of unemployment over the period shown. *(6 marks)*

(b) Using a trade cycle diagram to help you analyse the statement 'Unemployment is still increasing but will fall with the fluctuation of the trade cycle.' *(10 marks)*

(c) Using the passage and your own knowledge, analyse the adverse economic effects of unemployment. *(10 marks)*

(d) Evaluate the view that 'creating full unemployment should be the government's most important macroeconomic objective.' *(15 marks)*

How the macroeconomy works: the circular flow of income

This chapter will introduce you to the first of two **economic models** that we use to portray the workings of the macroeconomy.

The model that we study in this chapter is the circular flow model, to be followed in Chapter 13 by the aggregate demand aggregate supply model (AD/AS). The circular flow model starts with a simple illustration of the economy, to enable you to become familiar with the terms, and then builds into a more complex model of an economy like that of the UK involved in international trading.

💡 The circular flow of income

In Chapter 11 you became familiar with the idea that all economies have fluctuations in their levels of economic activity.

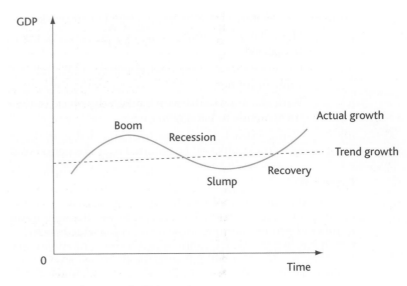

Figure 12.1 *A fluctuation in GDP over time*

Fig. 12.1 shows a fluctuation in GDP over time, which is known as the economic cycle. It is of varying duration and goes through a pattern of boom, **recession**, slump, recovery and boom. This happens to all economies though the severities of the booms and slumps obviously differ. At times a recession may be only a modest slowdown in the level of economic activity which may be hardly noticed; in others it may lead to high levels of unemployment and reduced economic activity, as the UK experienced in 1991. Similarly, a boom may simply be recognisable in that the firms have more difficulty in recruiting labour. At other times it may be accompanied by rapid inflation and a growing **balance of payments** deficit. There is agreement in economic circles that changes in aggregate or total expenditure cause changes in economic activity.

To study the **flows** and how they affect the economy, we will take a very simple model. In Fig. 12.2 there are four households, or families, that have been shipwrecked on a desert island. The supply of money in the economy is £5 and we assume that all the money will be used to buy

▨ Key terms

Economic models: these are used to show the essential characteristics of complicated economic conditions in order to analyse them and predict the result of changes of variables.

Recession: when an economy is growing at less than its long-term trend rate of growth.

Balance of payments: exports minus imports – a deficit means more is imported than exported.

Flow: measured over a specified period of time.

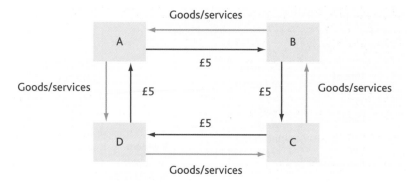

Figure 12.2 *Goods and services*

goods and services. Household A spends £5 and receives from household B goods and services in exchange. Household B then spends £5 on goods sold by household C and the process is repeated until all households have participated.

This model allows us to examine certain outcomes from this simplified economy. The **stock** of money in the economy is £5, which flows round the economy from household to household. If the £5 changes hands more than once during the period under consideration income earned will be greater than the amount of money in the economy. The stock of money creates a flow of goods and services as each household has produced £5 of output. If we assume that the four households comprise the total economy then:

- the value of the national output or GDP is £20 (4 × £5 for each household)
- each household has earned £5 so the value of the national income is £20
- each household has spent £5 so national expenditure is £20.

Thus in this simplified model GDP = National Output = National Income = National Expenditure. Not only is this correct in the simplified model but with a few statistical adjustments it holds true for the UK economy.

In a more sophisticated economy households do not trade with each other and in order to make the model more realistic firms are introduced as is shown in Fig. 12.3.

This diagram is somewhat more sophisticated as it shows a distinction between firms and households. Firms hire factors in order to produce goods and services. The owners of the factors are assumed to live in households so the diagram shows the four factors of production being hired from households. The factor services hired are land, labour, capital and entrepreneurial talent. In return for their work the factors are paid their factor price rent, wages, interest and profit. This is shown on the left-hand side of the diagram.

The flow of money and income is circular as:

- the income earned by the households allows them to buy the goods and services that are sold by the firms
- the firms use the factors of production to produce goods and services
- households buy the goods with the money they have earned in working for firms
- the money passes from firms to households and then back again.

■ **Key terms**

Stock: a quantity measured at a particular point in time.

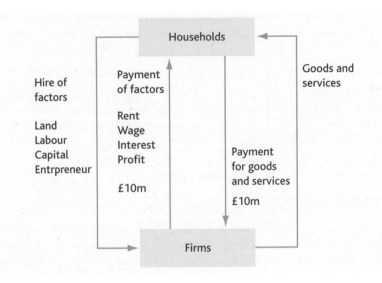

Figure 12.3 *Households and firms*

If we assume that factors are paid a total of £10m and they spend all their money on the products of domestic firms and that domestic firms spend all of the £10m on hiring factor services then the economy will stay at equilibrium of £10m and national income will remain unchanged. Economists distinguish between the money flows in the economy, which they refer to as the monetary sector and the flows of goods services and factors of production that they designate the real economy.

But in reality households and firms do not spend all of their income on the products of domestic firms and firms do not spend all their revenue hiring domestic factor services and so in Fig. 12.4 we see a more realistic situation.

Fig. 12.4 shows households and firms are linked together to represent the circular flow of income through the economy. Coming in on the left-hand side of the diagram is an arrow labelled **injections.** Increases in injections increase the level of national income.

> ■ **Key terms**
>
> **Injections:** money that originates outside the circular flow and so will increase national income/ output/expenditure.

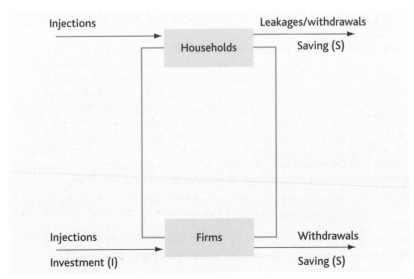

Figure 12.4 *Circular flow of income through economy*

On the right-hand side of the diagram is an arrow labelled leakages or **withdrawals**. Increases in withdrawals reduce the size of the national income.

This type of economy is often referred to as a two-sector economy as there is only **investment (I)** and **savings (S)** to consider.

Investment represents an addition to the circular flow as it is revenue for firms that does not arise from the spending of households. From the point of view of the circular flow investment is only carried out by firms.

Savings is seen as a withdrawal as it is money put aside by both households and firms to meet future expenditure and is not passed on in the circular flow to domestic firms or households. Savings are expected to grow as income increases and fall as income falls. They are **income induced**. Since the act of saving implies reduced consumption by households and reduced expenditure by firms we would expect aggregate demand in the economy to decrease. This economy will be in equilibrium when injections equal withdrawals or in the case of the two-sector economy where investment equals saving.

If injections and leakages are not equal the economy is said to be in disequilibrium. Disequilibrium can occur as a result of differences in the plans of both consumers and firms. If consumers ex-ante plan to save more and therefore spend less producers will find themselves with unsold stocks. If as a result labour becomes unemployed the incomes of consumers will be reduced, leading to less spending and the economy will contract. The level of national income will fall and as it falls savings will decline as we assume that the amount that is saved depends on the level of income. This will bring about an ex-post equilibrium where realised saving equals realised investment.

💡 If planned or ex-ante investment is greater than planned saving the economic system is in a state of disequilibrium. The extra investment injects additional income into the economy and the economy grows through the **multiplier effect** that increases both income and savings bringing about an ex-post equilibrium where realised investment equals realised savings.

In summary:

- ▨ If planned saving > planned investment then national income falls.
- ▨ If planned saving < planned investment then national income increases.
- ▨ If planned saving = planned investment national income is in equilibrium.

There is considerable evidence to suggest that an injection into the economy will cause a multiplier effect to operate and that the increase in national income is likely to be larger than the initial injection. Assume that a business decides to invest in new machinery. This provides income for workers in the capital goods industry who will receive the payment for making the machinery and they will spend this money on consumer goods and services that will create further employment. Those newly employed workers in other businesses will receive money, which they will spend, so the initial injection will continue to generate demand and have an effect far greater than the original injection. It will not continue forever as at each stage some of the money will be withdrawn, in the form of taxes, savings, or spent on imports by those who receive it.

An alternative way to look at equilibrium in this two-sector economy is by looking at total planned expenditure or aggregate demand. In our two-

■ **Key terms**

Withdrawals: any money not passed on in the circular flow and has the effect of reducing national income/output/expenditure.

Investment (I): spending by firms on buildings, machinery and improving the skills of the labour force.

Savings (S): a withdrawal from the circular flow.

Income induced: will increase as income increases and decrease as income decreases.

Multiplier effect: where an increase or decrease in spending leads to a larger than proportionate change in the national income.

AQA Examiner's tip

Do not confuse the economists' definition of investment with the use of the term 'investment' by non-economists who refer to it as the purchase of financial assets.

sector economy aggregate demand is the sum of planned consumption plus planned investment. If aggregate demand (total planned spending) is greater than the level of national income the economy will grow and national income will increase. If aggregate demand is less than national income the economy will contract and national income will fall.

In a two-sector economy equilibrium occurs where:

- planned injections = planned withdrawals
- investment = savings
- aggregate demand = income, i.e. where $AD = C + I$.

Case study

Savers cash in on squeeze

Savers are being offered the best rates for six years as banks rattled by ongoing turmoil in the financial markets attempt to attract them. The best fixed rate savings deals yesterday topped 7 per cent for the first time since 2001. Attractive rates of saving are more likely to persuade consumers to reduce their borrowing and increase their saving.

Rates have surged in the past fortnight as banks try to head off the effects of the credit crunch. While the market crisis has seen the cost of borrowing rise for mortgage owners, analysts last night said it had also led to 'a great, great time' for savers. They predicted that the increased savings would lead to a slow down in consumption and a reduction in economic activity.

The credit crunch arose after banks stopped lending to each other in the financial markets while they wait to assess the fallout of troubles in America's sub-prime mortgage market.

Banks and building societies are desperate to raise money and feel that savers represent a much more attractive market than borrowers in the current climate.

Mark Dampier, head of fund research at Hargreaves Lansdown, said with the base interest rate likely to go down next year, the fixed rate savings deals would continue to be a good deal. And he predicted the current situation would continue until banks regained their confidence.

Source: adapted from Ben Farmer, 'Savers cash in on squeeze', *The Daily Telegraph*, 14 September 2007

In Fig. 12.6 the analysis has been extended to a three-sector economy as the government sector has been introduced. The government is active in terms of injections, government expenditure and leakages, taxation. We view government expenditure (G) as an injection as it does not arise through the spending of households. It may benefit firms that win government contracts or receive income as a result of government spending. Government spending may benefit households through employment in the government sector or through transfer payments. For example, if you are a Year 12 student your parents should be receiving child allowance for you!

Taxes (T) affect both firms and households and reduce the amount that both households and firms have to spend. They represent a leakage from

Figure 12.5

Activity

The incomes of the factors of production in a closed economy are made up of:

- Rent   £10m
- Wages   £60m
- Interest   £15m
- Profit   £25m

The economy is in equilibrium as savings equals investment at £5m.

1. Construct a diagram showing the circular flow of income and the appropriate injections and withdrawals.

2. Explain why a planned increase in investment of £10m will lead to disequilibrium in the economy.

3. Explain how the economy will return to equilibrium.

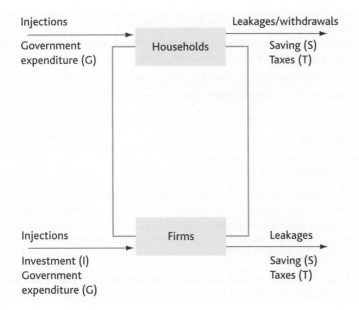

Figure 12.6 *The three-sector economy*

the circular flow. The result of government spending on national income will depend on **net government spending**, i.e. whether governments spend more in the economy than they take out in the form of taxes. This is announced in the Budget where the Chancellor of the Exchequer explains the relationship for the coming year between government spending and taxation. In a three-sector economy equilibrium occurs where:

Planned injections = Planned withdrawals

i.e.

Investment + Government Expenditure = Saving + Taxes

or where

Aggregate Demand = Income

i.e. where

$$AD = C + I + G$$

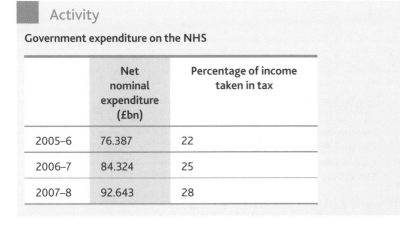

Activity

Government expenditure on the NHS

	Net nominal expenditure (£bn)	Percentage of income taken in tax
2005–6	76.387	22
2006–7	84.324	25
2007–8	92.643	28

Key terms

Net government spending: the difference between government spending and taxation.

1 Using the figures explain the difference between nominal and real.

2 With the help of a circular flow diagram explain the likely effects on the likely level of increased expenditure on the NHS.

3 Using column 3 outline the likely effects of the increased percentage of income taken in tax on the economy.

■ **Case study**

Increased taxes reduce income

The Chancellor admitted that taxes have risen while he has been running the Treasury. His admission came as research showed that families have less money to spend at the end of each month than at any time in the past four years, thanks to increased taxes and soaring household bills.

The Chancellor agreed that tax, as a percentage of national income, was higher than it had been under the last government if National Insurance was included. But he made no mention, in an interview with the BBC, of council taxes, which were reported yesterday to have increased by three times the rate of inflation, during the years Labour has been in power.

Fig. 12.7 is the full four-sector economy as foreign trade in the form of exports and imports has been included. It is also no longer a closed economy but has now become open as it is involved in international trade. Imports (M) are shown as a withdrawal as they represent spending by both domestic firms and households that is not passed in the circular flow. Exports (X) are an injection as they originate outside the flow and increase the size of the national income.

The overall effect of foreign trade on the economy will depend on the overall balance. If exports exceed imports the effect will be to increase

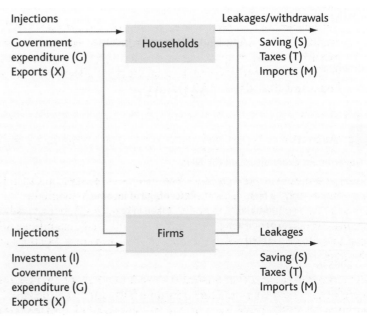

Figure 12.7 *The four-sector economy*

national income, whereas if imports are greater than exports national income will tend to decrease. In a four-sector economy the overall level of economic activity depends on:

- Whether the sum of injections = the sum of withdrawals then national income is in equilibrium.
- If Aggregate demand = income where AD = Consumption expenditure + Investment expenditure + Government expenditure + (Exports minus imports). This is usually shown by the expression $C + I + G + (X - M)$.
- If the sum of injections > the sum of withdrawals then the level of national income is rising.
- If the sum of withdrawals > the sum of injections then the level of national income is falling.

AQA **Examiner's tip**

You should ensure that you are familiar with what the injections and withdrawals are and how changes in them can lead to changes in the level of national income.

Case study

The destination of UK food exports

Exports to the European Union made up 68.8 per cent of all overseas food and drink sales, with Poland and Estonia seeing the biggest growth in demand for UK produce. The total drink market rose 7.4 per cent in 2005, with whisky being by far the biggest export – accounting for about a quarter of all sales, with a value of £2.526bn.

Meat exports increased by 4 per cent to $746m, with lamb making up the largest share of that by value. However, it was the bounce back of demand for beef, after a 10-year export ban was lifted, that grabbed analysts' attention.

'As British beef finally returns to overseas menus, we have seen our food and drink exports reach an all time high,' said Food From Britain chief executive David McNair. 'This heralds the end of a difficult decade, which we emerge stronger from, and with a solid and more diverse platform for future growth and employment,' he added.

But he warned that competition from other export giants such as France, Germany and the US was fierce. 'We need to recognise exporting as a strategic route to long-term growth and benefit from such experience to allow us to compete more effectively both at home and abroad,' Mr McNair said.

Figure 12.8

Source: adapted from 'UK food and drink exports surge', 999 Today – Business and Commerce, 20 April 2007

Some of the items in the circular flow such as consumption expenditure, investment and saving, imports and exports are at the whim of households and firms so it is possible that there could be quite volatile changes in aggregate or total demand. This potential instability could lead to quite large changes in national income and cause fluctuations in the economic cycle.

Governments could if they wished try to counterbalance changes taking place in the private sector. Thus if income falls, due to an increase in withdrawals in the private sector, governments could increase their own expenditure or reduce taxes to offset the outcome.

AQA **Examiner's tip**

It is essential when answering a question about a change in any of the components of injections or withdrawals that candidates bear in mind that changes in them will affect the level of national income. The circular flow theory is an essential part of your economist's toolkit.

In contrast, if incomes rise, due to changes in the private sector, the government can try to reduce the effect if it so wishes. This manipulation of government expenditure and taxation is called **fiscal policy**.

Changes in aggregate demand may occur as a result of a change in injections or withdrawals or a change in consumer expenditure. Changes in the monetary economy, for example a fall in the rate of interest, lead to changes in consumption and investment that affect the real economy and lead to a change in the level of national income and the economy's position on the economic cycle.

An increase in expenditure will lead to an increase in the level of employment that will further increase expenditure, business expectations will improve, the future will look good, and businesses will increase their investment.

Increased aggregate demand can also lead to an increase in the levels of inflation if aggregate demand grows more rapidly than the amount that the economy can produce – aggregate supply. Increasing levels of income and inflation can lead to an increase in imports that may result in a balance of payments deficit. If inflation rises rapidly then under such circumstances the government may decide to slow down the rate of growth in the economy. The effect of this change in expenditure will have an effect on the level of economic activity that we looked at on the economic cycle diagram.

A reduction in aggregate demand due to an increase in withdrawals, reduction in injections or a fall in consumption expenditure will have the reverse effect and as the level of national income decreases firms will begin to reduce their output as not as many goods are being purchased. They will 'lay off' labour and unemployment will begin to rise. Business expectations will change from positive to negative. The amount spent on imports will fall and firms will try to export more to make up for the loss of business at home. The government's income from taxes will fall and its expenditure on job seekers allowance and social security will increase.

💡 The importance of consumption

Private consumption expenditure accounts for about 60 per cent of aggregate expenditure. Consumers, after they have paid the statutory deductions of tax and national insurance, are left with their **disposable income,** which may be even further reduced if they enter into pension and mortgage commitments. What is left can either be spent or saved; usually a combination of both. In general we find that a higher percentage of income is consumed when income is lower, i.e. those on low incomes spend a larger proportion of their incomes than those on high incomes. Conversely, those on higher incomes can save a larger proportion of their income.

Changes in consumption

There are a number of factors that cause changes in the level of consumption:

- *The wealth effect* Consumers will change the level of consumption if they see a change in the level of their wealth. So if the value of a person's house rises they may decide to borrow against it in order to increase the level of their expenditure. Experience in the 1980s as house prices rocketed upwards and borrowing increased rapidly was that when house prices fell consumers/borrowers felt worse off and reduced their consumption, which started a recession. A change in the value of financial assets can also cause a wealth effect.

- *Inflation* Expectations of inflation should lead to consumption increasing as consumers recognise that goods will be dearer in the future and so buy now in advance of price increases. This is known as anticipatory buying. If the inflation continues or rises it has a negative wealth effect, i.e. it reduces wealth, and consumers often react by saving more and spending less in order to try and restore the value of their wealth.

- *The rate of interest* Changes in the interest rate change the cost of borrowing and this will affect the level of consumption that occurs. We would expect consumers to borrow more as the interest rate falls and borrow less as the rate of interest rises.

- *Expectations* The consumer's view of the future has a marked effect on what they do with their income. Positive expectations are said to occur when the consumer expects the future to improve, e.g. the likelihood of promotion at work will probably increase consumption, while fears of unemployment, which create negative expectations, are more likely to increase saving.

AQA Examiner's tip

The evaluative part of a question is unlikely to include a specific mention of the circular flow model but it can be used for analysing and then evaluating the issues posed by the question.

Stretch and challenge activity

1. a Why do economists refer to a 'flow' of goods and services but a 'stock' of money?
   b Explain why national expenditure = national income = national output.
   c What do you understand by the term 'multiplier effect'? Explain the effect assuming increased withdrawals.

2. a Define the terms 'injection' and 'withdrawal'.
   b Explain why we refer to withdrawals as being income induced.
   c Distinguish, using an example, between ex ante and ex post.

3. a List three injections and three withdrawals.
   b Apart from income what factors are likely to affect consumption?
   c Explain what will occur in the macroeconomy if $I + G + X > S + T + M$

✔ After completing this chapter you should:

- understand why economists use economic models

- understand and be able to recognise the fluctuations that economies have in their levels of economic activity

- understand what is meant by injections and withdrawals and recognise the importance of changes in them for the macroeconomy

- understand what is meant by equilibrium and disequilibrium in the macroeconomy

- understand what makes up aggregate demand

- understand the role and importance of the multiplier

- be able to build up the circular flow model from a two-sector to a four-sector economy.

AQA Examination-style questions

1

Continuing high levels of retail sales have also been matched by high levels of consumer borrowing. Analysts suggest the increased value of housing plus the below trend interest rates and the continuing benign economic outlook have all contributed to consumers' increasing desire for credit. Consumer borrowing in real terms increased each year between 1992 and 1998, from £0.6 billion to £15.6 billion, and then remained fairly level to 2000. That levelling was followed by sharp increases in 2001 and 2002. Mortgage equity withdrawal, the part of borrowing secured on houses that is not invested in the housing market but is spent on other goods and services, has also been strong in recent years.

(a) Using Figure 1 identify two features of the rate of growth of consumer borrowing over the period. *(5 marks)*

(b) Figure 1 refers to 'borrowing in real terms'. Explain the term *real* and any other way in which borrowing could have been stated. *(4 marks)*

(c) Figure 1 refers to consumer borrowing. Explain and analyse two determinants of consumer borrowing. *(8 marks)*

(d) Using the data and your economic knowledge, outline the importance of consumer borrowing in achieving a high level of national income in the UK . *(10 marks)*

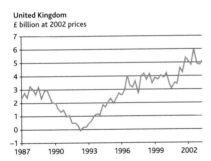

Figure 1 *Net borrowing by consumers in real terms*

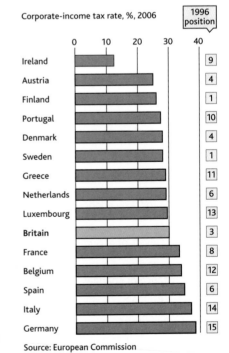

Source: European Commission

Figure 2 *Downwardly mobile*

2   **Extract A**

First and most important, ordinary voters have grown less grateful for the long period of sustained economic growth over which Mr Brown has presided. Small wonder, since household budgets have been squeezed recently by higher inflation and rising taxes. During Labour's first five years in office, real disposable income per person increased by 3% a year, faster than in the previous two decades. Since 2001, however, it has been rising by only 1.5% a year, and most recently by less than 1%.

On the eve of the budget, official statisticians analysing the latest Retail price index figures revealed that retail prices, the broadest measure of inflation, increased in the year to February by 4.6%, the highest rate since August 1991 and ahead of average earnings, which have been growing by 4.2%.

Businesses constitute the second group that needs wooing. Businessmen have become increasingly disgruntled by Mr Brown's tax-grabbing ways, especially since his budget in 2002 pushed up employers' national-insurance contributions. Firms may not have votes but their bosses' disenchantment undermines Labour's crucial claim to combine social justice with a business-friendly regime. Furthermore, companies can vote with their feet, and more are threatening to move to countries with greater tax appeal.

After an early period of austerity when he made much of his caution, Mr Brown turned into a big spender, proclaiming in 2000 that he had been 'prudent for a purpose'. The resulting surge in spending, together with a run of disappointing tax revenues, sent the budget deep into the red as government expenditure exceeded its income from tax.

adapted from © The Economist Newspaper Limited, London (2007)

(a) Using extract A, define carefully the term real disposable income per person.

(b) Using Figure 2, compare the current and 1996 international position of the UK in terms of corporate taxation. All other things being equal, suggest the likely effects on business investment.

(c) Paragraph 2 in extract A refers to the Retail Price Index (a) explain what you understand by the term 'index'.

(d) Using your own knowledge and a circular flow diagram, explain the likely effects on the level of national income of the information given in extract A.

13 Aggregate demand and aggregate supply

At the start of this book you learnt about demand and supply analysis, where demand referred to the individual or the household and the supply was the goods or services of a particular industry. When considering the macroeconomy we use aggregate demand (AD) and aggregate supply (AS) to consider *total* demand and supply in the economy. We are considering the total amount of demand that is operating in the economy together with the total supply of all goods and services.

The meaning of aggregate demand

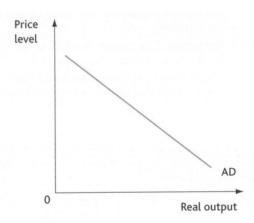

Figure 13.1 *The axis and the AD curve*

Note that the *y*-axis is labelled 'Price level' and the *x*-axis is labelled 'Real output'.

You will notice that the *AD* curve slopes down from left to right. This is due to the following factors:

- When prices fall consumers experience a wealth effect, they feel better off because their incomes will buy more goods or services. The wealth effect will increase consumption so more will be purchased at lower prices.

- A fall in the price of UK goods also lowers the price of UK exports so more will sell abroad. Also, imports will become more expensive so the demand for domestically produced goods will increase.

- Expectations – if consumers expect prices to rise in the future they will increase their consumption now but if they expect prices to fall they will buy later.

A movement along the *D* curve will be caused by a movement of the aggregate supply curve.

Shifts of the aggregate demand curve

Any factor that changes aggregate demand will cause the *AD* curve to shift. An increase leads to a rightward shift, while a decrease leads to a leftward shift. Aggregate demand is made up of consumption plus investment plus government expenditure plus net exports (exports minus imports). This is abbreviated to the equation or identity $AD = C + I + G + (X - M)$.

An explanation of the factors affecting (determinants of) aggregate demand

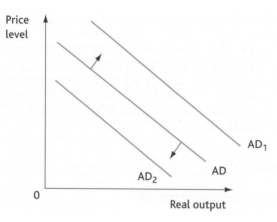

Figure 13.2 *Factors affecting aggregate demand*

Investment

We have seen in Chapter 12 that investment is defined as firms investing into capital equipment machinery and premises. The decision to invest is affected by a number of factors:

■ The rate of interest – a fall in the rate of interest will shift the AD curve to AD_1 as borrowing will be cheaper and firms will wish to invest in new equipment to maintain or improve their competitive position. An increase in the rate of interest will deter some investment and the AD curve will shift to AD_2.

■ Business expectations – if the rate of interest is falling, businesses will expect more sales in the future as consumer demand will increase. Such **positive expectations** are likely to increase investment, shifting the AD curve to the right from AD to AD_1 all other things being equal. On the other hand, **negative expectations** – fewer sales in the future – will lead to a fall in aggregate demand from AD to AD_2.

■ The rate of technical progress – new equipment and technological development are likely to lead to increased business investment as firms 'without state of the art' equipment will lose sales to those that have it. A case in point is this computer that is being used to write this chapter. It is operating Windows XP and though perfectly satisfactory, at some stage it will need to be upgraded as it will not be able to handle the new Vista software.

■ The rate of change of income – this will affect firms' demand, and an increase in demand, if firms are producing at virtually full capacity, will lead to an increase in investment expenditure as firms will want to be able to cater for the increased consumption. As the price of the required machinery is likely to be much larger than the value of the individual goods it produces, investment expenditure will be quite a large injection into the circular flow, shifting the aggregate demand curve from AD to AD_1 and producing a multiplier effect. This reaction of investment to the rate of change of income is called the **accelerator effect** and coupled with the multiplier effect could lead to sizeable

■ Key terms

Positive expectations: businesses expect the future sales and profits to improve due to factors like increased aggregate demand.

Negative expectations: businesses expect future sales and profits to be less due to factors like falling aggregate demand.

Accelerator effect: the relation between the change in new investment and the rate of change of national income.

AQA Examiner's tip

Investment is a demand-side factor that will initially shift aggregate demand but in the longer term should increase aggregate supply.

■ Links

For an explanation of the multiplier effect, see Chapter 12.

■ Key terms

Privatisation: sale of government-owned assets to the private sector.

■ Links

For further information on public and merit goods see Chapter 8.

fluctuations in demand. A slowdown or fall in consumer expenditure is likely to lead to a large fall in investment that will slow the growth of the macroeconomy.

Government expenditure

This is mainly spending on public and merit goods and local government services. Over the last 50 years government spending has fallen as **privatisation** has transferred previously nationalised industries to the private sector. Governments have also reduced their spending in order to reduce the rates of taxation and their own levels of borrowing. Government investment into areas like schools and hospitals will shift the AD curve to AD_1, while a cut in government spending will shift aggregate demand to AD_2. Over the past five years UK government expenditure has begun to increase and a view on this can be seen in the following case study.

■ Case study

Public expenditure in the UK

Britain's ballooning public sector will grow bigger than Germany's next year for the first time since the early 1970s. The Organisation for Economic Cooperation and Development figures show public spending in the UK will overtake that of Germany in 2007. The OECD says state spending will hit 45.3 per cent of gross domestic product next year, compared with 45.1 per cent in Germany. Britain's public spending remains far above that of other major economies including the US, where it will be 36.9 per cent of GDP next year, and Japan, where it will be 36.2 per cent. But it is far below France's state expenditure, which will be 53.5 per cent.

The OECD figures show the rise in the UK's tax burden over the next two years will be the fourth-biggest in the Western world.

Net exports (X – M)

■ UK exports depend on aggregate demand in its major trading partners so if the European economies are growing, demand for UK exports should increase, shifting the aggregate demand curve from AD to AD_1. On the other hand, if the UK's major trading partners are in recession we would expect the aggregate demand curve to shift from AD to AD_2.

■ Exports and imports are affected by the value of the pound sterling. If sterling has fallen in value against the euro, UK exports will be cheaper in Europe and sales should increase, shifting AD to AD_1. If sterling increases in value UK exports will become more expensive and AD will shift to the right to AD_2.

■ If the UK economy is growing and incomes are rising consumers are likely to spend more on imports and this will shift the aggregate demand curve to the left from AD to AD_2. The same effect will occur if the value of sterling rises as imports will appear cheaper in the UK and consumers will purchase more of the cheap imports.

AQA Examiner's tip

Keep an eye on media coverage of things such as trends in unemployment and inflation.

1 A fall in the value of sterling is likely to lead to:

   a an increase in imports

   b an increase in the current account deficit

   c increased investment by UK firms

   d an increase in exports.

2 Construct aggregate demand diagrams to show the effect of the following:

■ A fall in the rate of interest

■ A shift in business expectations from positive to negative

■ A fall in the value of the dollar in relation to sterling

■ Increased foreign direct investment into the UK economy

■ The election of a government committed to reducing public expenditure

■ An increase in economic growth rates in the European Union.

🔘 Aggregate supply

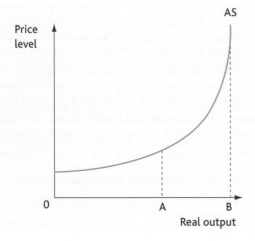

Figure 13.3 *Aggregate supply curve*

This curve slopes upwards from left to right and shows the total output that the economy can produce using available factors of production at a given price level. Fig. 13.3 illustrates what we can consider to be an all-purpose aggregate supply curve. It shows that as prices increase firms will increase output and while there is labour available to be employed prices will increase by only a small amount as there is plenty of labour available at the existing wage rates. This is shown in Fig. 13.3 as the part of the aggregate supply curve from *O* to *A*. As the labour market tightens and the required labour becomes more scarce wages begin to increase and prices rise, as shown on the diagram between *OA* and *OB*. At some stage the economy reaches full employment and is unable to produce any more goods and services. This is shown at *OB* where the aggregate supply curve becomes vertical.

The diagram above could be referred to as a **Keynesian** aggregate supply curve as the Keynesian view was that wages would remain fairly stable up to full employment and then rise as labour became scarce.

There is an alternative view of aggregate supply, the **classical view**, which distinguishes between short-run aggregate supply and long-run aggregate supply. In the short run money wages remain constant and the price of all other factors in the economy remain fixed.

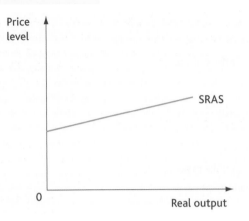

Figure 13.4 *Short-run aggregate supply curve*

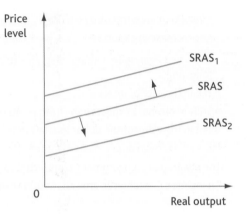

Figure 13.5 *A shift in SRAS*

Figure 13.4 shows a short-run aggregate supply curve (*SRAS*) where output increases but prices rise relatively slowly. We assume that in the short run firms can increase output, by paying their existing workers overtime. This will lead to earnings rising slightly but the increase in demand will have a larger effect on output than prices. The *SRAS* is drawn on the assumption that the firm's costs remain the same.

A shift in the *SRAS* will be caused by any factor that changes the firm's costs. So in Fig. 13.5 an increase in costs will shift the curve upwards from *SRAS* to *SRAS*$_1$, leading to a decrease in *AS* at every price, while a fall in costs will shift the curve downwards to *SRAS*$_2$ increasing *AS* at every price.

Factors affecting the short-run aggregate supply

■ An increase in the money wage rate will increase firms' costs and shift the curve from *SRAS* to *SRAS*$_1$.

■ An increase in the rate of interest will make it more expensive for businesses to borrow and will reduce aggregate supply shifting the curve from *SRAS* to *SRAS*$_1$.

■ A rise in the price of imported raw material will increase firms' costs and reduce aggregate supply shifting the curve from *SRAS* to *SRAS*$_1$.

■ An increase in corporation tax will increase firms' costs and shift the *SRAS* curve upwards, while a fall in taxation will shift the *SRAS* from *SRAS* to *SRAS*$_2$.

The long run

While it is fairly obvious that the aggregate supply curve becomes vertical when all factors of production are fully employed and the productive capacity of the economy is reached, classical economists believe that the **long-run aggregate supply** curve will become vertical and reach its productive capacity before full employment is reached. They reason that in the economy there will be some workers who would prefer not to work and to stay on benefits rather than work for low wages and so output will reach its maximum level of actual output before full employment is achieved and it reaches its potential output. In other words actual output may not reach the economy's productive capacity, its potential output. Fig. 13.6 shows a long-run aggregate supply curve (*LRAS*). Classical economists refer to these workers as voluntarily unemployed because they are not prepared to join the work force until they are offered a higher level of wages. This level of output where the *AS* curve becomes vertical is called the **natural rate of unemployment** and is the normal capacity output for the economy. This corresponds to the vertical part of the curve in Fig. 13.3 and shows that firms are unable to increase output as the economy is on the production possibility boundary.

Factors affecting the LRAS

The long-run supply curve can shift over time and this is shown in Fig. 13.7. A rightward shift shows rising real output and increasing economic growth.

Factors influencing the LRAS are as follows:

■ An increase in the amount of capital equipment will increase output in the economy and shift the curve in Fig. 13.7 from *LRAS* to $LRAS_1$. This increase in capital may have been caused by a lower rate of interest, which has increased investment. Natural disasters like earthquakes can wipe out capital stock and reduce the output and GDP of the economy that will also lead to rising levels of unemployment shifting the *LRAS* curve to $LRAS_2$.

■ Technology is also important as improved technology produces capital equipment that is more productive than previous capital equipment. Such capital equipment increases labour productivity, which means that more goods and services can be produced over the same amount of time leading to a shift to the right of the LRAS curve. Anything that increases labour output will also shift the curve to the right, so increased investment in education and training, more efficient working practices and better managerial techniques are beneficial.

■ Attitudes are important as an entrepreneurial culture where individuals are prepared to set up businesses can increase aggregate supply. This may be helped by the institutional structure of the economy and the economic incentives that it offers. For example, in the US economy the levels of income taxes are low and individuals who set up firms are able to benefit from their success with high profits and increasing levels of wealth. Contrast this with a society that has high levels of taxation and high social security benefits where the attitude is one of greater reliance on the state and those individuals who are enterprising will be seen as the exception rather than the norm.

■ Policies that persuade a larger proportion of the labour force to work will reduce the natural rate of unemployment and shift the *LRAS* curve to the right. To this end governments have reduced income taxes and the real value of unemployment benefits to encourage more labour to participate in the economy.

■ **Productivity** – increased productivity will increase the output of labour over time, which will shift the long-run aggregate supply curve to the right.

Case study

UK hammered over failure to meet worldwide challenge

Britain's manufacturing sector has had the worst performance of any G7 country in recent decades, a study from the Ernst & Young ITEM Club says.

AQA Examiner's tip

If you are an adventurous student you will hopefully read around the subject and you may encounter the terms neo-Keynesian and neoclassical. These are present-day economists whose current theories are rooted in either the classical or Keynesian tradition.

■ Key terms

Long-run aggregate supply: the economy's productive capacity.

Natural rate of unemployment: the rate of unemployment that is consistent with a stable rate of inflation.

■ Links

Natural rate of unemployment is an A2 topic.

Figure 13.6 *Long-run aggregate supply curve*

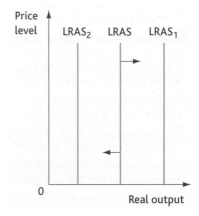

Figure 13.7 *A shift in LRAS*

High wage inflation, allied with high public spending, has made it extremely difficult for manufacturers to make ends meet, according to the study, which charts the decline and fall of the sector in the UK.

Peter Spencer, chief economic adviser to the highly respected institution, said manufacturers had to improve their productivity and efficiency or face possible extinction.

'UK manufacturers have been suffering', he said. 'This is partly the side effect of Labour's fiscal expansion, which has kept interest and exchanges rates relatively high.'

But the main problem is that employers have failed to control their labour costs. 'So their salvation lies not in a fiscal retrenchment and lower real exchange rate, it lies in their own hands.'

Professor Spencer's conclusion that low productivity is largely responsible for the fall in manufacturing output shatters the widely held view that industry has been hit hard by a rise in the comparative expense of sterling.

Source: adapted from Edmund Conway, 'UK hammered over failure to meet worldwide challenges, *The Daily Telegraph,* 16 June 2006

💡 Macroeconomic equilibrium

Fig. 13.8 shows the macroeconomic equilibrium where $AD = AS$ at price level OA and real output OB.

Some examples of model use are shown below and they can be adapted to whatever is being tested.

An increase in *AD*

Increased consumption, investment, government expenditure or exports will shift the aggregate demand curve to the right. This is shown in Fig. 13.9 where AD shifts from AD to AD_1 moving from A to B on the diagram, along the $SRAS$ curve and changing the macroeconomic equilibrium. Output will increase, as unemployment falls and existing workers may do overtime. Output will increase from OV to OX and prices will rise slightly. A larger increase in aggregate demand would shift the curve to AD_2 giving a new macroequilibrium at C, output OZ. Any further increases in aggregate demand at this full capacity output would not lead to increased output but purely an increase in the level of prices. As key labour would be scarce firms would increase wages to get extra workers, and workers feeling in a strong position would push for wage increases that would further contribute to rising prices.

The result of this increase in demand has been inflation, if the economy expands beyond its normal capacity output. This can be seen in Fig. 11.1, output OB in Chapter 11. To close this inflationary gap, governments can try to reduce the level of aggregate demand by cutting government expenditure or increasing the level of taxes. But unless the gap was very large the government is likely to use monetary policy and leave it to the **Monetary Policy Committee** of the Bank of England to increase the level of interest rates.

Activity

Construct diagrams to show how the following factors will affect aggregate supply – assume an increase in all cases:

1. The money wage rate.
2. The stock of capital equipment.
3. The rate of interest.
4. The price of imported raw materials.
5. The state of technology.
6. The size of population of working age.
7. The preference for leisure.
8. The replacement ratio (ratio of benefits to wages – a replacement ratio of 75 per cent means that benefits are equal to 75 per cent of wages.

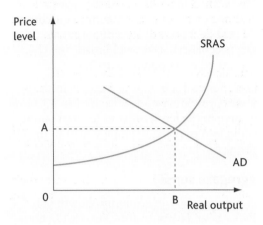

Figure 13.8 *Macroeconomic equilibrium*

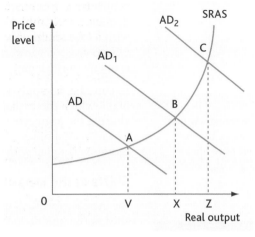

Figure 13.9 *AD shifts*

A decrease in *AD*

Fig. 13.10 shows the effect of a fall in aggregate demand. The *AD* curve shifts to the left from *AD* to AD_1 moving from *A* to *B* on the diagram along the *SRAS* curve. If the normal capacity output was *OX* the economy is now operating at underemployment as output has fallen from *OX* to *OZ*. Demand deficient unemployment has occurred due to the fall in aggregate demand and prices have fallen from *P* to P_1. This situation corresponds to output *OA* in Fig. 11.1 of Chapter 11.

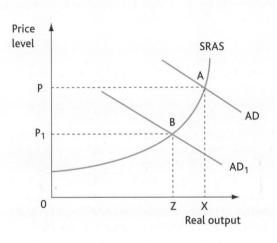

Figure 13.10 *A fall in aggregate demand*

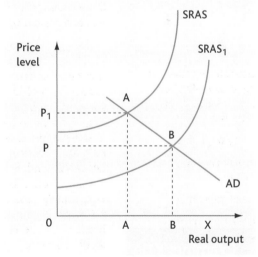

Figure 13.11 *An economy in macroeconomic equilibrium*

Governments facing this situation of a deflationary output gap can try to increase the level of aggregate demand by increasing government expenditure or reducing the level of taxes. However, in today's climate they are more likely to leave it to the Monetary Policy Committee who are likely to reduce the level of interest rates.

Shifts in the short-run aggregate supply

Fig. 13.11 shows an economy in macroeconomic equilibrium at *A* where the price level is OP_1 and real output is *OA*. An increase in aggregate supply leads to a movement from *SRAS* to *SRAS*₁ down the aggregate demand curve from *A* to *B* leading to a new macroeconomic equilibrium with a lower level of prices *OP* and an increased level of output at *OB*. Increased aggregate supply is beneficial as it would make the UK economy more competitive compared to its trading partners.

In contrast, a **supply-side shock**, for example a steep increase in the price of oil, which increased firms' costs would have the effect in Fig. 13.11 of shifting the aggregate supply curve to the left leading to reduced output and increased prices. This would lead to rising unemployment in the UK economy coupled with increasing prices.

Shifts in the long-run aggregate supply

An increase in LRAS represents an increase in economic growth or a shift of the production possibility boundary outwards. Fig. 13.12 shows the *LRAS* shifting to the right to *LRAS*1 leading to lower prices *P*₁ to *P* and increased output *OA* to *OB*. Measures to increase aggregate supply have been targeted by governments since the late 1970s and they aim to accelerate the rate at which GDP increases.

A fall in LRAS is likely to come about as a result of a natural disaster like an earthquake, where productive capacity is wiped out or by economic mismanagement. In Fig. 13.12 a shift of the *LRAS* curve to the left from *LRAS*₁ to *LRAS* decreases output from *OB* to *OA* and prices rise from *OP* to *OP*₁. This will lead to reduced employment, increased inflationary pressure and an economy that is less competitive internationally.

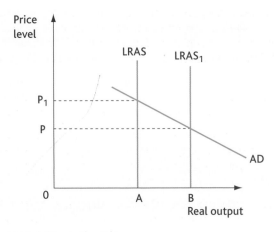

Figure 13.12 *LRAS shifting to the right*

Activity

Stretch and challenge

1 a Construct an AD/AS diagram showing an increase in aggregate demand.

   b Explain the likely effects of an increase in aggregate demand on the macroeconomy if the economy is below its trend output.

   c 'An inflationary output gap requires an increase in aggregate supply.' With the aid of a diagram explain this statement.

2 'The price of oil could soon reach $100 per barrel.'

   a Construct an AD/AS diagram to show the effect on the economy.

   b Analyse the likely effects on (i) inflation and (ii) the balance of payments.

3 'Investment affects both aggregate demand and aggregate supply but in the short term could be inflationary.'

a Construct an AD/AS diagram showing increasing investment and its long-term effect on the economy.

b Explain two of the likely causes of increased investment expenditure.

c Explain under what circumstances in the economic cycle investment is likely to be inflationary.

■ Case study

The cost of disasters

The costs associated with natural disasters have risen astronomically in the most recent decades, according to research released by the World Bank.

The amount spent on clearing up and repairing regions hit by events such as hurricanes, earthquakes or floods is now some 15 times higher than in the 1950s, and more than tripled in the 1990s alone to $652bn (£370bn).

The key reasons for such a dramatic increase are that more people have moved to urban areas that are at particular risk, and that the prevalence of disasters such as floods has risen markedly in recent years, the authors of the report said.

These findings are of particular relevance given that recent disasters, including the Asian tsunami and Hurricane Katrina have been some of the most costly in history. Katrina killed 1,422 people and caused some $75bn in damage, while the tsunami killed 224,000 people and cost $7bn.

He said that while the cost for disasters was borne by both rich and poor countries, the effect on smaller economies was much more profound.

'Losses from natural disasters have averaged nearly 15pc of the gross domestic product in the world's poorest countries in the past two decades, a time during which more than 4bn of the world's people were directly affected', said Mr Thomas.

Insurance companies have also been hit extremely hard by the growing incidence of disasters, with last year's hurricanes Katrina, Rita and Wilma costing an estimated $80bn to the industry alone.

Source: adapted from Edmund Conway, 'Bills flood in as global disasters multiply', *The Daily Telegraph*, 22 April 2006

✓ *After completing this chapter you should:*

- understand the meaning of aggregate demand and aggregate supply
- understand that aggregate demand can change if any of the components of $C + I + G + (X - M)$ change
- understand what causes shifts in aggregate demand and aggregate supply
- understand how to use aggregate demand and supply diagrams and link them with trend output and actual output and the possibility boundary diagrams

■ understand the difference between long run and short run

■ understand the difference between Keynesian and classical long-run aggregate supply.

AQA Examination-style questions

1 **The operation of monetary policy**

The Monetary Policy Committee (MPC) did a sound job for the first eight years of its life with the help of tame inflation worldwide. While we hesitate to criticise an icon there is no doubt that it reacted hastily when it cut interest rates prematurely when the money supply and aggregate demand was growing very rapidly. We now have an inflationary problem nearly two years later, not to mention high levels of personal debt levels. The MPC has at last acted and raised interest rates three times since August, RPI inflation is running at 4.8 per cent and credit has been growing at nearly 15 per cent.

Source: adapted from Damian Reece, 'Rates must rise to put inflation genie back in bottle', *Telegraph*, 24 April 2007.

(a) Using the RPI figure of 4.8 per cent explain what is meant by the term inflationary problem. *(5 marks)*

(b) Using an AD/AS diagram analyse the likely effect on the UK economy of credit growth of nearly 15 per cent. *(8 marks)*

(c) The extract refers to the Monetary Policy Committee having 'at last acted and raised interest rates three times since August'. Using AD/AS analysis analyse the likely effect of this on the UK economy. *(8 marks)*

(d) Evaluate the view that the growth of credit is likely to have an adverse effect on the UK's macroeconomic performance. *(25 marks)*

2 **The progress of the economy**

Continuing high rates of interest in the UK and the decreasing value of the dollar has led to an increase in demand for sterling and the pound hit its highest levels for more than a quarter of a century after a prediction of a 6 per cent interest rate. This means that UK residents can expect to see import prices fall as the stronger pound will mean that it can be exchanged for a greater amount of foreign currency, thus making imports cheaper. Analysts are predicting a surge in imports. The corollary of a strong pound for exports is that they will be more expensive and UK firms will face falling sales. Firms will need to find ways to cut costs.

Levels of employment in the economy may be increasing but the data is confusing as the government's two measures of unemployment pointed in opposite directions. For the eighth time in nine months the number of people out of work claiming benefits was down. While the other measure suggested that more people were looking for work even though they were not claiming benefit. Unemployment is a prime example of wasted resources in the economy.

(a) Explain the meaning of the statement 'the pound hit its highest levels for more than a quarter of a century'. *(2 marks)*

(b) Use an AD/AS diagram to help you explain the effect on UK firms of an increase in the value of the pound. *(8 marks)*

(c) The extract refers to two measures of unemployment. Using an AD/AS diagram explain how the government could reduce the level of unemployment in the economy. *(12 marks)*

(d) Evaluate the view that an increase in the value of sterling would have a beneficial effect on the UK's macroeconomic performance. *(25 marks)*

14 Macroeconomic policy objectives

Key terms

Policy objective: government's major macroeconomic objectives.

Policy instrument: techniques used to achieve policy objectives.

Links

You will study policy instruments in Chapters 18–20.

This chapter is about what the government wants to achieve for the macroeconomy in order to increase the economic welfare of its citizens. In this chapter we will look at why governments want to achieve full employment, economic growth, control inflation and achieve a sustainable balance of payments. This chapter builds on what you started to study in Chapter 11 and uses the toolkit that you became familiar with in Chapters 12 and 13.

Policy objectives, policy instruments and policy indicators

Policy objectives are the targets or goals that the government wants to achieve, and economists see these in terms of full employment, economic growth and higher living standards, control of inflation and a satisfactory balance of payments.

Policy instruments are the techniques or weapons that the government uses to achieve its policy objectives. An example may be monetary policy – if inflation is expected to increase beyond the target level (the objective) the authorities may use monetary policy (the instrument) by raising the rate of interest to reduce aggregate demand.

Table 14.1 *Policies*

Policy objectives	Policy instruments	Policy indicators
Full employment	Monetary policy	Claimant count figures
		ILO statistics
	Fiscal policy	
	Supply-side policy	
Economic growth	Monetary policy	GDP
	Fiscal policy	
	Supply-side policy	
Stable prices	Monetary policy	RPI
	Fiscal policy	CPI
	Supply-side policy	
Balance of payments	Monetary policy	% of GDP
	Fiscal policy	ONS figures
	Supply-side policy	

Policy indicators are the indicators that you studied in Chapter 11 and include GDP, RPI and CPI that allow us to measure changes in economic performance.

Table 14.1 indicates the four objectives in the left-hand column and the instruments that could be used to achieve it in the central column. The right-hand column suggests what policy indicators could be used to monitor changes.

■ Full employment

Unemployment in an economy represents a waste of a scarce factor of production that could be increasing economic welfare by producing goods and services. Governments want to promote full employment because it leads to an increased standard of living and reduces human misery as those unemployed are likely to suffer from greater economic, social and health problems than those who are employed. From a financial aspect full employment is likely to give governments a healthy level of income through income tax payments, while at the same time reducing their expenditure on benefits, leaving them with more funds to spend on public and merit goods that may increase long-run aggregate supply.

Governments could achieve full employment by increasing aggregate demand. Diagrammatically an increase in employment can be shown by moving the aggregate demand curve to the right as shown in Fig. 14.1.

An increase in AD from AD to AD_1 will increase employment with some price increases. An increase in AD to AD_2 will take the economy to the full employment level, while any increase beyond that AD_3 will cause an increase in the level of inflation. In the past, government activity, using a Keynesian approach to create full employment by promoting demand-side expansion, has caused both inflation and a balance of payments deficit as the inflation made UK goods internationally uncompetitive and domestic consumers purchased cheaper imports. This is an example of a policy conflict as one policy has conflicted with others. Governments in the 1960s and 1970s tried to trade off by reducing unemployment until inflation and the balance of payments deficit were too high and then reversing their policies. This became known as a **boom/bust policy**.

Diagrammatically we can also show how employment could be increased by shifting the long-run aggregate supply curve to the right by the use of supply-side policies. Suffice it to say that such policies try to make labour more employable and flexible to undertake numerous roles in the labour market. The emphasis is more on making labour employable for the jobs that are on offer by giving them the right skills rather than governments trying to increase aggregate demand to create jobs that would otherwise not exist.

Fig. 14.2 shows a much healthier situation as output is increasing, which will create more employment at the same time as prices are falling, reducing inflation and making the UK economy far more competitive. This approach is more likely to reconcile the policy conflicts that full employment will generate without creating the trade-offs at the full employment level seen in the Keynesian technique of increasing aggregate demand.

While over the past decade the UK has been extremely successful in reducing the levels of unemployment it has not had the same success in increasing the rates of labour productivity, which remains lower than France, the USA or Germany. Labour productivity is expressed as a percentage of output per man hour. Increased productivity usually results from increased investment in both human and physical capital

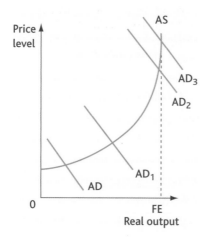

Figure 14.1 *Moving aggregate demand curve*

■ Key terms

Boom/bust policy: the government using macroeconomic tools to stimulate and then contract the economy.

■ Links

You will study supply-side policies in Chapter 20.

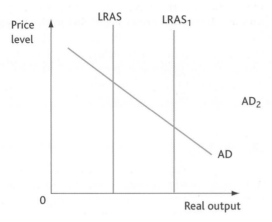

Figure 14.2 *Output increasing*

(**total factor productivity**) allowing the same amount of workers to produce more in a given time or releases workers to increase productivity elsewhere.

Case study

Poor show

The Chancellor has long wished to close Britain's productivity gap, the UK's output per hour with other countries. It is proving a long haul as output per hour is 19 per cent higher in France, 15 per cent higher in the USA and 5 per cent higher in Germany than it was in Britain. Why is Britain finding it so hard to reach the same productivity levels as other advanced economies? A recent survey by the OECD highlighted failings in skills, innovation and transport.

Long-standing deficiencies in education mean that the British workforce has a much higher share of low-skilled people than is the case in most developed countries. That may explain why Britain has not wrung as much extra efficiency from its investments as America.

Innovation is especially important in propelling productivity in advanced countries. But across a range of indicators – including spending on research and development, and securing new patents – Britain compares poorly with the best-performing countries.

A clogged transport system caused by years of underinvestment also seems to be harming productivity. Britain has the most congested roads in the European Union. This adds to business costs while making it difficult to exploit just-in-time methods. Unreliable trains take their toll of commuters.

Source: adapted from © The Economist Newspaper Limited, London (19 January 2006)

Economic growth

This is the situation where an economy is able to produce more goods and services over time and represents an increase in the economy's productive capacity. As you saw in Chapter 11 growth was cumulative and measured in terms of real GDP. You also came across the fact that trend growth and actual growth could be different producing output gaps in the economy. The actual growth achieved may fall below the productive capacity of the economy as illustrated by the long-run aggregate supply. Actual output may be below potential output and the economy may be inside the production possibility boundary. Growth is often both stated as a percentage for the economy or in terms of GDP per capita and measured in nominal and real terms.

"Slow down a bit Jenkins - give the economy a chance to catch up."

Figure 14.3 *Jenkins cartoon*

Case study

'Fast economic growth' in Africa

The economic outlook for Africa is improving after a decade of growth of 5.4% for the continent that matches global rates, the World Bank has said. But the bank's latest report, Africa Development Indicators 2007, says ongoing investment is needed to sustain long-term development on the continent. Otherwise, a split may grow between affluent nations and stagnant ones.

The report looked at more than 1,000 indicators covering economic, human and private-sector development, governance, the environment and aid. It concludes that growth in many African countries appears to be fast and steady enough 'to put a dent on the region's high poverty rate and attract global investment'.

The World Bank's chief economist for Africa, John Page, said he is 'broadly optimistic' that there's a fundamental change going on in Africa. 'For the first time in about almost 30 years we've seen a large number of African countries that have begun to show sustained economic growth at rates that are similar to those in the rest of the developing world and actually today exceed the rate of growth in most of the advanced economies,' he told the BBC.

The key, said Mr Page, was that 'Africa has learnt to trade more effectively with the rest of the world, to rely more on the private sector, and to avoid the very serious collapses in economic growth that characterized the 1970s, 1980s and even the early 1990s.'

However, poor infrastructure and the high cost of exporting from Africa compared to other regions of the world has been holding the continent back rather than any failures of African enterprise or workers. Volatility in sub-Saharan Africa has dampened investment, the report says. Corruption is also a factor that may limit needed investments in education and health.

'Perhaps the easiest illustration of that is in the resource-rich economies where the resources often accrue to a small number of corporations and to government,' said Mr Page.

Source: adapted from © bbc.co.uk/news

Governments pursue economic growth because they believe that it increases the standard of living of the population, by increasing the output of goods and services, increasing GDP per head. At this stage it might be the time to introduce the idea of whether or not rapid rates of economic growth are sustainable. In terms of environmental considerations is our pursuit of faster growth going to have a deleterious effect on future generations? Are we going to pass on to them an environment that is as good as ours? Are we increasing our own economic welfare at their expense? Putting these concerns aside until we revisit them in A2 we can show the relationship between actual and trend growth in Fig. 14.4.

At output *OA* actual growth is above trend leading to inflationary pressure in the economy. There is at this point a policy conflict because while the authorities are desirable of growth, too rapid a rate of growth will create inflationary pressure and lead to an increase in imports. At present the authorities are using monetary policy via the Monetary Policy Committee to restrain aggregate demand when inflation exceeds 2 per cent CPI. It is likely that this policy would be employed at *OA* in an attempt to reduce actual growth back to the trend level. At *B* actual growth is below trend and the MPC is likely to reduce the rate of interest if it considers that aggregate demand is too low. Unemployment will be higher than the authority desires, leading to increased expenditure on benefits and reduced government income from taxes.

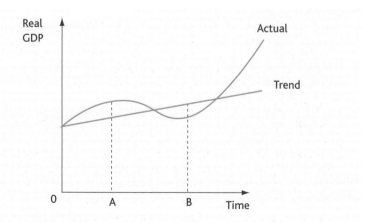

Figure 14.4 *Relationship between actual and trend growth*

💡 While the explanation given above may seem to indicate that the best that can be hoped for is that growth can be kept at its trend level and that this will allow reasonable attainment of the other objectives, it must be remembered that the trend rate of growth can be increased. This has already been shown in Fig. 14.2 with the movement of the LRAS curve to the right. Going back to Chapter 1 you will recall that growth can also be shown by an outward shift of the production possibility boundary.

Economists consider that it is supply-side factors that are likely to cause economic growth and while governments cannot directly affect all of the causes, they put policies in place to try encourage the private sector in the right direction.

■ Inflation

Inflation is a persistent rise in average prices in an economy. The UK has an inflation target of 2.0 per cent CPI, which is thought to be beneficial to the economy. UK experienced inflation of 23 per cent in the 1970s but some developing countries have seen hyperinflation in excess of 1,000 per cent per annum. You will study inflation in greater detail in Chapter 16 but here we will consider its detrimental effects and how it interacts with the government's other macroeconomic policy objectives.

■ In so far as governments try to achieve a reasonably fair distribution of income, inflation is extremely hard on some social groups like pensioners who are on fixed incomes and workers in a weak bargaining position.

■ Inflation redistributes income from lenders to borrowers as the interest rate may be below the rate of inflation so real rates are negative. Lenders will lose out and investment may slow down as funds will become more expensive, which will reduce growth rates in the economy.

Possibly the most disadvantageous aspect of inflation is that is distorts behaviour by economic agents:

1 Consumers indulge initially in anticipatory buying, to beat the inflation but in reality the increased aggregate demand adds further fuel to the inflationary fire. Continuing inflation brings fears of job loss leading to an increase in the savings ratio leading to a rapid fall in aggregate demand and the possibility of a recession.

2 Workers try to anticipate inflation by increased wage demands that increases cost inflation. In terms of an AD/AS diagram the SRAS curve would shift to the left.

3 Firms are likely to increase prices in order to cover wage and cost increases, which will increase inflation even more.

■ Unemployment is likely to increase as consumers will turn to relatively cheaper imports and demand for UK exports will fall as a result of the inflationary price increases.

■ The balance of payments is likely to become seriously adverse if the UK inflates more rapidly than its major trading partners as imports will increase relative to exports.

If inflation is as bad as we have painted above a reasonable question would be: why then is the inflationary target of the UK authorities not zero per cent rather than the 2 per cent targeted by the Chancellor?

A zero level of inflation would not take into account the improvement of goods and services over time and would mean that in real terms prices would be falling. This would not provide much of an incentive for producers to continually improve their products. The Japanese experience of **deflation** has shown us that it can lead to a situation where consumers hold off buying, expecting prices to fall further and eventually firms sell at a lower price in order to make sales. This reinforces consumers' views that prices will fall leading to a downward spiral of prices and rising levels of unemployment as firms go out of business.

Inflation beyond a certain level is disadvantageous for an economy as it will lead to a deteriorating balance of payments, rising levels of unemployment and eventually slower rates of economic growth. Controlling inflation may be seen as an intermediate objective that the authorities must achieve to be able to concentrate on other policy objectives like economic growth, full employment and a balance of payments surplus. Looked at from this perspective controlling inflation becomes the prime requisite for achieving other economic aims.

Key terms

Deflation: a situation where prices persistently fall.

Case study

The dangers of runaway inflation

It is hard to imagine that things could get any worse in Zimbabwe where the inflation rate has passed 2,200 per cent per annum; last week the national power company announced that it would ration electricity in cities, possibly to a meagre four hours per day, just as the southern hemisphere's winter is starting to bite. Residents of the capital have been rushing to get firewood and paraffin, though a domestic worker's monthly wages can buy only 5 litres of paraffin or 2 litres of cooking oil. Many companies already operating at about 40 per cent of capacity, say cuts will force them to reduce their working hours even more. 'The whole thing is a nightmare', says the boss of a small furniture making factory. 'We don't know when we will have power or when it will go and this is affecting our output. Then at home water runs out when you are bathing and the electricity goes when you are cooking'. Hospitals must use gas stoves, coal-fired boilers, fuel generators, solar power and candles.

Source: adapted from © The Economist Newspaper Limited, London (17 May 2007)

Activity

1. Construct a diagram to show inflation.

2. In the light of the case study consider why control of inflation is such an important objective.

Figure 14.5 *Weighing scales*

■ The balance of payments

Mention has been made in Chapter 11 of the UK's involvement in international trade and the balance of payments on current account, an annual measure of the relationship between the amounts spent on imports and that earned from the sale of exports. We can categorise the relationship as follows:

1 A balance is where what is imported equals the value of what is exported.

2 A surplus is where the income from exports exceeds expenditure on imports.

3 A deficit is where more is spent on imports than is earned from the sale of exports.

While either of the first two can be seen as an external policy objective of the authorities the third, which accurately represents the UK situation, indicates a policy conflict – the aim of increasing the numbers employed and in the short term increasing economic growth may clash with achieving a surplus in the balance of payments.

The reason for continuing deficits is attributed to a number of factors:

■ A shift in the economy away from manufacturing and into services with a continuing run-down of manufacturing output, which means we have to import manufactured goods which previously would have been domestically produced.

■ The UK's appetite for imported goods, as it is calculated that out of every extra £1 earned the proportion spent by UK consumers on imported goods exceeds 50p.

■ Rates of interest that are overly high when compared to our trading partners, which increase the value of sterling, making our exports less competitive abroad and making imports cheaper.

The problem facing the authorities in achieving their policy objectives in this area is one of conflicting objectives. They would, however, stress that policies to reduce inflation will increase UK competitiveness and that it makes economic sense to purchase goods from abroad if they are cheaper than they can be made at home.

However, if a country imports more than it exports it has to borrow to pay for the extra imports. At present for the UK this is not a problem as vast amounts of currency flow through the London market and overseas investors appear very happy to lodge currency with us. While the deficit is only a relatively small percentage of GDP foreign confidence is likely to remain as the UK authorities could reduce demand and thus the deficit if necessary.

A problem arises if the deficit suddenly starts to grow and/or overseas investors no longer wish to hold money in the UK and foreign banks and other lenders refuse to lend money. To overcome this lack of credit or '**credit crunch**' the UK government would have to cut domestic spending to reduce the demand for imports. This action would cause a policy conflict as it would lead to reduced economic growth and rising unemployment. As a result the authorities may have to indulge in a policy trade-off where the rate of growth and employment is restricted to a level that maintains an orderly balance of payments deficit.

■ Key terms

Credit crunch: where borrowing becomes more expensive or unavailable.

AQA Examiner's tip

■ Parts B and C of examination questions may require students to explain how a policy objective may be achieved.

■ Part D may ask for the evaluation or ranking or importance of the policy objectives or whether pursuit of one objective is consistent with achieving other objectives.

Activity

Stretch and challenge

1 a Define policy objectives and policy instruments.

   b What policy conflicts are likely in a positive output gap?

   c Why are stable prices seen as a key to achieving the other objectives?

2 a With the aid of a production possibility diagram explain the view that there is no opportunity cost to unemployment.

   b Explain why there is a trade-off between inflation and unemployment.

   c Justify and evaluate what you consider to be the most important macroeconomic objective.

3 a Construct an AD/AS diagram to show that actual growth may be less than potential growth.

   b Outline the factors that determine economic growth.

   c Explain why governments have to restrict the rate of economic growth.

💡✅ *After completing this chapter you should*

- be able to explain the differences between policy objectives, policy instruments and policy indicators

- be aware of the fact that governments' policy objectives have as their main aim the intention to improve economic welfare

- understand that there are policy conflicts some of which can be resolved, and where no resolution is possible trade-offs have to be accepted

- be aware that achieving one objective, e.g. control of inflation, may be necessary to achieve further objectives like economic growth and full employment

- be in a confident position to go forward and look at the policy objectives in greater depth together with the weapons to achieve them.

AQA Examination-style questions

1   **Not all as rosy as it seems**

The rising value of the pound seemed a fitting tribute to the UK's remarkable economic performance over the past decade. With unemployment lower than in Germany, France, Italy and the United States, the Prime Minister's future looked bright. Record rates of economic growth, at least for the UK, have occurred without the usual accompanying inflation. So pensioners and other people on fixed incomes have enjoyed an increase in their standard of living and pressure for wage increases has been held in check. The Chancellor has advised that a trend rate of 2.75 per cent is now possible without overheating the economy while actual variations are gradually becoming smaller. He attributed this 'economic miracle' to his own cautious policy and the use of supply-side techniques such as improving education and training and reducing the real value of benefits to encourage and enable people to take jobs.

Yet from the perspective of the informed observer not all is well; UK levels of productivity stay obstinately lower than our transatlantic and continental trading partners as our rates of investment in capital equipment, training and infrastructure are lower. The trade deficit shows no signs of getting smaller and is making its way rapidly towards 4 per cent of GDP. This alone should set alarm bells ringing at number 11 as the trade deficit is an increased withdrawal from the economy. While this will impact on manufacturing employment in the UK the increasing deficit may reflect the fact that standards of living are increasing and consumers are purchasing goods that are no longer made in the domestic market.

While the Monetary Policy Committee did not raise rates last month there are at least four members of the committee who think that the genie is easing his way out of the bottle and that rates need to move upwards. Hawks point to increases in the cost of the manufacturing index and increased lobbying by pensioner groups who want to restore the links between pensions and wages in order to increase their portion of the increased growth.

(a)	Using the passage and your own knowledge define inflation and identify two costs of inflation	(5 marks)
(b)	With the aid of a diagram explain the difference between trend and actual growth rates	(8 marks)
(c)	The extract says 'UK levels of productivity stay obstinately lower'. Explain what this statement means and analyse three ways in which productivity could be improved	(12 marks)
(d)	The extract refers to alarm bells ringing as a result of an increasing trade deficit. Evaluate the importance of an increasing trade deficit in terms of the other macroeconomic policy objectives	(25 marks)

2   **The UK economy**

	Real GDP £bn	% unemployed	Inflation % increase on year	Balance of payments % of GDP
2006	1296.1	5.2	1.6	−3
2007	1296.3	5.0	2.1	−3.5
2008	1298.0	3.5	3.1	−4.2

The expansion of the UK economy since 2006 has led to an increased standard of living as real GDP has risen for most groups in the economy as unemployment has fallen persistently throughout the period. While the Monetary Policy Committee have by judicious changes in interest rates managed to control inflation it has increased over the period and future projections suggest that the governor of the Bank of England may be writing to the Chancellor to explain why inflation has overshot its target. The Committee will have to form a view whether the increased GDP has fuelled demand or whether cost increases are the cause. Inflation, in addition to making the UK less competitive in international trade increases uncertainty for firms that wish to invest and individuals who wish to save.

The economy is showing signs of a positive output gap, which combined with a tight labour market and increasing demand, is likely to adversely affect the balance of payments. Firms seeing the domestic market growing may increase their supply to it rather than selling in more difficult markets abroad. Increasing incomes that occur in this stage of the economic cycle will further help to increase the deficit.

The problem faced by the authorities at any part of the cycle is that some of their macroeconomic objectives are being realised while others are not. The role of government is rather like that of a juggler trying to keep too many balls in the air at once. Finally one of them is dropped.

(a)	Define real GDP and explain the link shown in the table between GDP and the percentage unemployed.	(5 marks)
(b)	Inflation in the table is increasing. With the aid of a diagram and the extract analyse one cause of inflation.	(8 marks)

(c) Using the table, the extract and your own knowledge explain what factors may have caused the balance of payments figures shown in the table.

(12 marks)

(d) Using the table and the extract evaluate to what extent they indicate conflicting policy objectives and the subsequent need for trade-offs.

(25 marks)

Economic growth and the economic cycle

This chapter is about economic growth in both the short term and the long term and how growth is affected by changes that take place as the economy moves through its economic cycle. We will look at why growth is considered to be an important objective in most economies but also why some are arguing that the world pace of growth may need to slow down if growth is to remain sustainable.

💡 Economic growth – measurement and definition

Economic growth is seen to be an important policy objective as it increases the availability of goods and services to the population. Emergent economies that are now growing rapidly like the 'BRICs' – Brazil, Russia, India, and China – are extremely aware of the need to achieve high growth rates to end poverty and achieve a better state of economic well-being for their populations.

Chapter 11 referred to the trend rate of growth for the UK economy as about 2.5 per cent per annum and Chapter 12 introduced a diagram showing the difference between the actual and trend rates of economic growth. In this chapter the concepts will be considered in more detail and will start by referring to the figure of 2.5 per cent for the UK economy. This is reckoned to be the trend rate of growth; the annual average growth rate that has been calculated over a longer period than just a single economic cycle and is defined as the rate at which the economy can grow without exerting either upward or downward pressure on inflation. At 2.5 per cent growth rate the UK economy will remain stable. Under these circumstances growth can be seen as an increase in the productive capacity of the economy of about 2.5 per cent per year. Factors that increase an economy's productive capacity will allow the economy to grow at a more rapid rate and these will mainly be supply-side factors.

However, for an economy to grow there needs to be adequate demand that is capable of absorbing the extra goods and services that will be produced. This increased aggregate demand will create the right climate for entrepreneurs and business people to invest in new capital equipment and increase their firms' productive capacity.

Skills

One of the most important skills for you to master is constructing the diagrams and this needs to be done in a logical fashion – the advice below concerns an AD/AS diagram but can be adopted for most diagrams.

■ Construct the axes and correctly label them.

■ Draw in the AD and AS curve.

■ Draw in the horizontal and vertical lines that show price and real output levels.

■ Draw in whatever new curve is relevant and show the new equilibrium.

Short-term economic growth or economic recovery

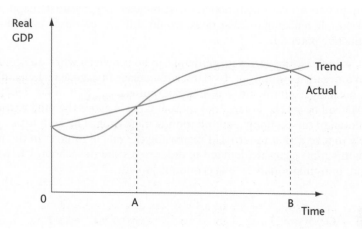

Figure 15.1 *Trend and actual growth*

> **Activity**
>
> **1** Explain the meaning of 2.5% and 8.2% when applied to a country's growth rate.
>
> **2** Construct a diagram to illustrate the rapid growth of the 'BRIC' economies.

Figure 15.1 is a diagram with which you should already be familiar, the relationship between trend and actual growth. Between *O* and *A* on the diagram actual growth is below trend, the economy is experiencing higher than expected unemployment and lower output levels. We are in a situation of a negative output gap as the actual GDP is below the economy's productive potential, i.e. its trend level of output. To see this in another way look at Fig. 15.2 showing the production possibility boundary of an economy.

In terms of our negative output gap we could argue that the economy is at point *A* inside the boundary – it is not reaching its productive potential that would be on the boundary showing that all factors of production are fully employed. A movement from *A* to the boundary would indicate economic recovery rather than economic growth. If you used AD/AS analysis to portray the same problem you would be likely to produce something very similar to Fig. 15.3 where AD has shifted from *AD* to *AD*₁ that is below the full employment output of the economy.

Any of the factors that will shift *AD*₁ back to *AD* or shift the output of the economy back to the production possibility boundary or close the negative output gap will restore the economy to its trend or potential growth rate. These factors that you encountered in Chapter 13 are

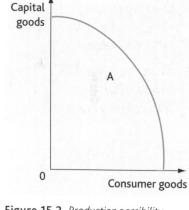

Figure 15.2 *Production possibility boundary*

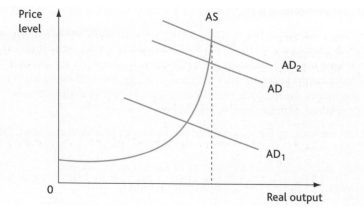

Figure 15.3 *AD has shifted*

> **Activity**
>
> Using Fig. 15.3:
>
> ▪ Explain why increasing levels of aggregate demand are important if economic growth is to take place.
>
> ▪ What happens when AD increases to *AD*₂.

the components of $C + I + G + (X - M)$. An increase in any of these factors will push the economy back to its trend level and create short-term growth. Government policies that increased aggregate demand, for example reducing interest rates, would shift the economy toward its productive potential.

Just as increases in aggregate demand can be beneficial when an economy is in a negative output gap, too large an increase in aggregate demand can push an economy into a positive output gap – A to B in Fig. 15.1 or AD will be at AD_2 in Fig. 15.3. Actual GDP is above the productive potential of the economy and inflation is increasing. The authorities are likely to take action in terms of increasing the rate of interest in the hope of dampening aggregate demand in order to restore the economy to its trend, non-inflationary rate of economic growth.

Activity

1 Which of the following policies would you recommend to influence aggregate demand and close a positive output gap in the UK:

a an increase in the rate of interest

b a fall in the value of sterling

c a cut in income tax rates

d an increase in government spending

2 Explain how an increase in exports might help to close a negative output gap.

💡 Long-term growth

Chapter 13 has considered the factors that affect the long-run aggregate supply of the economy, mainly supply-side factors that cause growth by increasing the economy's productive potential – i.e. they increase the trend rate of economic growth. What is essential for growth is that firms take up improved capital equipment and that they are able to increase both capital and labour productivity. This may require expanding markets, either domestically or overseas, in order that firms consider such investment worthwhile or government policies that are framed to encourage firms in the use and take-up of advanced capital equipment. Governments who tax profits at a level above other countries may find that some firms will leave and relocate in lower tax countries and those unable to move may be reluctant to increase their investment in the hope of increased profits if they consider business taxation levels to be punitive.

Fig. 15.4 illustrates the diagram that we use to show sustained economic growth in the long term. The LRAS has shifted to the right showing increased output and lower prices. This will mean that the economy will be more competitive in international markets and will assist our balance of payments. In the long run the aggregate supply is assumed to be independent of prices and is affected by:

■ an increase in the quantity of the factors of production – land, labour and capital

■ an increase in the productivity of factors of production

■ advances in technology and their take-up by firms.

In terms of land mass the UK is relatively small compared to some of the European economies. Some countries get high growth rates due to

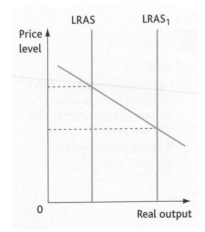

Figure 15.4 *Sustained economic growth*

their level of natural resources. Russia has huge deposits of both oil and natural gas that is allowing its economy to grow at rapid rates.

While it is not easy to expand the quantity of labour the case study below shows that immigration may help.

Case study

Second thoughts

When the European Union expanded in May 2004, just 3 of its existing 15 members welcomed migrant workers from Eastern Europe. Britain was the only large country to open its labour market. The decision was made that allowed eager Poles, among others, to fan out to vegetable fields, building sites, factories and restaurants across Britain.

The new wave of migration has certainly brought some impressive short-term benefits. The working-age population has recently been increasing at its fastest for over 20 years, which should feed through to faster GDP growth. Competition from so many keen jobseekers has helped to keep wage pressures at bay despite the leap in inflation caused by higher energy and commodity prices.

A former minister says that the new arrivals have halved wages for builders in his Southampton constituency. Other MPs also worry that the migrants will undermine attempts to get people off benefit and back to work. 'If you have a choice between hiring someone who has been on incapacity benefit with a mental health problem for five years, or a young, fit Pole, who are you going to go for?' they ask

Source: adapted from © The Economist Newspaper Limited, London (24 August 2006)

While importing labour from overseas can ease labour shortages especially if demographic changes mean that the population is ageing and less young people are entering the workforce, making the best of the labour available by increasing **participation rates** is also advisable. The last 30 years has seen a large increase in the participation of women in the economy as the tertiary sector has expanded and female expectations have changed.

In terms of increasing productivity the authorities are trying to increase the numbers that leave with a broad education – at least five GCSEs including English and Maths – while at the same time endeavouring to persuade more students to stay on and deepen their education. The government is worried about the low take-up at advanced level of hard subjects like maths and sciences that they see as important for future research and development and subsequent growth.

Labour flexibility is also related to education and is essential to increasing LRAS as workers are expected to be able to adapt to new tasks and ways of working as conditions change.

There is some talk of the school leaving age being raised to 18 as in Germany but this would require a modified curriculum in order to cater for those who want skill-based employment in the future. Despite the increased expenditure on education, industry often criticises government education policy on the grounds that it does not produce the type of

Key terms

Participation rates: proportion of the country's population that makes up the country's labour force.

labour that firms want to hire, thus reducing potential movements of the LRAS curve to the right.

Advances in technology are important as they reduce firms' costs of production – e.g. the nail gun and chain saw means that a roofing firm can cut the wood and build more rapidly and with less labour than if its workers had to use hand saws and hammers. New technology also leads to new products that generate the extra expenditure required to maintain economic growth. There is not always a measurable link between investment and growth as investment may be in areas that are declining or are not going to lead to increases in aggregate demand. Further investment in the Rover car company would have been unlikely to have generated increased demand for the vehicles. Investment needs to be into areas that are expanding rather than contracting.

■ Case study

Mobile phones and economic growth

You are a fisherman in Kerala, a region in the south of India. Visiting your usual fishing ground you bring in an unusually good catch of sardines, which means other fisherman will have done well so there will be plenty of supply to the local beach market; prices will be low and you may not be able to sell your catch. Should you head for your local market or go down the coast in the hope that other fishermen have not done well and your fish will fetch a better price? If you make the wrong choice you will not have time to visit another market because fuel is costly and markets are only open for a couple of hours before dawn – as fish are perishable you may have to dump your catch in the sea even though markets further round the coast are crying out for fish! Enter advanced technology in the form of the mobile phone. Fishermen can now call several local markets to find out the best price. Fish are no longer wasted and price variations have fallen dramatically.

Source: adapted from © The Economist Newspaper Limited, London (10 May 2007)

The case study above is a good example of how new technology helps to increase economic growth as it shows an increase in realised productive capacity. In the past unsold stocks were wasted but the phones mean that the fishermen no longer have to dump their catch back into the sea – they now add to the amount of food available in the area.

Take-up of new technology in the UK often lags behind both Europe and the USA. In the former case the argument is that businesses are too concerned in producing short-term profits to satisfy avaricious shareholders, whereas European businesses are free to concentrate on the long term due to different attitudes of shareholders. The USA is argued to benefit from lower taxes so firms are able to keep a greater proportion of their profits, making risky investment more worthwhile.

■ Economic growth and the production possibility boundary

The production possibility boundary in Fig. 15.5 shows the potential output of the economy.

Activity

1. Assess the relative importance of the factors that are likely to cause long-term growth.

2. Construct two diagrams that you could use in essays to show the effect of growth on an economy. Explain what the diagrams show.

AQA Examiner's tip

PPB diagrams and productivity are technical terms used in both Unit 1 and Unit 2 specifications so be ready to answer questions about or use them in either exam.

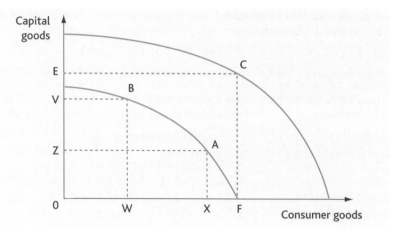

Figure 15.5 *Potential output of the economy*

The economy is producing two goods, capital goods and consumer goods. Assume the economy is at point *A* on the boundary where production is biased in favour of consumer goods. Production of consumer goods is *OX* while production of capital goods is *OZ*. Assume that as a result of an increased desire to save, the economy moves to point *B* on the boundary. This leads to a reallocation of the factors of production as capital goods production has increased from *OZ* to *OV*, while production of consumption goods has fallen from *OX* to *OW*. This increase in capital equipment should have the effect of increasing the economic growth of the economy that can be shown by an outward movement of the boundary. This reallocation of factors gives rise to the saying 'less jam today means more jam tomorrow'. In order to increase potential output the economy has had to sacrifice consumer goods (*WX*) today in order to produce extra capital goods (*ZV*) that will give more of both goods tomorrow. The opportunity cost of the extra growth is the *WX* consumer goods that have to be sacrificed today. But if the PPB moves outward then at *C* more of both goods are available and living standards should rise. Consumer goods have increased to *OF* and capital goods *OE*. While living standards may well increase in the future some groups may consider that the opportunity cost is too high. More elderly people who may not see the benefits of growth may prefer more now to later and those on pensions may fear that they would suffer from resource reallocation.

While we are on the subject of opportunity cost economists also stress that there are substantial costs to continuing growth and that increased growth will not necessarily increase living standards. Costs like increasing pollution, growth of urban slums, depletion of natural resources and damage to the environment are becoming areas of increasing public concern. This can be seen from the following case study:

Case study

Green shoots

China is not feted for its stewardship of the environment. One recent World Bank report found that 16 of the world's most polluted cities were in China; and a draft version puts the total economic cost of outdoor air and water pollution at around £50bn a year or 5.8 per cent of China's GDP. By some estimates China has now become the world's largest producer of greenhouse gases. The pollution that has resulted from China's growth is a huge problem in terms of the costs resulting from working days lost and the medical costs of treating respiratory ailments.

Source: adapted from © The Economist Newspaper Limited, London (19 July 2007)

There are also ethical issues in continuing rates of economic growth in that we may be destroying the environment in which we live and this is not a sustainable policy. It is argued that our actions will reduce the welfare of future generations and a study by the World Wildlife Fund concluded that 'the human race is plundering the planet at a pace that outstrips its capacity to support life'. The report warns that 'either consumption rates are dramatically and rapidly lowered or the planet will be no longer able to sustain its growing population'.

■ Activity

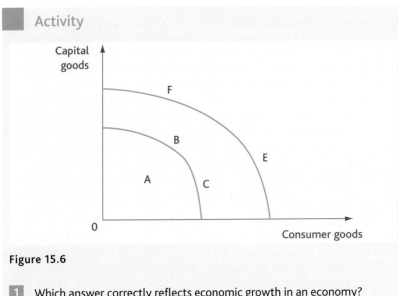

Figure 15.6

1 Which answer correctly reflects economic growth in an economy?

   a a to b

   b b to c

   c c to e

   d e to f

2 Which position on the diagram is likely to lead to increased economic growth in the future?

■ Economic growth and the AD/AS model

Fig. 15.4 indicated that economic growth can be shown by a movement to the right of the LRAS curve. Fig. 15.7 combines both AD and AS in a neoclassical diagram to indicate how an increase in investment could lead to an increase in economic growth. Initial equilibrium is at *A*, where aggregate demand, short-run aggregate supply and long-run aggregate supply are equal. An increase in investment shifts the AD curve to AD_1 and the increased prices will lead to an expansion of short-run aggregate supply. The economy will be in a positive output gap at *B*. (We are assuming that *A* is the full employment level for the economy.) The increased investment expenditure should lead to a shift of the long-run aggregate supply curve to point *C*, indicating lower prices and increased real output. The short-run aggregate supply curve should shift downwards (*SRAS* to *SRAS*₁) as the improved technology resulting from the investment expenditure should lower firms' costs. The new equilibrium output of the economy reflecting the higher potential growth rate will be at *C*. Remember that there is likely to be a time lag between the increase in investment and the increased growth rate in the economy.

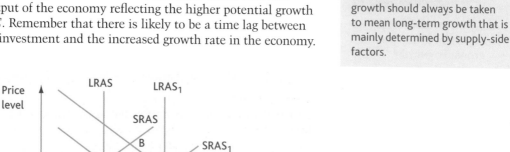

Figure 15.7 *AD/AS in a neoclassical diagram*

Output gaps and the economic cycle

In Chapter 12 we came across the fact that all economies have fluctuations in their levels of economic activity known as the economic cycle. These fluctuations are responsible for producing the output gaps in the economy. In Fig. 15.8 during the boom period the economy is growing strongly, has a positive output gap and GDP is exceeding the economies productive potential, which is shown by the trend growth line.

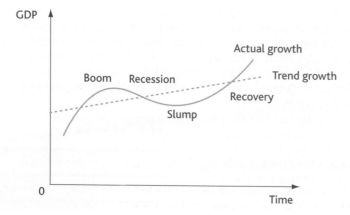

Figure 15.8 *Boom, trend growth line*

As the economy moves into a recession due to some factor sparking off a fall in aggregate demand GDP falls and the economy may even go into a slump. A slump is a situation of severe decline in the level of economic activity, such as the UK experienced in 1991–2. Application

Activity

Stretch and challenge

1 a What are the components of aggregate demand?

b Why is investment an important determinant of economic growth?

2 a Draw an AD/AS curve to illustrate long-term economic growth.

b Why might the immigration of young people benefit the economic growth of the UK?

3 a What do you understand by the term opportunity cost of growth?

b Using a PPB diagram show the opportunity cost of growth and the possible future benefits.

of the appropriate economic policy since then has been instrumental in avoiding such a reduction in economic activity but falls in aggregate demand can result in the economy going into a negative output gap where unemployment would be increasing, aggregate demand would be falling and GDP would be below the economy's productive potential. The severity of output gaps will be due to the size of the fluctuations of aggregate demand.

☑ *After this chapter you should:*

- be able to differentiate between the definition and measurement of economic growth

- be familiar with the terminology of actual growth and trend/potential growth

- be quite happy using PPB, AD/AS and trend actual growth rate diagrams to illustrate different aspects of economic growth

- realise that while demand-side factors are likely to cause short-term growth or recovery it is supply-side factors that affect long-term economic growth

- be aware of the role of the economic cycle in causing output gaps.

 Examination-style questions

1 **Extract A**

Economic growth, the increase in countries GDP can be a crude measure of an increasing standard of living. Those in developed countries who have relatively low rates of growth wonder at the double digit rates achieved by China and India. But it must be remembered that GDP growth is an increase in what went before and the older developed world has already reached a substantial standard of living so that while a small increase looks less impressive than a large one it does also depend on the standard of welfare the economy has already attained.

Despite differences in the rates of growth one fact stands out that growth is a cyclical and not a linear process. The table illustrates only too well the difference between trend growth 2.5% and actual growth that varies throughout the period. The cycle occurs as a result of changes in the level of aggregate demand often brought on by the actions of the Monetary Policy Committee aiming to stabilise inflation around 2% CPI. Changes in the level of aggregate demand produce output gaps where trend and actual growth diverge producing higher than expected unemployment and slow growth in a negative output gap and tight labour markets and a surfeit of imports in a positive output gap.

Growth still remains something of a symbol of international prestige, especially among the developed countries as it gives

Average GDP growth 1990 – 97 = 2.5%

Year	GDP growth %
1995	2.3
1996	3.5
1997	1.9
1998	2.4
1999	2.8

the policy makers the prestige of managing the macroeconomy correctly. However, there are increasingly voices that argue that further growth will endanger the very existence of the planet and that demand and consumption need to be seriously reduced. Those in the opposite camp argue that society expects consumption to increase and not fall and they see growth as the most important macro-objective. Their view is that the government's most important macroeconomic objective should be to increase consumption and ignore all restrictions on growth and do all they can to increase it.

(a) Use a diagram to help you explain the difference between trend and actual growth. *(5 marks)*

(b) In 1996 GDP growth was at 3.5%. Briefly explain why some economists might argue that this is unsustainable. *(8 marks)*

(c) Explain what factors may have caused the fluctuations in the economic cycle in the table. *(12 marks)*

(d) The writer states that 'the government's most important macro economic objective should be to increase consumption and ignore all restrictions on growth and do all they can to increase it.' Examine and evaluate the likely effect on the macroeconomy of following the writer's suggestion. *(25 marks)*

2 It is a matter of some concern as to why Africa a huge continent rich in mineral resources, with an abundant population of young people has not grown as rapidly as Asia. Both have a profusion of factors in terms of land and labour and some especially in Africa have vast mineral resources.

While trend growth rates in Asia, even allowing for the unreliable statistics published by the Chinese, have been about 8%, Africa struggles to achieve 1% and for certain countries the GDP figures are a minus number.

Asia has readily embraced the international market and has found ways to ensure that its goods are internationally traded, whereas some African countries are landlocked and in dispute with their neighbours, which makes transportation and entry to world markets difficult. However, some of Africa's politicians also have a remarkably parochial view of the world and do not actively encourage international trade.

However, when all is said and done growth may not be all that it is cracked up to be. Asian cities are growing at fantastic rates and slums plus their accompanying degradation and crime are a massive problem. Perhaps it is easier to live in a slow-growth or no-growth country.

(a) Using the passage and your own knowledge, explain why developing economies are likely to have more rapid growth rates than developed economies *(5 marks)*

(b) The passage refers to the trend growth rate – explain how this could (i) be measured and (ii) defined *(8 marks)*

(c) Use an AD/AS diagram to help you explain the meaning of the statement in the passage that 'increasing aggregate demand is an essential precondition for economic growth'. *(12 marks)*

Inflation, deflation, employment and unemployment

Links

In Chapter 11, inflationary pressure was defined and also measured using index numbers and figures from the RPI.

Key terms

Demand pull inflation: where aggregate demand exceeds aggregate supply leading to an increase in the level of prices.

AQA Examiner's tip

Make sure you are aware of the subtlety of the definitions.

This chapter explores in more detail two of the government's macroeconomic objectives and the possible difficulties of achieving them both simultaneously. The current view of reconciling the problem is considered together with both the causes of inflation and unemployment.

Inflation and deflation

Inflation is a persistent increase in the level of prices. Don't forget that it is possible to have a 'declining rate of inflation'; the economy still has inflation but it is growing less rapidly. Do not confuse a declining rate of increase with deflation, which is strictly defined as a persistent fall in the price level.

Causes of inflation

Inflation can be caused by both demand- and supply-side factors. Demand-side factors lead to **demand pull inflation** – the excess demand pulls the prices up. Demand-side factors are anything that causes an increase in aggregate demand: an increase in consumption, investment, government expenditure or an increase in exports can exert inflationary pressure on the economy. Increases in any of these components will have different effects at different times in the business cycle. An economy that has a negative output gap will positively benefit from an increase in aggregate demand, while the same economy if it has a positive output gap will find that an increase in aggregate demand will fuel inflation. This can be seen in Fig. 16.1.

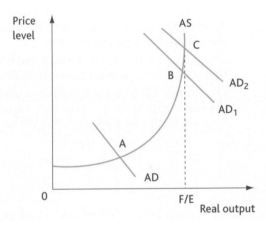

Figure 16.1 *Aggregate demand*

The diagram shows that AD and AS are in equilibrium at *A*, which is below the full employment level. An increase in aggregate demand to *AD*₁ takes the economy to *B*, the full employment level, and is accompanied by a rise in the price level as the labour market begins to tighten. Any further increase in aggregate demand will cause demand pull inflation as an increase that takes the economy to point *C* leads to an increase in monetary rather than real GDP.

One of the most recent examples of this has passed into economic history as 'The Lawson boom' (named after the Chancellor of the Exchequer at the time) at the end of the 1980s, where aggregate demand was allowed to expand too rapidly. The operational independence of the Bank of England in terms of setting the interest rate is an attempt to 'head off' increases in aggregate demand before they exert inflationary pressure.

The second cause of inflation is known as **cost push inflation**. Here prices can be pushed up by increases in the costs of production:

- A rise in the cost of imported raw materials.
- An increase in wage levels due to a **tight labour market** or powerful trade unions pushing up wages.
- A rise in indirect taxes or measures imposed by government on firms that increases their costs, e.g. increased costs associated with a stricter health and safety regime.

Figure 16.2 *Nigel Lawson*

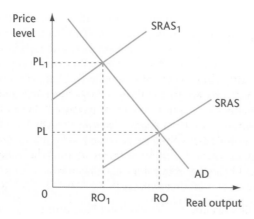

Figure 16.3 *Aggregate supply curve*

 Key terms

Cost push inflation: where increased costs of production result in firms increasing their prices leading to an increase in the general price level.

Tight labour market: where firms have to increase wages to attract the labour that they require.

In Fig. 16.3 the aggregate supply curve has shifted to the left as a result of a cost increase, leading to a higher level of prices PL to PL_1 and a lower level of real output which has fallen from RO to RO_1. Cost push inflation will lead to increasing levels of unemployment.

While economists refer to these types of inflation separately they can easily become linked. A rise in the general level of prices caused by excess demand can quickly give rise to wage claims from groups who think that increased prices has reduced their standard of living.

 Activity

1 All other things being equal demand pull inflation is more likely to result from:

a an increase in income taxes

b an increase in investment

c an increase in imports

d a decrease in government spending

2 Cost push inflation is most likely to be caused by:

a an increase in exports

b a fall in the rate of interest

c OPEC reducing its level of output

d a reduction in income tax

3 Construct one AD/AS diagram for the UK economy to reflect the following statements:

■ UK government expenditure on public and merit goods increases creating a multiplier effect in the economy.

■ An increase in the $ against the £ increases UK import costs of essential raw materials.

■ Explain the effects of these changes on the UK economy.

■ Case study

Zimbabwe – ripping the heart out of the heartlands

The meeting of the 14-member states of the Southern African Development Community (SADC) in Zambia last week provided scant hope for the people of Zimbabwe. Few details emerged from behind the closed doors, but Zambia's President Levy Mwanawasa, who currently chairs the regional body and had previously compared Zimbabwe to a sinking Titanic, declared that problems in the neighbouring country were 'exaggerated'. With 80 per cent unemployment, inflation that could now be over 10,000 per cent, and severe shortages of the most basic goods, many Zimbabweans may disagree. Over 3 million of them are thought to have left the country, and the UN refugee agency is working on contingency plans in case the exodus worsens.

Another UN agency, the World Food Programme, reckons that 4 million Zimbabweans – about one-third of the population – will need food aid by the beginning of next year.

A school was set up on one of the farms, and one of the teachers now lives in the main house. Nearby, two of his pupils are staring up a tree, slingshots in hand. They are hunting a monkey, their only chance of eating meat. The youngest, wearing shorts that reveal his bony legs, says they manage two meals a day: tea and bread, when available, for breakfast, and maize porridge later in the day. His battered shoes are far too big and the laces are tied around his ankles to keep them from flying off. He lives 4 km (2.5 miles) away and walks to school.

Source: adapted from © The Economist Newspaper Limited, London (23 August 2007)

■ Full employment and the measurement of unemployment

It would appear quite logical, using the figures showing the relationship between the numbers of registered unemployed and the number of job vacancies, to argue that when they are equal full employment has occurred. Unfortunately this ignores the fact that our measures of unemployment are not completely accurate and may exclude some groups, for example older retired workers who fail to register as they feel it unlikely that they will obtain jobs.

One of our macro policy objectives is full employment – the full use of all labour resources so that the economy can produce at the limits of its potential GDP, or on its production possibility boundary.

In reality 100 per cent employment cannot be achieved as there will always be some unemployed people due to labour turnover, movement between jobs and incapacity to work. Structural changes where jobs are lost in industries that are declining and increasing in areas that are growing will require people to be mobile and transfer between jobs. So if full employment is not 'full employment' in the sense that everybody is employed, how do we define it? It is best explained as the situation that is occurring when the aggregate supply curve becomes vertical. This can be seen in Fig. 16.1 in the present chapter or in Fig. 15.7 in the previous chapter where full employment is shown by the long-run aggregate supply curve.

In Fig. 16.1 if aggregate demand increases beyond AD_1 the labour market will tighten as there will be a scarcity of labour in the economy and prices will begin to increase. If the authorities take steps to restrict aggregate demand to AD_1 the full employment level is restricted by the level of inflation that the government deems acceptable. So if the government sets the inflation target for the Monetary Policy Committee at 2 per cent then full employment will be lower than if they had set the inflation target at 3 per cent.

A further complication with the definition of full employment is that even at B and beyond in Fig. 16.1 there may be unemployed labour in the economy because the skills that the labour possesses are not those required by expanding firms. The level of unemployment that represents full employment may fall over time as over the past decade unemployment has fallen in the UK without increasing inflationary pressure. The normal economic cycle variations of the economy will mean that there will be fluctuations around the level of full employment. One of the factors that would improve the supply of labour to the economy is welfare reform, as shown in the next case study.

Links

At A2 we will consider the Phillips curve that will provide a deeper analysis of the relationship between employment and inflation.

Activity

1. Explain why the term 'full employment' can never mean what it seems to imply.

2. Evaluate the likelihood of a conflict between objectives.

Case study

'Workshy must lose benefits, says minister'

Jobless people who refuse to accept help to return to work could lose welfare benefits, the Work and Pensions Minister warned yesterday. In the latest 'crackdown' on the 'can't work, won't work' minority, the minister said that hard-working families could not be expected to pay for those refusing to take jobs.

He told the Institute for Public Policy Research think-tank that there was a 'small group' of claimants in areas with plenty of jobs who were physically able to work. There should be stronger incentives to persuade people into work as well as more help for individuals with mild alcohol problems, mental health difficulties or skills deficiencies.

'If we are to break the cycle of benefit dependency, we need to ask whether we should expect more from those who remain on Jobseeker's Allowance for long periods of time in return for the help we provide', he said.

'More active steps to get back into the labour market; more involvement in programmes that could increase the prospect of getting a job. And for those who won't do so, then there should be consequences, including less benefit or no benefit at all.'

Source: adapted from George Jones, 'Workshy must lose benefits, says minister', *The Daily Telegraph*, 20 December 2006

Unemployment and inflation

From the previous paragraph and a study of Fig. 16.1 it can be seen that there is some possible conflict between the macro policy objectives of full employment and stable prices and choice of an inflation level of 2 per cent CPI may mean that the levels of employment would be lower than the authorities would like.

Falling unemployment is likely to lead to increased wages as workers will feel in a stronger position and firms will offer higher wages to retain and attract the best workers. This will increase inflationary pressure that will make UK goods and services less competitive, assuming that UK goods were competitive before the inflation took place. The dilemma that then faces the government is that reducing the inflationary pressure will create rising unemployment, while allowing the economy to expand will reduce unemployment but create inflationary pressure. In the past, governments, committed by their manifestos to full employment, would often try to resolve the problem by letting the economy expand until inflationary pressure was unacceptable and then slowing it down until the levels of unemployment were undesirable and then repeating the process again. This policy was referred to as a boom/bust policy.

Modern economic thinking starts from the view of keeping inflation down to acceptable levels. If inflation is kept at a level equal to or below our major trading partners then UK goods and services will remain competitive, which will lead to increasing sales. This expansion of demand will lead to falling rates of unemployment and will continue as long as inflation is kept in check. While there is no doubt that in the short term there exists a trade-off between inflation and employment levels, in the long term the cause of full employment may be better served by inflationary pressure that is kept under control.

Before you conclude that control of inflation will thus ensure UK competitiveness abroad remember that this only holds if we actually have the manufacturing capacity to produce the products and that in some areas despite inflation control we are unable to compete with 'cheap labour' countries.

AQA Examiner's tip

If you are thrown by this question it may help you to draw an AD/ AS diagram with the lines drawn in showing the price level and the real output.

Activity

1. An economy's short-run aggregate supply curve is upward sloping. Following an increase in aggregate demand, what is most likely to happen to inflation and unemployment in the short run?

	Inflation	Unemployment
A	increase	increases
B	decreases	increases
C	decreases	decreases
D	increases	decreases

2 In a situation of a positive output gap:

  a Both inflation and unemployment will be falling

  b Inflation will be increasing while employment will be falling

  c Inflation will be increasing and unemployment will be falling

  d Inflation will be falling and employment will be falling

3 Use an AD/AS diagram to help you explain why a trade-off between inflation and unemployment may be required.

Demand-side causes of unemployment

Increases and decreases in the factors that comprise aggregate demand set up movements in the economy that we refer to as the economic cycle. This cyclical pattern leads to increases and decreases in the rates of unemployment. Such unemployment is known as **cyclical unemployment** or **demand deficient unemployment** as it is caused by a deficiency of aggregate demand in the economy. We can show it diagrammatically by using Fig. 16.1. At A cyclical unemployment would occur because the level of aggregate demand was below the full employment level as the economy was experiencing a negative output gap. There is insufficient demand in the economy to employ the available factors of production. The remedy is for the authorities to increase aggregate demand, which is likely to occur if the Monetary Policy Committee reduces the rate of interest. At AD_2 the operation of the economic cycle would lead to very low unemployment as the economy would be in a positive output gap. At this point the danger is inflation if aggregate demand continues to grow. The response of the Monetary Policy Committee would be to increase the rate of interest to offset increasing demand-side pressure.

These demand-side changes are likely to lead to fluctuations around the full employment level.

However, aggregate demand is made up of a number of factors including consumption, investment, government expenditure and net exports and while consumption may be important the other determinants need to be considered. Government expenditure can have a major effect on employment as can be seen from the increases in employment in both the NHS and education due to government expenditure over the past five years. Demand for UK exports is important for the manufacturing sector and deindustrialisation due to overseas competition reduces employment in the UK. Investment as a component of aggregate demand is dwarfed by consumer expenditure but it is important for creating growth and jobs.

Supply-side causes of unemployment

Frictional or **search unemployment** occurs as people leave one job and may be temporarily unemployed while they explore what the job market has to offer. It is called frictional as the labour markets do not operate immediately to match the supply of labour to the demand for labour. Some of this frictional unemployment may be seen as **voluntary unemployment** as some people may leave their current jobs and search for a better one. In other cases frictional unemployment is involuntary as they may have been made redundant from their current job.

Structural unemployment is more long term than frictional unemployment as it is associated with changes in the structure of industry as some industries close down and the workers are then left

Key terms

Cyclical unemployment: demand deficient unemployment that occurs as a result of the economic cycle.

Demand deficient unemployment: insufficient aggregate demand in the economy to employ the available labour.

Frictional/search unemployment: people between jobs.

Structural unemployment: unemployment caused by a change in the demand side or supply side of the economy.

Voluntary unemployment: workers who are not prepared to take a job at current wage levels.

Activity

Go into national statistics online (www.statistics.gov.uk) and find out the various percentages of GDP of the constituents of aggregate demand. This information will assist you in evaluating their importance as determinants of aggregate demand.

1 Use an AD/AS diagram to help you examine the effect on unemployment of a fall in the rate of interest.

2 Explain why increased government expenditure and the resulting multiplier effect is likely to reduce unemployment.

AQA Examiner's tip

Question 2 above does not explicitly ask you to draw an AD/AS diagram but it will enhance your analysis if you do.

jobless. It occurs when both the demand and supply patterns of the economy change. The UK coal mining industry is an example; demand was changing as power stations and domestic consumers were switching to gas and coal could be obtained far more cheaply from Australia and South America, leaving UK coal miners without jobs. Structural unemployment can be caused by both technological change and foreign competition and lead to a decline in the demand for the products of domestic industries. Overcoming structural unemployment requires considerable occupational retraining for the workforce, financial grants to try to attract foreign industries to fill the gap left by domestic industries and/or assistance to workers to move to areas where jobs are available.

In terms of an AD/AS diagram, Fig. 16.4 shows the economy in equilibrium at A at price level OP and output OE. Structural unemployment caused by the shutting of an industry can be shown by shifting the short-run aggregate supply curve from $SRAS$ to $SRAS_1$ leading to a reduced level of output OF and a higher level of prices OP_1. Disasters like earthquakes or tsunamis that destroy capital equipment lead to the long-run aggregate supply curve shifting to the left, indicating that the potential output of the economy had fallen.

Both frictional and structural unemployment are present in the UK as there are always people between jobs and competition from abroad and fast changing technology is likely to lead to structural unemployment. Firms relocating to cheaper areas of production and to escape high taxes are also likely to create unemployment.

In evaluation of supply-side causes students might like to consider government response to structural unemployment in terms of retraining schemes. Doubtlessly there will be some who are too old to retrain and for those that can there needs to be jobs available, i.e. there needs to be sufficient aggregate demand for the economy to employ them. Also, as they are starting at the bottom they may have to accept a substantial wage reduction that may mean they are better off receiving benefits. Finally, are governments well placed to judge the needs of the private sector or is the result likely to be government failure?

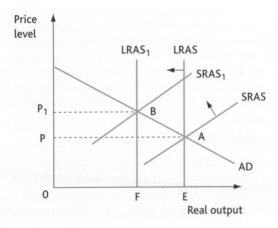

Figure 16.4 *Positive output gap*

■ Unemployment and output gaps

In Fig. 16.5, O to A shows a positive output gap and at this stage in the cycle we would expect that unemployment will be low and that the labour market will be tight as cyclical unemployment will be falling due to increasing aggregate demand. However, bearing in mind the supply-side causes of unemployment there are likely to be units of labour who remain unemployed as they have the incorrect skills for the jobs on offer or are still searching for a better level of wages than they are currently being offered.

Those searching for better jobs will be able to remain unemployed longer and extend their search if the level of benefits paid to the unemployed is high, relative to the level of wages. A lower level of benefits that persuaded the frictionally unemployed to return to work more rapidly would reduce some of the tightness of the labour market that occurs during a positive output gap. Similarly, with structural unemployment the more rapidly unemployed workers can be retrained and returned to the labour market the greater the benefit for the economy.

From *A* to *B* Fig. 16.5 shows a negative output gap where decreasing levels of aggregate demand will have increased cyclical or demand deficient unemployment augmenting those who are already unemployed due to supply-side causes. Some labour may become **discouraged workers** during this period of the cycle thinking that they are unlikely to be able to find a job. These workers may permanently withdraw themselves from the labour market.

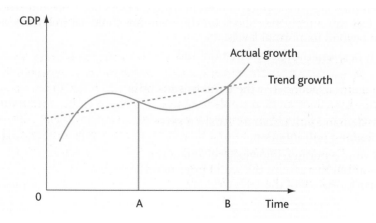

Figure 16.5

☑️ *After completing this chapter you should:*

■ understand that a potential conflict exists between inflation and unemployment

■ understand how the authorities deal with the conflict between controlling inflation and reducing unemployment

■ understand that both demand- and supply-side factors influence employment and unemployment and that the government has different strategies in dealing with them

■ understand the difference between cost push and demand pull inflation

■ understand how to use AD/AS diagrams to illustrate these macroeconomic objectives.

Key terms

Discouraged workers: workers who leave the labour market because despite numerous attempts they are unable to find a job.

Activity

1 With the aid of a diagram analyse what techniques the authorities could employ during a negative output gap to overcome unemployment.

2 Evaluate the view that a positive output gap will remove unemployment from the economy.

Activity

Stretch and challenge

1 a Explain the terms demand pull and cost push inflation.

  b Outline the main causes of cost push unemployment.

  c Construct an AD/AS diagram to show cost push inflation – explain what would result.

2 a Explain how the UK measures unemployment.

  b Outline the costs of unemployment.

  c Construct an AD/AS diagram to show the effects of an increase in UK immigration of skilled Polish workers.

3 a Give two demand-side reasons for unemployment.

  b Explain the term structural unemployment.

  c Evaluate the difficulties the authorities face in reducing cyclical unemployment.

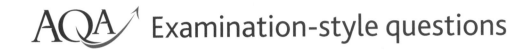

AQA⁄ Examination-style questions

1   While the Chinese economy is suffering from increasing inflationary pressure the Japanese
    are gradually overcoming their decade of deflation. Banks have been restored to health due
    to government-imposed mergers and bad loans have been removed from their balance sheets
    by government appointed agencies. Consumer demand is increasing and beneficial but if it
    continues the authorities will face demand pull inflation. Trade with China is growing rapidly
    stimulating the economy by export-led demand.

    In the USA increasing levels of imports and the ability of low-cost Chinese goods to destroy
    virtually any industry has given rise to talk about a negative output gap in the US economy.
    While most observers think that this is over-hyping the problem the mood of Congress is
    becoming more anti-Chinese imports.

    Across the pond in the UK, while individual industrialists may fume about the low-cost
    competition from China, the government takes a very relaxed attitude to it viewing low-cost
    imports as a strategic ally in reducing inflation. The "Westminster view" is that the UK is
    a predominantly service-based economy and Chinese competition is unlikely to have much
    effect; a view borne out by the statistics. What does appear to bother the UK government is
    the possibility of a substantial increase in the price of oil following OPEC's decision to restrict
    production. The authorities feel this supply-side shock on the economy could set in chain events
    that would increase inflation beyond its normal levels.

    (a)   Distinguish carefully between the terms 'inflation' and
          'deflation'.   (5 marks)

    (b)   With the aid of a diagram explain what the writer means by a
          negative output gap.   (8 marks)

    (c)   The source refers to demand pull inflation. Analyse two
          possible causes of demand pull inflation.   (12 marks)

    (d)   Using the data and your economic knowledge evaluate the
          impact that a "substantial increase in the world price of oil
          might have on the performance of the UK economy.   (25 marks)

2   While most of Europe and the USA have not seen a recurrence of mass unemployment since
    the 1980s and techniques to manage cyclical unemployment have become more sophisticated,
    structural unemployment continues to give governments headaches. Demand-deficient
    unemployment is managed in most countries by ensuring that aggregate demand remains at the
    correct level to maintain what economists have come to call "non-inflationary full employment".
    The responsibility to manage demand is usually placed on the shoulders of the central banks;
    in England the Bank of England, in the USA the Federal Reserve and in Europe the European
    Central Bank. All of their respective governments believe that inflation control leads to full
    employment and long-term growth.

    But even within the cosy definition of full employment developed economies suffer from
    structural unemployment, which has been aggravated by globalisation and technological changes
    as it has speeded the process up. Very few industries or sets of workers can be sure that some
    newly emergent country or new process will not render them too expensive and then redundant.
    Modifying educational systems, improving training and promoting industrial investment in order
    to counter structural unemployment has become a major objective of governments.

    While structural unemployment remains a problem, employers in the UK have found it difficult
    to obtain labour due to demographic changes as the labour force ages. Traditional suppliers of
    labour, like Ireland for the building industry have grown extremely rapidly and the legions of
    labourers and builders have dried up; a serious problem for a government determined to increase
    the supply of social housing while also building Olympic facilities. Immigrants from Eastern
    Europe have filled the gap in both building and other industries.

(a) Explain the term 'non-inflationary full employment' as used in the passage. (*5 marks*)

(b) With the aid of an AD/AS diagram, explain one possible cause of demand-deficient unemployment. (*8 marks*)

(c) The source refers to structural unemployment. Analyse the likely causes of structural unemployment and suggest what actions could be taken by the authorities to remedy it. (*12 marks*)

(d) Evaluate the likely effects on the economy of an influx of workers from Eastern Europe on the UK's macroeconomic objectives. (*25 marks*)

17 The balance of payments on current account

During the last six chapters reference has been made to the UK's competitiveness when trading with other countries. This chapter will discuss the components of the current account and the annual balance of trade in goods and services between UK and the rest of the world.

💡 The items in the balance of payments on current account – an overview

In this introductory section we are going to look at one part of the balance of payments that is known as the current account, which refers to trade in goods and services. The other part of the balance of payments refers to capital flows, i.e. where the money comes from or goes to as a result of current account transactions. This part of the account, which you will study at A2, is known formally as the financial account.

The current account is in four parts:

- trade in goods
- trade in services
- investment income
- current transfers.

The table below shows that overall in 2006 the UK's balance of payments was in deficit:

💡 **Table 17.1** *Balance of payments on current account, 2006 – figures rounded to the nearest hundred million*

	Exports £ million	Imports £ million	Balance £ million	Brief description of components
Trade in goods	245,000	322,000	−72,000	Import and export of goods
Trade in services	125,000	95,000	30,000	Import and export of services
Investment income	240,000	221,000	19,000	Incomings and outgoings from past investments
Transfers	16,000	28,000	−12,000	Official and private transfers of money
Current account balance			**−35,000**	

These four items added together make up the balance on current account. While we have defined both exports and imports in previous chapters a useful way of recognising them is to look at the money flows. If sterling is being changed into foreign currency it is usually being spent on foreign goods and services and money is flowing out of the UK, which is characteristic of an import. When you go on holiday abroad you change your pounds into foreign currency and spend that money in your holiday destination. If, say, someone in Spain books a flight on British Airways from Madrid to the UK, euros at some stage must be changed into sterling to pay BA for their services

🛈 There are two other, rather dated, terms that you may encounter when reading about the balance of payments and these are '**visibles**' and '**invisibles**'.

In terms of each of the accounts noted above an export would add to UK's income and would be shown by a + in the accounts, while an import, which is money leaving the UK would be shown by a − sign. In general over the past decade, while certain parts of the current account have been in surplus, e.g. trade in services, the overall balance has been in deficit. When you look at the figures it will seem a huge amount but economists tend to consider the deficit in terms of its percentage of GDP and whether or not the size of the deficit or surplus is having an effect on the macroeconomy.

The balance of trade in goods

Notice the title of this subheading is 'the **balance of trade**'.

This is a technical term and you will come across the usage of the term both in the newspapers and on the radio and TV news. It is used when referring only to trade in goods. It only means visible trade and excludes the rest of the accounts that make up the current account. Countries like Germany with a large secondary sector and rapidly developing countries like China tend to have a very large surplus in terms of trade in goods. This may be due to the reputation that their goods have achieved for quality, reliability and innovation in the case of Germany or due to their advantages in terms of cheap labour that makes their goods comparatively cheap in terms of China.

Key terms

Visibles: exports or imports that are tangible, that you can see and touch as they cross international boundaries.

Invisibles: intangibles such as the provision of insurance or banking services.

Balance of trade: visible exports minus visible imports.

Figure 17.1 *Goods coming in and out*

The balance of trade is the result of the difference between visible exports and visible imports. If the UK exports more than it imports the balance of trade will be shown by a + sign and we refer to it as a 'trade surplus'. If, as is more likely the case the UK imports more than it exports we refer to it as a 'trade deficit' and it will be shown in the accounts by a minus sign. You may also come across the term 'trade gap', which is often used by journalists when reporting on the size of a trade deficit.

Key terms

Deindustrialisation: a fall in the proportion of national output accounted for by the manufacturing sector of the economy.

Globalisation: the ability to produce goods anywhere in the world and sell them in any country.

While the UK exports a number of manufactured goods like cars, ICT hardware, food and pharmaceuticals, we tend to import a large number of products. This is partly due to the fact that for many goods we can import them more cheaply than we can manufacture them ourselves and as a result of this the manufacturing sector of the UK has shrunk. This is referred to as **deindustrialisation**, the reduction in size of the manufacturing sector as the move to a tertiary economy has taken place. Our industrial structure together with that of other developed countries has changed due to the increase in **globalisation.**

Large firms that trade internationally have been able to manufacture in virtually any part of the world and they have moved their operations to areas where production costs can be minimised. This has meant that relatively high cost manufacturing countries are no longer competitive in manufacturing basic consumer products that can be produced using assembly line production. This has affected the UK's industrial structure, its balance of trade, its balance of payments on current account and also the macroeconomy.

It may seem confusing that we import goods such as cars, when we can make them in the UK but reasonably free international trade increases the standard of living for consumers as it allows them a greater range of choice than if they could only purchase products made in their own country. It also increases the competitiveness of domestic producers who have to keep up with and endeavour to beat the innovation of foreign producers.

Activity

Table 17.2 *UK exports and imports*

Year	UK exports £m	UK imports £m	Balance of trade £m
2002	187,000	234,000	−47,000
2003	188,000	237,000	
2004	191,000	252,000	
2005	212,000	280,000	
2006	245,000	329,000	
2007			
2008			

Using the website www.statistics.gov.uk find the statistics for 2007 and 2008 and answer the following questions:

1. Explain the trend of UK exports since 2002.

2. Explain the trend of UK imports.

3. Calculate the balance of trade over the period 2003–8 and explain what the figures mean for the UK economy.

Case study

Still behind

The final threat is a factor at the root of competitiveness itself – productivity! UK productivity as measured by GDP per worker is behind the average of all other G7 countries. The main reason put forward for the poor performance of the UK is lack of investment and in particular the low rate of investment in research and development.

Britain lags behind other developed economies in converting new ideas into industrial applications. With the exception of a few areas like pharmaceuticals UK businesses have not been effective in terms of creating new products and services and improving processes and practices. Similarly, British managers have been criticised for their failure to adopt the latest management practices. This contributes to the UK's poor performance on the balance of payments as UK residents are keen to purchase updated items from abroad that UK firms no longer supply, which also reduces their competitiveness in the international market place.

As Professor William Baumol argued in his book *The Free Market Innovation Machine: Analysing the Growth Miracle of Capitalism,* successful companies and successful economies no longer compete on the basis of low prices and low costs, but on the basis of continuous and sustained innovation.

Source: adapted from David Pierce, 'Labour productivity', *British Economy Survey* 34, spring 2006 and John Van Reenen, 'Productivity races', *Britain Today*, 2007

To improve our balance of payments and position of international competitiveness we need to increase our levels of research and development and investment, both public in areas like transport and infrastructure and private in terms of new technology. The penetration of Chinese and other developing countries' imports into the UK and world markets means we are less competitive in the production of basic goods. Supporting industries where our competitive position and strengths are waning does not make economic sense. Our advantage seems to lie in the areas of enterprise, the number of new 'products' designed by the financial institutions of the City of London for international consumption is extremely innovative and in the area of scientific research we lead the world in the number of citations and the number of papers published per head of population.

Why is our trade balance important?

- The effect on the macroeconomy – exports are an injection into the circular flow and boost the level of national income. The multiplier amplifies the effect of exports on the economy.
- Levels of employment in manufacturing industry are dependent on exports as a large percentage of manufactures are exported.
- While the South of England can be seen as primarily service based the Midlands and North of England have a larger percentage of manufacturing industries. A fall in export sales has a large effect on these regions and widens the regional income gap.

AQA Examiner's tip

- Data on our most popular exports and imports is likely to appear in data response questions in this part of the specification.
- Be aware that a change in the trade balance will have an effect on the macroeconomy through changes in aggregate demand.

Figure 17.2 *A container ship*

■ Trade in services

This account covers both the services that the UK exports and the services that we import. Probably our two most important export services could be summed up as financial services – banking, insurance – and tourism. We also provide and import other types of services like sea transport, both cargo and passengers, and civil aviation through firms like British Airways. Tickets on UK planes sold to foreign travellers are shown as credits in the services account, whereas our purchases of tickets from overseas airlines are recorded as debits. Services are also provided by nationals working abroad, so an employee of BP working in Saudi Arabia would be adding to UK service income.

The growth of service income tends to be a characteristic more of developed countries that have the education, skills and expertise to provide these services. The UK has moved closer toward a service-based tertiary economy and is well placed to offer such products. However, there is still debate among economists as to whether a service-based economy will be able to maintain a healthy balance of payments as without a flourishing secondary sector an economy is reliant on other countries to supply its manufactured goods. While this part of the account is usually in surplus, other developed countries also offer services in competition to the UK.

■ Activity

Table 17.3

Year	Exports services £m	Services imports £m	Services balance £m
2002	90,000	73,000	17,000
2003	97,000	78,000	
2004	108,000	82,000	
2005	115,000	91,000	
2006	125,000	95,000	
2007			
2008			

Using the website www.statistics.gov.uk find the statistics for 2007 and 2008 and answer the following questions:

1 Explain the overall trends in UK services exports and imports since 2002.

2 Calculate the balance of trade in services over the period 2003–8.

3 Calculate whether the balance in services is sufficient to overcome the deficit in goods.

When you have calculated the services balance you will appreciate its contribution toward the overall balance of payments in recent years.

Investment income

This part of the account measures earnings made from investments overseas minus income flowing abroad from foreign investments in the

UK. A flow of capital out of the UK economy such as banks giving loans to foreign nationals, the buying of shares in foreign companies and the setting up of new businesses abroad will generate future investment income for the UK. All of these activities lead to investment income in the form of interest, dividends and profits that flow back into the UK as a result of the previous outward capital flows. Alternatively, a flow of capital into the UK for any of the same reasons will lead to outward capital flows in the future in terms of interest profits and dividends.

💡 UK banks are active in overseas markets both in terms of retail and commercial lending and involved in mergers with other banks. Foreign banks have merged with UK banks and are active in the UK market.

The London Stock Exchange offers shares in company's worldwide and both domestic and foreign investors are large buyers, leading to shareholdings in numerous countries.

In terms of direct investment, companies such as Honda, Toyota and Datsun have established car plants in the UK, which have helped to reduce unemployment levels and make the UK a net exporter of cars. Profits made by these companies will be repatriated to their country of origin.

Activity

Lord Jones of Birmingham, the trade minister, has used his first major overseas trip to call on the Indian government to speed up the liberalisation of the country's financial services markets.

Launching a new trade lobbying body called the UK India Business Council in Mumbai yesterday, Lord Jones said that Britain's lacklustre exporting performance to India – the country receives only 1 per cent of British exports – was partly down to the City's inability to sell financial services.

'Mumbai is not opening up to financial services as quickly as it ought to be. Probably our greatest export is financial services. People say we only export 1pc to India. Well, one of the reasons is that we are not allowed to,' said Lord Jones, the former head of the business trade body, the CBI, who was asked to join the government by Gordon Brown in June. Lord Jones said he was reassured by senior ministers that India was 'committed to reform'. '[They said] it was just a question of time. I said "Fine, but globalisation does not give time."'

He also pressed government ministers to speed up approvals for energy exploration in India and to allow more competition from British law firms.

Source: adapted from Richard Tyler, 'Lord Jones urges India to open up financial services market', *Telegraph*, 28 September 2007

Answer the following questions:

1. Under which part of the current account would the 'City's' exports be found?

2. Explain the importance to the UK of this part of the account.

Case study

Talk is cheap

We all know what the Germans are good at. They do precision engineering: all those quietly humming washing machines and the cars with their sleek bodywork and gleaming chrome. We also know that Germany is a country in serious trouble, failing as it has to embrace the need for flexibility in the tough new global environment. We know this because Gordon Brown has told us many times over the past 10 years that the European model is washed up. Germany was so abysmally competitive last year that it ran a record trade surplus and was the biggest exporter of any country in the world.

But how has Britain fared when it comes to paying our way in the world? Britain still has a world-class pharmaceutical industry, and still makes a tidy sum from selling arms abroad, often to some pretty unsavoury regimes. Yet the deficit in visible trade in goods – stuff we make – was more than £60bn in 2006. That's around 5 per cent of GDP, far bigger than anything the UK has witnessed in the postwar period. Trade in services – accountancy, insurance, banking, architecture, advertising – brings the deficit down to around 4 per cent of GDP. But for the past decade, the only thing that has made the deficit manageable is that Britain has been earning more money on its investments abroad than foreign investors have made here.

The story as far as New Labour is concerned is that our failure in the second half of the 20th century to exploit the potential of higher consumer spending on cars, washing machines, hi-fis and personal stereos has actually left us better placed to exploit the sunrise industries of the 21st century – biotechnology, robotics, environmental protection, pharmaceuticals. Successful economies will require brains more than brawn, and Britain is full of smart people.

There is an element of smoke and mirrors in all this, however. It is true that as countries develop, the number of people employed in services tends to go up. The reason for this is that productivity growth in manufacturing is much faster than it is in services: it takes far fewer hours to make a car today than it did 100 years ago, but the same time to cut someone's hair. It is also true that each wave of capitalism since the industrial revolution has been based on a distinctive technology: coal and steam, then railways and electricity, then mass transportation and consumer goods. Although the vast numbers of poor people in India and China (let alone Africa and Latin America) suggest there will still be strong demand for consumer durables and machine tools for a good while yet, information technology and the human genome may be at the centre of the next long upswing.

Source: adapted from Larry Elliott and Dan Atkinson, *Fantasy Island,* Constable & Robinson Ltd, 2000

Table 17.4 *Transfers balance*

Year	Balance of transfers £m
2002	–9,081
2003	–10,122
2004	–10,949
2005	–12,008
2006	–11,899

Transfers

This account measures the transfers of money between countries. Private transfers of money refer to exchanges between individuals, for example money sent home to their families from Britons working overseas or money sent home from immigrants working in the UK.

The second element of this account is government transfers that include:

- grants to overseas countries
- UK contributions to the European Union budget
- contributions to international organisations, such as the International Monetary Fund, the World Bank and the World Trade Organisation

- maintenance of troops abroad
- maintenance of embassies and consulates.

While private transfers may vary, government transfers are always a deficit item due to expenditure overseas.

The transfers balance from 2002–06 is shown in Table 17.4.

Adding the three balances above to the trade in goods balance gives the current balance.

Using the figures for 2002 the balance of payments on current account would be as shown in Table 17.5.

The overall balance is usually negative as the UK has not experienced a surplus in recent years. It is this part of the account, which tends to be discussed on the radio and in the newspapers and a country's economic progress, is judged on the basis of it. Strong trading economies are expected to have a positive balance on their current account. Changes in a country's current account can come about for a number of reasons:

- Changes in the value of the currency can affect the prices of imports and exports and affect consumers' decisions.

- Changes in aggregate demand – a rise in UK national income is likely to lead to an increase in the trade deficit as consumers spend a large proportion of their income on imported goods. An increase in economic activity in our major trading partners is likely to increase expenditure on UK exports.

- A country whose macroeconomy is inflating faster than that of its trading partners will find that as its goods become more expensive they do not sell abroad. At the same time imports will grow as they will be relatively cheaper. This is a major reason to keep inflation under control.

- Increases in labour productivity will make a country more competitive and will have the effect of reducing the prices of goods and services, which will make a country's goods more attractive. If its productivity is lower than that of its trading partners firms may have difficulty reducing costs to a competitive level.

- Innovation will lead to new products that will increase a country's competitive position in world markets.

Maintaining international competitiveness is vital if a country is going to maintain either a surplus or a balance. A loss of competitiveness will mean a fall in demand for its goods and services, which is likely to increase unemployment and an increase in demand for more competitive imports. This is likely to make the UK more import dependent as firms are not sufficiently competitive to supply the overseas or domestic market and either shut down or relocate abroad.

The benefits for a country's citizens of a current account deficit is that they are able to consume extra goods and services as they are in effect consuming more than they are producing themselves. However, in the longer term in order to move into surplus they are going to have to reduce their levels of consumption below the levels of current production in order for exports to exceed imports. A country with a surplus, on the other hand, is consuming less goods and services than it produces. The benefit is that in the long term they are building up assets, which will allow them to consume more than they currently produce.

Table 17.5 *Balance of payments on current account*

	£m
Trade balance	−47,705
Services balance	16,830
Investment balance	23,376
Transactions balance	−9,081
Overall balance	−16,580

Examiner's tip

- Do not confuse a balance of payments deficit (imports > exports) with a budget deficit (government spends more than it raises in taxes).

- Note that you may be asked to define the current account and the main items in that account.

- In order to keep up to date use the website www.statistics.gov. uk

Activity

Briefly explain the difference between the balance of trade and the balance of payments on current account.

The current account and the AD/AS model

Both exports X and imports M are components of aggregate demand. A current account deficit or surplus will therefore affect the macroeconomy through changes in aggregate demand. With a surplus, foreign demand will increase aggregate demand for UK goods, increasing exports. If domestic consumers are buying less imports and more domestic produce imports will fall.

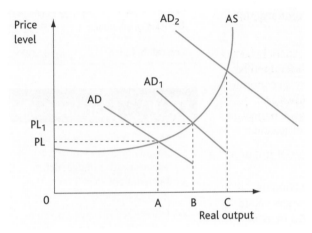

Figure 17.3 *Current account surplus*

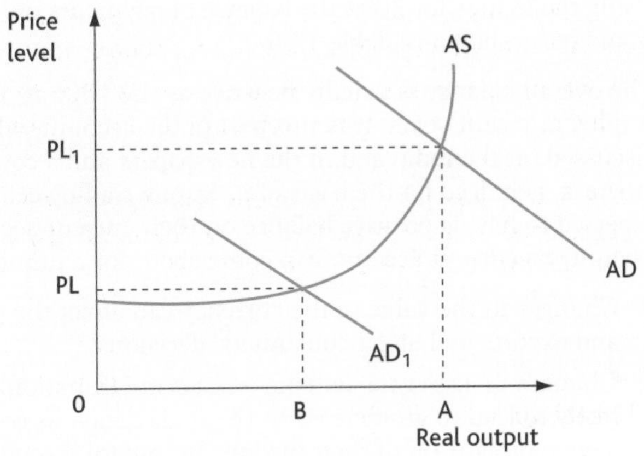

Figure 17.4 *A fall in aggregate demand*

In Fig. 17.3 a current account surplus has shifted AD from AD to AD_1 and there has been an increase in both real output OA to OB and the price level OPL to OPL_1. If exports increase AD beyond AD_2 inflation will occur as the economy is pushed into a positive output gap. Increased exports will benefit the economy when there is a negative output gap but will add to inflationary pressure in a positive output gap.

A balance of payments deficit will have the reverse effect as AD will fall; either because exports are not selling so foreign demand for UK goods has fallen or UK demand for imports has increased reducing AD for domestic goods. This will reduce both real output and the price level. If the economy is experiencing inflation a fall in exports will reduce aggregate demand and inflationary pressure.

In Fig. 17.4 a fall in aggregate demand from AD to AD_1 has reduced prices from OPL_1 to OPL and output from OA to OB reducing inflationary pressure in the economy.

The UK authorities would like to achieve **current account equilibrium** because this would lead to a greater level of stability in the macroeconomy as a disequilibrium situation of either surplus or deficit impacts on aggregate demand. Equilibrium is usually taken to mean that the current account will be at zero, so the amount imported equals the amount exported and there will be no impact on the macroeconomy.

Does a deficit balance matter?

Those economists who believe that a deficit is of little importance tend to argue that:

- due to capital movements if a country wants to operate with a current account deficit then there is no problem as long as foreign capital flows in to finance it; as the UK has attracted large amounts of inward

Key terms

Current account equilibrium: where the current account exercises no effect on the domestic macroeconomy.

investment in recent years it has been able to finance its current account deficit

- the deficit will be self-correcting if it is due to strong consumer demand as the economic cycle will at some point reduce demand
- some of the deficit may be due to imports of new capital equipment that will increase UK productivity.

However, some economists argue that:

- the deficit may indicate that the UK has lost competitiveness in foreign markets due to insufficient investment, low productivity and loss of comparative advantage to other countries
- continuous excess of imports over exports leads to withdrawals from the circular flow that will eventually lead to reduced levels of output and employment
- those who lose jobs in the manufacturing sector may not readily be employed in the service sector. The UK needs growing export markets in order to maintain full employment.

Activity

Using the figures you have acquired from the website www.statistics.gov.uk draw an AD/AS diagram to show the effect on the macroeconomic equilibrium of a balance of payments deficit and a balance of payments surplus on both a positive and negative output gap.

Activity

Stretch and challenge

1 The UK has the following transactions on its current account:

Manufactured exports £22bn; UK tourist spending abroad £10bn; Repatriation of funds by East European workers £3bn; UK firms receiving income from overseas subsidiaries £8bn; Foreign payments to UK banks for financial services £4bn; UK residents' payments to foreign-owned insurance companies £4bn; UK firms' payments to foreign ship-owners £5bn; Income from UK nationals working abroad £8bn; Foreign tourist expenditure in the UK £8bn; Income from UK sea transport and civil aviation firms £11bn; UK food imports £10bn; UK government subscriptions to international institutions £6bn; UK oil imports £8bn; UK imports of cars and trucks £6bn; Profits and dividends paid to foreign firms £6bn.

   a Work out which of these items are (i) visible exports (ii) visible imports.

   b Which items go into the following accounts: (i) trade in services (ii) investment income (iii) current transfers.

   c Calculate (i) the balance of trade (ii) the balance of payments on current account.

   d All other things being equal explain the likely effect of the current account balance that you have calculated on the macroeconomy.

   e How would your answer to question (d) have been different if the price of oil had risen by 50 per cent?

2 a Go onto the website www.statistics.gov.uk and find the latest current account figures.

   b *Ceteris paribus* (other things being equal) draw an AD/AS diagram to show their effect on the macroeconomic equilibrium.

💡✅ *After completing this chapter you should:*

- be able to recognise and explain the components of the current account
- be able to explain the meaning of the balance of trade in goods and appreciate its importance to the UK economy

- understand the importance of the contribution of services to the UK current account
- understand the role of investment and transfers and their contribution to the current account
- from given figures, be able to calculate the balance of trade and the balance of payments on current account
- be able to use the AD/AS model to show the effect of changes in the current account on the macroeconomy.

AQA Examination-style questions

1 **A new age for British exports**

Improvements in the trade balance with the EU27 are extremely welcome as a few years ago America was our biggest export market, but the strong pound isn't doing us any favours. Now we probably sell more to Turkey. We also supply Romanian and Bulgarian markets, and a little into east Asia. We listen very carefully to what customers want and to what our suppliers can do and as the government says, 'we need a steep rise in exports'.

'Competition with the Chinese is tough but their insatiable demand for capital goods has also helped British and European exporters to fill their order books and keep EU citizens in work. It's an echo of probably the biggest single change in the structure of British industry in the past 20 or 30 years – its drift into foreign ownership. Such moves have played a significant part in securing the UK's position as one of the world's favourite destinations for investment, which leads to repatriation of investment funds in the future.

While this improvement in the trade balance is extremely welcome, overall the balance is still in deficit, unlike the services balance that manages a consistent surplus. Yet there are still success stories that are more unequivocally 'Made in Britain'. GSK is the world's second-largest pharmaceutical company; Rolls-Royce is one of the two biggest makers of aero engines; JCB's earth-moving equipment is used to dig holes just about everywhere; British Aerospace, despite its problems (or because of them), makes a substantial contribution to the balance of payments.

Adapted from the *Independent*

(a) Explain the terms 'biggest export market' and 'capital goods'. (*5 marks*)

(b) With the aid of a diagram, explain the effect on the UK economy of a 'steep rise in exports'. (*8 marks*)

(c) With reference to the data and your own knowledge, explain what you understand by the services account and the transfers account. (*8 marks*)

(d) Evaluate the statement that a balance of payments deficit no longer matters (*25 marks*)

2 **The Productivity problem**

Why is Britain finding it so hard to reach the same productivity levels as other advanced economies? A recent survey by the OECD highlighted failings in skills, innovation and transport.

Long-standing deficiencies in education mean that the British workforce has a much higher share of low-skilled people than is the case in most other developed countries. That may also explain why Britain has not wrung as much extra efficiency from its investments in technology as America.

Innovation is especially important in propelling productivity in advanced countries. But across a range of indicators – including spending on research and development, and securing new patents – Britain compares poorly with the best-performing countries. Low productivity levels are likely to lead to a deterioration in Britain's trade balance.

The UK needs to improve its competitiveness and this is dependent on further improvements to the supply side of the economy such as productivity, skills and investment.

(a)   Explain what you understand by the term 'productivity'.   (3 *marks*)

(b)   Explain the connection made in the passage between low
       productivity levels and Britain's trade balance.   (6 *marks*)

(c)   With the aid of a diagram analyse the effects of a
       deteriorating trade balance on the macro-economy.   (8 *marks*)

(d)   Using the data and your economic knowledge evaluate
       the effects on the UK trade balance in goods and services of
       'further improvements to the supply side of the economy'.   (15 *marks*)

Monetary policy

■ **Links**

The determination of interest rates is covered in detail at A2 Level.

Policies that aim to influence an economy's aggregate demand are designed either to stabilise the level of output and employment or to stabilise the price level. Monetary policy plays a dominant role as one of the three major categories of policy used to manage the UK economy today, along with fiscal policy and supply-side policies, as outlined in the following chapters.

💡 The meaning of monetary policy

Monetary policy involves controlling the macroeconomy through changes in monetary variables such as the money supply or interest rates. In the last two decades it has become the principal strand of macroeconomic policy, and since 1997 it has been independently managed in the UK by the Monetary Policy Committee (MPC) of the UK's **central bank**, the Bank of England. The operational independence of the Bank of England granted in May 1997 is significant as it aims to remove political influence from the process of meeting the inflation target, though the Bank is responsible for achieving price stability and stability in financial markets.

In contrast, fiscal policy uses changes in levels of government spending and taxation to control the economy. Indeed, while fiscal policy can be used to influence aggregate demand in the macroeconomy, it can also be used to 'fine-tune' the supply side of the economy at a microlevel, affecting the efficiency of markets and incentives to work, invest and be entrepreneurial. Thus we can also say that there is a great deal of overlap between modern fiscal and supply-side policies.

■ The rate of interest and monetary policy

In recent years the prime instrument of monetary policy has been the **interest rate**. Through the interest rate, monetary policy affects aggregate demand. At higher interest rates, firms are less willing to spend on investment and households spend less on consumption. This is partly because, when the interest rate is relatively high, the cost of borrowing becomes high and people are discouraged from borrowing for investment or consumption purposes.

There is no unique rate of interest in the economy. For example, we can distinguish between savings rates and borrowing rates. However, interest rates tend to move in the same direction. For example, if the Bank of England cuts the base rate of interest then we expect to see lower mortgage rates and lower rates on savings accounts with banks and building societies.

The **real interest rate** is often important to businesses and consumers when making spending and saving decisions. The real rate of return on savings, for example, is the money rate of interest minus the rate of inflation. So if a saver is receiving a money rate of interest of 5 per cent on his savings, but price inflation is running at 2 per cent per year, the real rate of return on these savings is only +3 per cent.

💡 Monetary policy and aggregate demand

There are several ways in which changes in interest rates influence aggregate demand. These are collectively known as the **transmission mechanism of monetary policy**. One of the main channels that the MPC can use to influence aggregate demand, and therefore inflation, is via the lending and borrowing rates charged by the market. When the Bank's base interest rate rises, high street banks will typically increase the rates charged on loans and the interest that they offer on savings. This tends to discourage businesses from taking out loans to finance investment and encourages the consumer to save rather than spend, and so reduces the growth of aggregate demand. Conversely, when the Bank's base rate falls, banks tend to cut the market rates offered on loans and savings, which will tend to stimulate aggregate demand. Changes to the level of interest rates take time to have an impact on overall economic activity, i.e. there is a time lag involved. These time lags, understood to be up to 2 years in duration, combined with uncertainty about future economic events, mean that the MPC need to build statistical probability into the effects of current and past interest rate changes. Thus the Bank of England makes use of so-called 'fan diagrams' as shown in Fig. 18.2. These highlight the expected path of CPI inflation and output, based on judgements about the most probable outcome (indicated in the central path of the 'fan'), and increasing uncertainty surrounding those central projections further ahead.

A change in interest rates can have wide-ranging effects on the economy. A key influence played by rate changes is the effect on confidence – particularly the confidence of households about their financial circumstances.

Impacts of changes in interest rates on aggregate demand

1. *The housing market* Higher interest rates increase the cost of mortgages and hence influence the demand for most types of housing. This will slow down the growth of household wealth and put a squeeze on mortgage equity withdrawal (MEW – consumers borrowing off the back of rising house prices).

2. *Disposable incomes of mortgage payers* If interest rates increase, the disposable income of homeowners who have variable-rate mortgages will fall, leading to a decline in their purchasing power. The effects of a rate change are greater when the level of existing mortgage debt is high, leading to a rise in debt-servicing burdens for homeowners. However, a rise in interest rates boosts the disposable income of people who have paid off their mortgage and who have positive net savings in bank and building society accounts.

3. *Consumer demand for credit* Higher interest rates increase the cost of servicing debt on credit cards and should lead to a slow-down in the growth of retail sales and spending on consumer durables, the extent of which depends on the impact of a rate change on consumer confidence.

4. *Consumer and business confidence* The relationship between interest rates and business and consumer confidence is complicated, depending on economic conditions. For example, when businesses and consumers are worried about the risk of a recession, an interest rate cut can boost confidence, and hence aggregate demand, acting as a reassurance to the public that the Bank of England is alert to the dangers of a downturn in economic activity. It is possible, however, that a cut in rates could undermine confidence, e.g. if the Bank of

Figure 18.1 *The Bank of England*

▉ Key terms

Monetary policy: controlling the macroeconomy via changes in monetary variables such as the money supply or interest rates.

Central bank: the financial institution in a country or group of countries typically responsible for issuing notes and coins and setting short-term interest rates.

Interest rate: the cost of borrowing or the reward for saving.

Real interest rate: the money rate of interest minus the rate of inflation.

Transmission mechanism of monetary policy: how changes in the base interest rate influence the components of aggregate demand.

AQA Examiner's tip

Candidates should focus mainly on interest rates as the main instrument of monetary policy. The money supply should be treated as an indicator of whether the monetary policy implemented by the Bank of England is 'on course'.

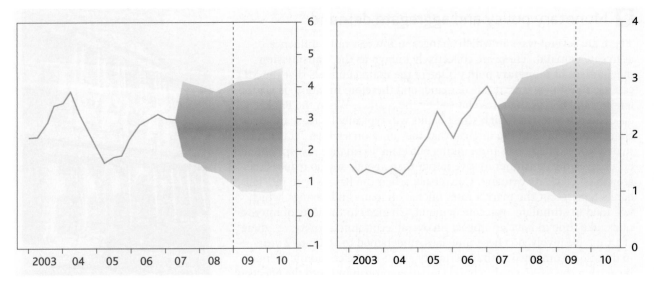

Figure 18.2 *Fan diagrams: GDP and CPI inflation projections based on market interest rate expectations*
Source: Bank of England Quarterly Inflation Report, August 2007

England cut interest rates too quickly, sending a message to firms and consumers that the Bank is concerned about the prospect of a recession. Thus interest rate setting often calls for a finely balanced judgement.

5 *Business investment* Firms take the actual and expected level of interest rates into account when deciding whether or not to undertake new capital investment spending. A rise in short-term rates may dampen business confidence and lead to a reduction in planned capital investment. However, many other factors influence investment decisions, including consumer trends, exchange rates and expectations of future profitability.

6 *Effects upon the exchange rate* Higher UK interest rates might lead to a strengthening of the exchange rate of the pound, particularly if UK interest rates rise relative to those in the Eurozone and the United States attracting inflows of so-called 'hot money' into the British financial system. A stronger exchange rate will reduce the competitiveness of UK exports in overseas markets because it makes our exports appear more expensive when priced in a foreign currency, thereby leading to a decline in export volumes. It also reduces the price in pounds of imported goods and services leading to lower prices and rising import volumes. If the trade deficit in goods and services widens, this is a net withdrawal of demand from the circular flow and acts to reduce aggregate demand in the economy.

Usually a UK interest rate cut will tend to weaken the pound as it makes it less attractive for foreign investors to hold their money in Britain. When the pound rises, British exports become more expensive, while imported goods from abroad become cheaper. So a strong pound, compared to other currencies, leads to a fall in demand for UK exports and a fall in demand for domestically produced goods that compete with imports from overseas. A relatively strong pound therefore reduces aggregate demand, and so can depress the rate of inflation.

How monetary policy affects real output and the price level in the AD/AS model

Suppose the government believes that the economy is close to full employment and is in danger of overheating. Overheating could push prices up without any resulting benefit in terms of higher real output. This is the classic case of demand pull inflation, i.e. too much aggregate demand in the economy relative to the supply capacity. An increase in the interest rate will lead to a fall in aggregate demand, thereby relieving the pressure on prices. This is illustrated in Fig. 18.3, where the initial position has aggregate demand relatively high at AD_1, with price level P_1 and real output at full employment level Y_1. An increase in interest rates shifts aggregate demand to the left, to AD_2. Real output falls slightly to Y_2 and the equilibrium price level falls to P_2. Thus monetary policy can be used to control demand pull inflationary pressure in the economy. A reduced price level, other things being equal, could help to make UK goods and services more competitive overseas, which may improve our balance of payments position.

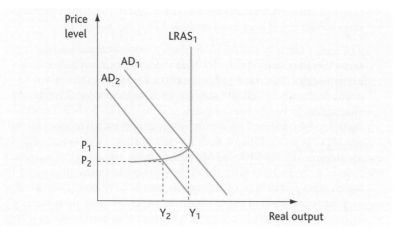

Figure 18.3 *Using monetary policy to manage aggregate demand*

Conversely, a reduction in interest rates can be used to boost aggregate demand. If there is some spare production capacity in the economy, e.g. at real output Y_2 in Fig. 18.3, increased AD could boost the equilibrium level of real output to Y_1, though with little spare capacity available in the economy as a whole, inflationary pressure may result, increasing the price level from P_2 to P_1.

Of course, the management of aggregate demand alone is only half the story and monetary policy exercised through the use of interest rates has been criticised as something of a 'blunt instrument'. In recent decades, more use has been made of policies to improve aggregate supply in tandem with demand management.

Links

These policies are outlined in Chapters 19 and 20.

Case study

Economists agree MPC will hold rate

Interest rates will stay at 5.75 per cent on Thursday. That is the conclusion of a Reuters survey last week of 61 economists, none of whom expects the Bank of England's Monetary Policy Committee to raise its main rate. Despite the unanimity, the avowed ambition of Mervyn King, Bank governor, to make monetary policy 'boring' has failed this year, with the MPC gaining a reputation for surprise decisions.

In January, 50 out of 51 economists polled by Reuters were caught off guard when the MPC raised rates. In June, financial markets were once again surprised by how close the MPC had come to raising again, after four members – including Mr King – voted for another increase. Mr King admitted in May that the central bank was 'clearly' failing to explain how it was likely to respond to economic data. The MPC seems to be split in their approach to interpreting economic data and subsequently tackling inflationary pressure. None of the groups has a majority, hence the tendency for more erratic outcomes as interest-rate decisions are based on a majority vote. Broadly speaking, Tim Besley, Andrew Sentance, Mr King and Sir John Gieve, deputy governor for financial stability, wonder whether the Bank has raised interest rates sufficiently to slow consumer spending and control inflationary pressures. David Blanchflower and Rachel Lomax, deputy governor for monetary policy, argue that rate changes take time to work through the economy and that raising interest rates too far could lead to an undesirably sharp slowdown.

Theories as to why the MPC appears to have become more unpredictable include the idea that the economic outlook is exceptionally uncertain, giving rise to a spread of judgements about outcomes. Michael Saunders of Citigroup says: 'This is shaping up to be the year of greatest division on the MPC since Bank independence. The nature of the economic challenges facing the MPC is more difficult than usual and this is the source of arguments.' David Miles of Morgan Stanley agrees: 'The enormous run-up in household debt, the huge increase in house prices and the big changes in the type of mortgages people have been taking out – in many ways each of these events is, in terms of modern history, unprecedented. So it is not surprising that it is hard to judge where consumer spending, and with it demand pressures, is going in the light of recent interest rate rises.'

Source: adapted from an article by Scheherazade Daneshku in the *Financial Times*, 30 July 2007

💡ℹ️ Monetary policy in the UK: inflation targeting and the role of the Bank of England

Since May 1997, responsibility for meeting the government's inflation target has lain, operationally, with the Monetary Policy Committee (MPC) of the Bank of England. The group comprising the MPC meet monthly to decide what interest rate should be set, in their view, to meet the government's inflation target. Initially the government's stated inflation target was set at 2.5 per cent as measured by a variant of the retail price index (RPI), known as **RPIX**, but was amended in 2004 as measured by the Consumer Price Index (CPI), at 2.0 per cent, plus or minus 1 per cent. The move to a CPI target was designed to be more in line with the European Central Bank's target measure.

Broadly, if the MPC considers that inflation is likely to rise above the target over the next two years, interest rates will be raised to reduce any

---

■ Activity

Read the case study.

1. Define monetary policy (paragraph 2).

2. Using an appropriate diagram in each case, explain how an increase in interest rates affects:

   a aggregate demand

   b aggregate supply.

3. Explain why David Blanchflower and Rachel Lomax (paragraph 3) might urge caution about 'raising interest rates too far'?

■ Key term

RPIX: a measure of the price level that excludes payments to service mortgage interest from the Retail Price Index measure. Used as the target measure for inflation by the government and MPC until the end of 2003.

inflationary pressure. If the MPC feel that inflationary pressures have weakened, a rate cut might well follow. If the economy is on course to meet the 2.0 per cent target, the MPC will leave the interest rate unchanged.

Operationally, the MPC sets the interest rate at which it makes short-term loans to monetary institutions such as banks. This is known as the **repo rate**, which is short for 'sale and repurchase rate'. High street banks tend to use this rate as their own base rate, from which they calculate the rates of interest that they charge to their borrowers.

As Fig. 18.4 shows, by May 2007, the MPC had made over 30 adjustments in 10 years. In that time there has been a cycle of small changes in interest rates. They have varied from 3.75 per cent (in the late autumn of 2003) to 7.5 per cent in the autumn of 1997. Generally though, the UK economy has experienced a sustained period of low interest rates over recent years, which has had important effects on the wider economy. Interest rates in the UK have been low by historical standards but have tended to be above the levels in the Eurozone and also in the USA.

If the MPC fails to keep CPI inflation within the target boundaries, the Governor of the Bank of England must write an open letter of explanation to the Chancellor of the Exchequer. It is fair to say that the arrangement of operational independence has been highly successful in maintaining economic stability, particularly in terms of the price level, though in April 2007, inflation missed the target for the first time, at 3.1 per cent exceeding the upper limit by 0.1 per cent.

■ **Key terms**

Repo rate: the interest rate that is set by the Monetary Policy Committee of the Bank of England in order to influence inflation. Short for 'sale and repurchase rate'.

CPI (Consumer Price Index): a measure of the price level similar to the HICP (Harmonised Index of Consumer Prices) used widely in the Eurozone. Used since 2004 as the target measure for inflation by the government and MPC.

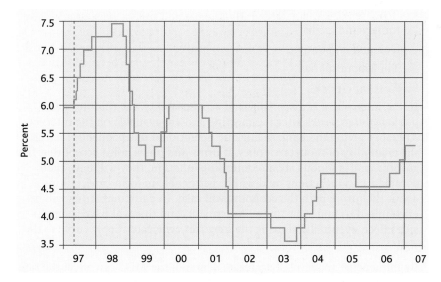

Figure 18.4 *Bank of England base rate, 1997–2007*

Fig. 18.5 shows the movements of the base interest rate and the **CPI** measure of inflation. As you can see, inflation has remained within the target range since the introduction of this target, except for April 2007. It is quite difficult to discern a relationship between interest rates and inflation. This may be due to the effects of time lags and reflects the fact that the MPC takes into account a wide range of factors when deciding whether or not to alter the rate of interest. One criticism of the CPI target is that it does not include major categories of expenditure of the typical citizen, including housing-related costs, and might therefore be considered an inaccurate measure of inflationary pressures in the economy. Employees thus tend to use the RPI as a basis for wage-negotiation, a price index that has tended to exceed the CPI measure.

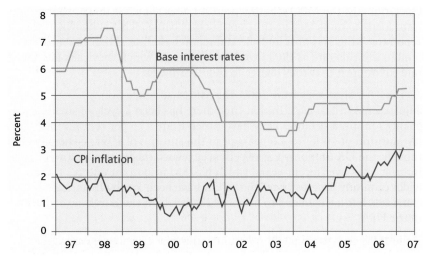

Figure 18.5 *The MPC's track record*

A typical set of minutes of a monthly meeting will reveal that the Committee consider the following factors:

- Financial markets
- The international economy
- Money and credit
- Demand and output
- The labour market
- Costs and prices.

In the interests of transparency and accountability, the minutes are published two weeks after the meeting and are available on the internet. Arguably, giving the Bank of England operational independence increases the credibility of monetary policy. If firms and households accept that the government is serious about controlling inflation, they will have more confidence in its actions, and will be better able to form expectations about the future path the economy will take. In particular, firms will be encouraged to undertake more investment, and this will have a supply-side effect, eventually shifting the long-run aggregate supply curve to the right.

By influencing the level of aggregate demand, the MPC can affect the rate of inflation so as to keep it in the target range, although the effects are not likely to take immediate effect.

The Bank of England prefers a 'gradualist' approach to monetary policy, i.e. it believes that a series of small movements in interest rates is a more effective strategy rather than sharp jumps in the cost of borrowing money. Their aim is not to shock consumers and businesses to control their spending, but to gradually increase the cost of borrowing money and increase the incentive to save, so that the pace of growth moderates and the economy can continue to grow without causing rising inflation.

It is important to note that monetary policy in Britain is designed to be proactive and forward-looking. This means that the MPC is aware that

Figure 18.6 *Mervyn King, Governor of the Bank of England, and Chair of the MPC*

changes in interest rates take time to work through the economic system. Making decisions on interest rates on the basis of today's inflation data simply does not make sense. The teams of economists at the Bank must make regular forecasts of inflation and consider whether the current level of UK interest rates is appropriate in order to meet the inflation target. The reaction of consumers and businesses to interest-rate movements is uncertain, as are the time lags arising from a change in interest rates. So the Bank of England undertakes a rigorous assessment of conditions in the economy, together with forecasts from its own economic model to find an appropriate rate of interest for the economy as a whole.

Activity

Prospects of a further interest rate rise were heightened yesterday as the deputy governor of the Bank of England said that current rates were too low to curb credit and demand growth. Explaining his decision to vote for a rate rise this month, MPC member Sir John Gieve, also the Bank's deputy governor for financial stability, said the danger of a loss of economic growth was preferable to taking a risk with inflation and the Bank's credibility.

Sir John acknowledged that the full impact of the Bank's four rate rises since August 2006 had not yet been felt. However, he was 'not convinced that current rates would be sufficient to bring credit growth and [aggregate] demand back to their long-term sustainable path'. The risks were that 'we may increase interest rates too fast or push them up too far, with an unnecessary loss of growth, and second, that we may raise rates too slowly with a cost in higher inflation and potentially higher interest rates and a sharper slowdown in the end'.

Sir John and Mervyn King, the Bank's governor, were outvoted this month when the nine-member monetary policy committee left its main rate unchanged at 5.5 per cent after a five-four split.

1. Why might the Monetary Policy Committee (MPC) of the Bank of England have increased UK interest rates 'four times since August 2006' (paragraph 2)?

2. Analyse the possible disadvantages of the MPC 'raising interest rates too slowly'.

▪ Other aspects of monetary policy: the money supply and the exchange rate

The money supply

So far, we have focused on the use of interest rates as the key tool of monetary policy, which, indeed, they are. The government does have other monetary instruments at its disposal – influencing the **money supply** and the **exchange rate** of the pound – though has used these in the past with mixed results. Problems have arisen, arguably, from an incomplete understanding of their impacts and a rapidly changing financial environment.

> Prior to 1992…perhaps the most controversial frameworks took the form of commitments to meet targets for growth in the money supply. They were meant to act as rules, which would tie the hands of politicians, but they proved ineffective, not least because the underlying economic relationships broke down.

Source: 'The MPC comes of age', speech by Deputy Governor Rachel Lomax at De Montfort University, February 2007.

▪ Key terms

Money supply: the total amount of money in an economy.

Exchange rate: the price at which one currency, e.g. the pound, exchanges for another, e.g. the US dollar.

■ Key terms

Narrow money: notes, coins and balances available for normal transactions.

Broad money: money that is held in banks and building societies but that is not immediately accessible.

AQA Examiner's tip

Really, the money supply is seen these days as more of a policy indicator than a policy objective or instrument.

Defining the money supply is, in practice, a complicated affair. Clearly, any definition must include notes and coins, though arguably we are moving towards a 'cashless society' with an increasing number of transactions involving debit cards, credit cards, personal cheques and other electronic transfers. People are making payments using money balances held in their name at banks and building societies, whilst using cards or cheques to transfer some of their bank balance to the payee's account. Obviously these bank balances are serving as money and are therefore counted as part of the money supply. The total of all currency in the form of notes and coin, plus balances available for use in normal transactions is known as **narrow money**. Beyond this amount of money, there is an additional, vast amount of balances at banks and building societies that are not so readily accessible (less 'liquid' in financial jargon) and not available for use in normal transactions. This is usually referred to as **broad money**.

> The willingness of banks to relax lending criteria in recent years...[is] the best example of a potentially dangerous rise in money supply, akin to a helicopter drop of extra notes. ...What we need to be concerned about today is the creation of extra money through the banking system and the way that happens is through the granting of credit to willing borrowers who borrow to spend.
>
> *Source: Sir John Gieve, Deputy Governor of the Bank of England, June 2007*

Some economists view the excessive growth of the money supply as a prime cause of inflation, particularly where this has come from excessive printing of notes by monetary authorities. Changes in the money supply will indirectly affect aggregate demand, i.e. if the supply of money increases, perhaps due to a relaxation of limitations on personal borrowing, people will have more spending power and subsequently demand more goods and services. Aggregate demand will increase, shifting the AD curve to the right. This will put pressure on suppliers, bottlenecks will appear and prices will rise. Some would argue, therefore, that money supply should be restricted to keep inflation at a low level. However, it is worth noting that no definition of the money supply seems adequate when trying to establish a causal link to changes in the price level. This would appear to be as true now as it was in the 1980s.

■ Case study

'Crunch' time?

During September 2007, developments in global financial markets finally had significant repercussions in the UK, with the Bank of England taking the unprecedented step of rescuing the high street bank, Northern Rock, from an apparent shortage of funds.

The unravelling of the market for home loans on the other side of the Atlantic, in America's so-called 'sub-prime' mortgage market (which involved many US home-buyers being unable to repay the loans on their new homes as US interest rates steadily increased throughout 2007), was a key sign of a 'credit crunch'. A credit crunch is caused when borrowers are unable to afford to make repayments on loans and other credit agreements, usually because credit was taken when borrowing rates were favourable, or conditions relaxed, as in the 'sub-prime' case. This has significant damaging effects upon consumer spending and subsequently on business investment.

In a matter of a few days, in scenes that caused some commentators to reminisce about 'runs on the bank' from the days of the American 'Wild West', customers queued outside branches of Northern Rock to withdraw savings estimated to total around £3bn.

The Bank of England made a substantial credit facility available to Northern Rock in an attempt to alleviate the fears of savers and shareholders and thus to try to restore confidence in the credibility of UK financial markets in a bid to avoid a similar credit crunch in the UK.

Exchange rates

The exchange rate of a currency is the rate at which one currency can be exchanged for another. For example, we might assume that £1 can be exchanged for US$1.90 or €1.50 at a particular time on the foreign exchange market. We can also say that the exchange rate is the price of one currency expressed in terms of another currency.

Foreign exchange is needed because of the nature of international trade. If a UK citizen buys an item that has been produced in the US and imported into the UK, currency exchange must take place. This is because the US producer will require payment in their own currency, i.e. US dollars. The buying and selling of foreign currencies takes place on the foreign exchange market (Forex). Governments are largely powerless to influence the enormous volume and value of foreign transactions occurring on the foreign-exchange market, but governments can influence the exchange rate through interest rates. A relatively high interest rate offered in UK banks will tend to attract so-called '**hot money**' used for speculative purposes by individuals and firms looking to increase financial returns by placing their money in banks in countries offering relatively high interest rates. This will tend to increase demand for pounds and lead to a 'stronger' pound, i.e. the pound will be worth relatively more of other currencies.

Advantages of a strong pound

1 *Cheaper imports for consumers* A strong pound leads to lower import prices that boosts the real living standards of consumers, at least in the short run. For example, an increase in the real purchasing power of UK residents when travelling overseas or the chance to buy cheaper computers from the United States.

To use a numerical example, if a UK consumer wished to buy a $1,000 laptop computer made in the US, with an exchange rate of £1 = $1, the consumer would pay £1,000. However, if the pound strengthened to £1 = $2, the UK price would fall to £500, assuming the US manufacturer did not alter their dollar price in response.

2 *Lower production costs for producers* When the pound is strong it is cheaper to import raw materials, component parts and other inputs. This is advantageous for businesses that rely on imported components or who are wishing to increase their investment of new technology from overseas. Falling import prices have the effect of causing an outward shift in the short-run aggregate supply curve. If a country can now import more productive technology, the LRAS curve may shift out.

3 *Lower inflation* A strong pound helps to control the rate of inflation because domestic suppliers now face stiffer international competition from cheaper imports and will feel pressure to cut their costs and prices accordingly in order not to suffer from a loss of international

competitiveness. Cheaper prices of imported foodstuffs and beverages will also reduce the rate of consumer price inflation.

4 *Interest rates may be lower*, given low inflation than if the exchange rate was weaker, and cheaper money will eventually stimulate higher consumer spending and capital spending in the circular flow.

Disadvantages of a strong pound

1 *Increase in the trade deficit* The lower price of imports will tend to lead to consumers increasing their demand that can cause an increase in the trade deficit. In addition, exporting firms lose price competitiveness because they will find it more expensive to sell in foreign markets and face losing market share, which can damage profits and employment in some sectors and industries.

To use another numerical example, if the pound exchanges at £1 to €1, a UK car manufacturer can sell a £10,000 model for €10,000 in Belgium. However, if the pound strengthens to £1 = €1.50, the car will now cost €15,000 assuming the UK firm does not alter their pound price. The UK firm would certainly enjoy increased profits if sales volume remained the same, but the higher price in the Eurozone is likely to reduce sales, depending upon price elasticity of demand.

A high exchange rate has damaged employment in Britain in sectors such as textiles and clothing, car manufacturing and semiconductor production as production has shifted away from the UK towards countries with lower production costs.

2 *Slower economic growth* If exports fall, this causes a reduction in aggregate demand and reduces the short-term rate economic growth as measured by the percentage change in real GDP. A strong exchange rate may threaten output, employment and living standards more in some regions than others, especially in those that are more dependent upon markets for exported goods.

3 *Impacts upon business confidence and capital investment* Because investment is partly dependent on the strength of demand, reduced demand in export markets will tend to discourage business willingness to invest.

Activity

Using '£ reaches $2 level!' as your title, write a newspaper column to a general audience outlining and explaining the likely winners and losers of a relatively strong pound. You should make reference to UK consumers, UK firms (who may engage in import and export) and UK economic performance overall.

☑ *After completing this chapter you should:*

- be able to define monetary policy and explain the key instruments
- be able to explain the role of monetary policy in helping to achieve price stability
- be able to analyse the impacts of changes in monetary policy, in particular interest rates, upon macroeconomic performance using AD/AS analysis
- be able to explain how changes in interest rates can influence the exchange rate of the pound.

Examination-style questions

1   'When economic conditions look gloomy, interest rates may be cut to make borrowing cheaper and encourage spending.'
The policy measure described above is an example of a
(a)   supply-side policy
(b)   monetary policy
(c)   budgetary policy
(d)   fiscal policy.

(AQA, 2006)

2   A rise in the general level of interest rates is most likely to cause a fall in the
(a)   savings ratio
(b)   level of investment
(c)   level of unemployment
(d)   exchange rate.

(AQA, 2006)

3   Expansionary monetary policy is most likely to
(a)   shift the long-run aggregate supply curve to the left
(b)   result from a reduction in taxation
(c)   cause a surplus on the current account of the balance of payments
(d)   shift the aggregate demand curve to the right.

4   **UK Debt**
Study Extracts A, B and C, and then answer all parts of the question that follows.

Extract A: UK inflation and the base rate of interest, 1997–2004
See Fig. 18.5 on page 210.

Extract B: Is the UK in debt danger?
UK households are now amongst the biggest borrowers in the world. However, there needs to be a balanced view adopted of the impact of such borrowing. At the moment, borrowing seems comfortably affordable and the level of spending that it helps to finance can provide a welcome boost to aggregate demand. However, the potential problems cannot be denied. For example, increased imports are likely. There may be difficulties for families when mortgage payments cannot be met and houses are repossessed. The economy may also be at risk if the public do not respond to interest rate rises, designed, of course, to control aggregate demand and thereby reduce inflation. None of the difficulties is inevitable. These difficulties may, nevertheless, create a climate of uncertainty and declining confidence, which will eventually harm the economy.
Source: adapted from © bbc.co.uk/news

Extract C: Bank of England raises interest rates
Demand is already high relative to the supply capacity. Consumer borrowing continues at high levels. Strong growth is likely to be maintained and this could lead to inflationary pressures. Against this background, the Monetary Policy Committee (MPC) of the Bank of England judged that an increase of 0.25 percentage points in the rate of interest to 4.75% was necessary to keep inflation on target. Economic theory predicts that rising interest rates might discourage consumer spending and business investment, encourage saving and raise the exchange rate.

Source: adapted from the Bank of England press release, 5 August 2004, www.bankofengland. co.uk, accessed on 9 August 2004

1   Using Extract A, compare the changes in the base rate of interest with
    those in the rate of inflation for the period January 1997 to January 2004.   *(5 marks)*

2   Outline two determinants of business investment (Extract C)   *(8 marks)*

3   With the aid of a suitable diagram, explain two ways in which interest
    rate rises might help 'to control aggregate demand' (Extract B, line 8).   *(15 marks)*

4   Using the data and your economic knowledge, evaluate the
    significance of increasing levels of consumer borrowing for UK
    macroeconomic performance.   *(25 marks)*

Fiscal policy

Links

This will be outlined in more detail in Chapter 20.

Links

For further information on merit goods and public goods, see Chapter 9.

Fiscal policy is one of the three main categories of macroeconomic policy used in the UK today, the others being monetary policy and supply-side policies. Many areas of fiscal policy are likely to have direct impacts upon aggregate demand whilst also affecting aggregate supply. The government will need to be keenly aware of the impacts upon both sides of the economy when deciding upon its approach to fiscal policy.

💡 The meaning of fiscal policy

Fiscal policy is the term used to describe changes in taxation and government spending to meet macroeconomic objectives. It has been used in the past to influence the level of aggregate demand in the economy, though it is becoming an increasingly important tool used to influence aggregate supply, recognising how changes in taxation and government spending create incentives for firms and individuals.

In contrast, monetary policy is aimed squarely at influencing the level of aggregate demand in the economy, using the interest rate as the principal policy tool. Whilst fiscal policy is used alongside monetary policy, it is fair to say that fiscal policy has been given a much less important role in influencing the demand side of the economy today. Indeed, fiscal policy is mainly used for 'fine-tuning' the supply side of the economy at a microeconomic level.

Fig. 19.1 shows the UK government's forecast sources of income for 2007–8. Fig. 19.2 shows the UK government's forecast expenditures for the same financial year.

Often, changes over time in the levels and forms of government spending and taxation arise from changes in government policy. This may be connected to changes in the macroeconomic performance of the economy coupled with a particular government's views about what is best for society. Arguably, the government also has a public responsibility to provide products that would otherwise be underprovided, if at all, i.e. merit goods and public goods, as well as to correct externalities. With this in mind, it may change its spending in areas such as health, education and defence, or alter indirect taxes on alcohol, tobacco and fuel.

An upturn in economic activity will tend to boost employment and reduce unemployment; the subsequent increases in economy-wide income and consumer spending will automatically generate more revenue for the government in the form of income tax, excise duties and Value Added Tax (VAT). Reduced unemployment leads to the government needing to pay out less social security benefits, including Job Seeker's Allowance. These features of fiscal policy are known as automatic stabilisers.

The key date in the year for fiscal policy is the day of the Budget, which occurs in March each year. The Budget gives a forecast of government spending and taxation for the coming financial year, outlining spending totals and tax rates, as well as reviewing outcomes for the tax year about to end. The other key date is in November or December when the Chancellor presents his Pre-Budget Report, giving another forecast of government spending and taxation.

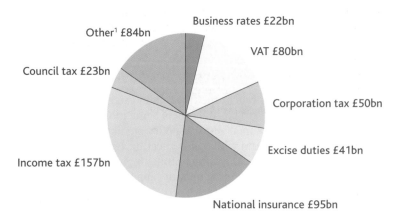

Other¹ £84bn

Business rates £22bn

VAT £80bn

Council tax £23bn

Corporation tax £50bn

Income tax £157bn

Excise duties £41bn

National insurance £95bn

**Total receipts
£553 billion**

¹ Other includes capital taxes, stamp duties, vehicle exise duties, and some other tax and non-tax receipts (e.g. interest and dividends).

Source: HM Treasury, 2007–08 projections. Figures may not sum to total due to rounding.

Figure 19.1 *UK government's forecast sources of income 2007–8*

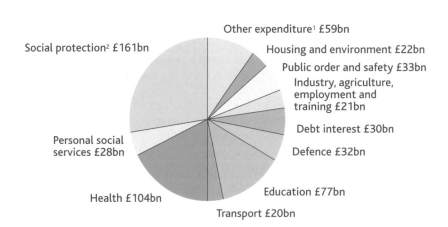

Other expenditure¹ £59bn

Social protection² £161bn

Housing and environment £22bn

Public order and safety £33bn

Industry, agriculture, employment and training £21bn

Debt interest £30bn

Personal social services £28bn

Defence £32bn

Education £77bn

Health £104bn

Transport £20bn

**Total managed expenditure –
£587 billion**

¹ Other expenditure includes spending on general public services; recreation, culture, media and sport, international co-operation and development; public service pensions; plus spending yet to be allocated and some accounting adjustments.

² Social protection includes tax-credit payments in excess of an individual's tax liability.

Source: HM Treasury, 2007–08 near cash projections. Figures may not sum to total due to rounding.

Figure 19.2 *UK government's forecast expenditures 2007–8*

Figure 19.3 *Gordon Brown presents one of his early budgets as the then Chancellor of the Exchequer*

💡 Taxation and fiscal policy

Taxation is the key source of government revenue. Key types of tax that may be manipulated are income tax rates along with personal allowances; social security payments such as National Insurance contributions; VAT; and excise duties (e.g. on alcohol, tobacco and petrol). On the expenditure side of fiscal policy, an increase in any area is likely to impact upon aggregate demand, though increases in some areas may have a greater impact upon aggregate supply. Increased expenditure on a nuclear submarine will add little to the productive capacity of the nation, while improvements to infrastructure such as a new airport will be a substantial boost.

■ Government spending and fiscal policy

A large proportion of national income is spent, on your behalf, by the government. In Chapter 9 we identified the need for spending on public goods, but much other spending is largely a normative matter. The difficulty is in deciding how much government spending is necessary to promote an optimum allocation of resources.

Government spending can be divided into three categories: **current spending**, **capital spending** and **transfer payments**. Current spending is concerned with the day-to-day running of public sector activities including purchasing raw materials as used in schools and hospitals as well as the wages of public sector workers. Improving the productive capacity of the economy involves capital spending, which includes investment in infrastructure such as roads and railways, along with building more schools and hospitals. Government spending involves expenditure on transfer payments such as Jobseeker's Allowance and disability benefits, as part of its welfare commitment.

Figure 19.4 *Widening the M1, an example of capital spending*

■ Fiscal policy and budget deficits and surpluses

A **budget deficit** occurs whenever government spending exceeds revenue from taxation and other sources, such as the sale of government services. Conversely, a **budget surplus** occurs when government revenue exceeds expenditure. A third possibility is a **balanced budget.**

A budget deficit can be eliminated by cutting public spending or by raising taxation, both of which can balance the budget or move it into surplus. If a deficit persists, it must be financed by borrowing. The borrowing that finances the deficit of the whole of the public sector is known as the public sector net cash requirement (PSNCR). In contrast, a budget surplus, or public sector debt repayment (PSDR) means that the government can use the excess revenue over expenditure to repay previous borrowing.

The amount that the government has to borrow is largely determined by what is happening in the economy as a whole. For example, a slowdown or recession has the effect of reducing tax revenues from direct and

Links

See Chapter 9, pages 102–114.

Key terms

Current spending: government spending on the day-to-day running of the public sector, including raw materials and wages of public-sector workers.

Capital spending: government spending to improve the productive capacity of the nation, including infrastructure, schools and hospitals.

Transfer payments: government payments to individuals for which no service is given in return, e.g. state benefits.

Balanced budget: where government receipts equal government spending in a financial year.

Budget deficit: where government spending exceeds government receipts in a financial year (PSNCR).

Budget surplus: where government receipts exceed government spending in a financial year (PSDR).

Links

In-depth coverage of the use of borrowing to finance a deficit is not required at AS Level.

indirect taxes whilst at the same time boosting government spending on welfare and causing a higher level of borrowing. Government finances have moved from surplus in the late 1990s to a deficit of over 2 per cent of GDP in recent years. The emergence of a rising budget deficit has been due to a slightly weaker economy and the effects of substantial increases in government spending on priority areas such as health, education, transport and defence. Both current and capital spending are rising in real terms.

Economists used to talk about discretionary budgetary policy. In the late 1990s, Gordon Brown, as Chancellor of the Exchequer, replaced discretionary budgetary policy with budgetary rules.

The government's budgetary position and the economic cycle

The government's budgetary position, i.e. surplus, deficit, or balanced budget, is likely to change over the course of the economic cycle. For example, during the upturn phase, the following will be true:

1. *Tax revenues* When the economy is expanding rapidly the amount of tax revenue increases, which takes money out of the circular flow of income and spending.

2. *Welfare spending* A growing economy means that the government does not have to spend as much on means-tested welfare benefits such as income support and unemployment benefits.

Thus, during an upturn, the government might well be able to run a budget surplus, or at least reduce a deficit. Conversely during a slowdown or a recession, the government normally ends up running a larger budget deficit. This means the government should (in theory at least) be able to balance its budget over the course of the economic cycle, as any period of budget deficit is countered by a period of budget surplus.

■ Demand-side fiscal policy

Discretionary fiscal policy

Discretionary fiscal policy involves deliberate changes in direct and indirect taxation and government spending, for example a decision by the government to increase total capital spending on road building or to increase the allocation of resources going direct into the NHS.

If it wishes to stimulate aggregate demand, perhaps to remedy a downturn in economic activity, the government essentially has two options. It can either look to cut taxes, or it can increase expenditure. In either case, the overall effect is the same and would be termed **expansionary fiscal policy**. Households will have greater real incomes than before, consumer spending will rise and aggregate demand will increase, as shown in Fig. 19.5, with the AD curve shifting to the right (AD_1 to AD_2). That is to say, a reduction in income tax would mean that large sections of the population receive more take-home pay. It can be expected that a large proportion of this increased income will be spent, though the proportion will depend upon the marginal propensity to consume. As a result, consumer spending will rise. Since consumption is the largest single component of AD, this can have a significant expansionary effect.

Alternatively if, for example, the government increases its expenditure on national road-building, the pay of civil engineers and construction workers will increase. Again, we can expect that a large proportion of this increased income will be spent, therefore leading to an increase in overall consumer spending. However, in manipulating levels of taxation and expenditure, the government must be careful not to stimulate AD too much.

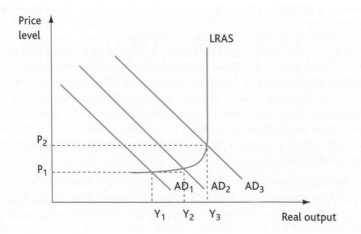

Figure 19.5 *Increasing government spending or reducing taxation will boost aggregate demand, shown by a rightward shift in the AD curve (AD₁ to AD₂)*

If AD is boosted too much (e.g. AD_1 to AD_3), however, in relation to the level of production capacity, as given by the long-run aggregate supply curve (LRAS), demand pull inflation could result, increasing the price level from P_1 to P_2. Matters are made more difficult when one also considers the multiplier effect.

To slow down economic growth, e.g. during a boom, when aggregate demand outstrips the productive capacity of the economy, **contractionary fiscal policy** can be used to counter the associated inflationary pressure. In this case, the government will reduce spending and increase taxation. The overall withdrawal from the circular flow of income should reduce aggregate demand, augmented by the multiplier effect.

Key term

Contractionary fiscal policy: increasing levels of tax revenue relative to government spending, appropriate during a boom in economic activity.

Activity

1. All other things being equal, a government would be undertaking a contractionary fiscal policy if it reduced:

   a government expenditure

   b interest rates

   c taxation

   d the exchange rate.

2. The UK government wants to lower the rate of inflation in the economy but this is likely to conflict with some of its other policy objectives in the short run. Which one of the following is most likely to deteriorate as a result of using contractionary fiscal policy?

   a The current account position

   b The unemployment figures

   c Export volumes

   d UK international competitiveness.

Key term

Supply-side fiscal policy: changes in the level or structure of government spending and taxation designed to improve the supply side of the economy through influencing incentives to save, to supply labour, to be entrepreneurial, and to promote investment, which are largely microeconomic in nature.

The multiplier

In his famous *General Theory*, John Maynard Keynes suggested that there may be multiplier effects in response to certain types of expenditure. Suppose that the government increases its expenditure by £1bn, perhaps by extending an existing motorway. The effect of this is to generate incomes for households, for example for contractors hired to build the road. In turn, those contractors will spend part of their additional income, providing an additional income stream to shopkeepers, newsagents and café owners, who in turn spend part of their income, and so on. Thus the original increase in government spending triggers further income generation and subsequent spending, causing the multiplier effect. Overall, then, equilibrium output may change more than the original increase in expenditure. An initial reduction in expenditure or increase in taxation can lead to a downward multiplier effect, working to reduce equilibrium output by a greater than proportional amount.

💡 The size or value of the multiplier depends most importantly on the size of withdrawals or leakages from the circular flow of income, i.e. how much of any addition to income UK households save, pay in income taxes or spend on imported goods. An increase in the propensity or tendency towards withdrawals or leakages from the circular flow will reduce the size of the multiplier. In very simple terms, if the value of the multiplier is 2, then for every £1bn injection into the circular flow of income, there will be an overall £2bn increase in equilibrium national income.

💡 Supply-side fiscal policy

Whilst fiscal policy can affect aggregate demand, there may also be an impact upon aggregate supply. Changes to fiscal policy can affect the supply-side capacity of the economy and therefore contribute to long-term economic growth. The effects tend to be longer term in nature and stem from 'fine-tuning' at a microeconomic level.

1 *Labour market incentives* Income tax cuts might be used to improve incentives for people to actively seek work and also as a strategy to boost labour productivity. Other things being equal, a cut in income tax will mean that workers are able to take home more pay per hour, which may be an incentive to work harder. The counter-argument is that workers could actually work fewer hours for the same take-home pay as before! Certainly, incentive effects of tax cuts will vary between individuals and there are competing theories about which will tend to dominate. Arguably though, many workers are unable to choose the number of hours they work. Some economists argue that welfare benefit reforms are more important than tax cuts in improving incentives – in particular to create a 'wedge' or gap between the incomes of those people in work and those who are in voluntary unemployment.

2 *Capital spending* Government capital spending on the national infrastructure, e.g. improvements to our motorway network or an increase in the building programme for new schools and hospitals, contributes to an increase in investment across the whole economy. Lower rates of corporation tax and other business taxes might also be used as a policy to stimulate a higher level of business investment and attract inward investment from overseas

3 *Entrepreneurship* Government spending might be used to fund an

expansion in the rate of new small business start-ups, e.g. on suitable grants.

4   *Research and development and innovation* Government spending, tax credits and other tax allowances could be used to encourage an increase in private business sector research and development – designed to improve the international competitiveness of domestic businesses and contribute to a faster pace of innovation and invention.

5   *Improvements in human capital* Increased government spending on education and training (designed to boost the human capital of the workforce) and increased investment in health and transport can also have important supply-side effects in the long run. An improved transport infrastructure is seen by many firms as crucial if the UK is to remain competitive within the European and global economy.

As shown in Fig. 19.6, the desired effect of supply-side fiscal policy is to shift the LRAS curve rightwards ($LRAS_1$ to $LRAS_2$), i.e. increasing the productive capacity of the economy. Since output rises in line with aggregate demand, we can avoid inflationary pressure and prices may fall in some markets (P_1 to P_2) as the economy can produce goods and services more efficiently.

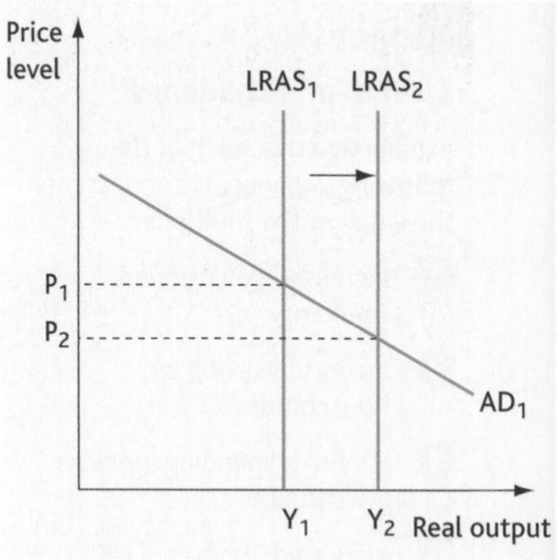

i Free-market economists are normally sceptical of the effects of government spending in improving the supply side of the economy. They argue that lower taxation and tight control of government spending and borrowing is required to allow the private sector of the economy to flourish. They believe in a smaller-sized state sector so that in the long run, the overall burden of taxation can come down and thus allow the private sector of the economy to grow and flourish. However, targeted government spending and tax decisions can have a positive impact even though fiscal policy reforms take a long time to take effect. The key is to help provide the right incentives for individuals and businesses, e.g. the incentives to find work and incentives for businesses to increase employment and investment.

Figure 19.6 *The effect of supply-side fiscal policy*

AQA   Examiner's tip

Candidates should clearly distinguish between the effects of demand-side fiscal policy and supply-side fiscal policy, along with a recognition that the former is focused primarily on the macroeconomy, whereas the latter works primarily, through the microeconomy.

Case study

Benefit 'will not provide work incentives'

Only between 30,000 and 45,000 families are likely to be tempted back to work by the government's new flagship benefit for the low paid, the Working Families Tax Credit (WFTC), the independent Institute for Fiscal Studies said yesterday. The WFTC is intended to increase the attractions of work as opposed to living off state benefits. As the government launched the bill to replace family credit with WFTC, the Institute said most of the gain from the new, more generous credit would go to people already in work, thereby strengthening the so-called **unemployment trap**.

Relatively few individuals are likely to be tempted into the labour market, despite the estimated £1.5bn extra cost of the credit, because for those on housing benefit the combined means-tests will still not leave them markedly better off, the Institute said. While people who do not receive housing benefit will make significant gains, those who do will lose 89p of each extra £1 they earn as they start to pay tax and national insurance and begin to lose WFTC itself and housing and council tax benefit as their earnings rise. Under the present system they lose 92p in the £1. Alan Duncan, a

Key term

Unemployment trap: where individuals receive more in benefit payments than they would be paid if they were in a job.

Activity

Read the case study 'Benefit "will not provide work incentives"' and answer the following questions:

1   Explain the supply-side justifications for the Working Families Tax Credit (WFTC).

2   Outline the criticisms and uncertainties surrounding the WFTC.

Activity

Stretch and challenge

Explain whether each of the following will increase or decrease the value of the multiplier:

1. increased government spending

2. increased saving by households

3. UK firms spending more on investment

4. increased imports of UK citizens

5. government reducing individual tax-free allowances.

senior researcher at IFS, said some further reform to housing benefit and its interaction with the new credit would be needed to provide bigger work incentives. The estimates have been made for the Bank of England's Monetary Policy Committee, which wanted to know the likely labour market effects of the new credit.

Source: adapted from N. Timmins, 'Benefit "will not provide work incentives"', *Financial Times*, 27 January 2007

☑ *After completing this chapter you should:*

- be able to define fiscal policy
- understand the role of fiscal policies in managing aggregate demand
- understand the supply-side effects of fiscal policy.

AQA Examination-style questions

Read Extract A, refer to Figs. 19.1 and 19.2 from earlier in this chapter and answer the questions that follow.

Extract A

The Government's objective is to build a strong economy and a fair society, in which there is opportunity and security for all. The 2007 Pre-Budget Report sets out the Government's future priorities, including:

- Maintaining macroeconomic stability as an essential foundation for achieving its objectives, since this underpins the economy's ability to raise productivity and increase investment;
- Strong growth of real GDP;
- Continuing the sustained investment in the NHS, with resources increasing from around £90 billion in 2007/8 to £110 billion by 2010/11, an average of 2.1 % per year in real terms;
- Simplifying the tax system to make it fairer, simpler and more efficient;
- Taking steps to protect the environment, including reforms and increases to the tax regime for aviation.

Source: 2007 Pre-Budget Report and Comprehensive Spending Review (adapted)

1   Using Figs 19.1 and 19.2, explain whether the government was expected to have a budget surplus or deficit in 2007/8 *(5 marks)*

2   (a)   Taxation is a leakage from the circular flow. Identify the two other leakages. *(2 marks)*

  (b)   Define:

  (i)   Real GDP (Extract A, line 6) *(3 marks)*

  (ii)   Investment (Extract A, line 5) *(3 marks)*

3   Using an aggregate demand and aggregate supply diagram, analyse the
     effects of an increase in government spending on an economy.   (*12 marks*)

4   Comment upon the effectiveness of using fiscal policy to meet the
     Government's macroeconomic objectives.   (*25 marks*)

20   Supply-side policies

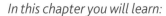
Links

A wide range of supply-side policies are available, many of which could also be considered fiscal in nature, as outlined in Chapter 19.

Supply-side policies are one of the three main types of policy used to manage the UK economy, alongside monetary and fiscal policy. However, it is worth noting that many improvements in the supply side of the UK economy result from the private sector, e.g. firms seeking to boost productivity to reduce unit costs in order to remain competitive or increase profitability. Chapter 13 indicated that the position of the aggregate supply curve depends primarily on the quantity of factor inputs available in the economy, and on the efficiency with which those factors are utilised. Supply-side improvements therefore focus on affecting the determinants of aggregate supply in order to shift the LRAS curve to the right.

◼ The meaning of supply-side policy

Supply-side policies are usually defined as those policies designed to increase the economy's aggregate supply and hence shift the long-run aggregate supply curve to the right. When combined with policies to manage aggregate demand they provide an effective means for allowing governments to meet their stated macroeconomic objectives.

In reality, many of today's improvements in the supply side of the economy arise from the private sector, rather than as a direct result of government policy. For example, private firms may seek to boost labour productivity in order to remain competitive. There are a number of ways of doing this, including increased training budgets and investment in the latest capital equipment. Thus, to bring things up to date, we might talk more of supply-side improvements rather than supply-side policies. The role of government, arguably, is to promote the ideal conditions in which such improvements can flourish, helping to remove market imperfections and restrictions so that the economy can operate in a more efficient manner.

Supply-side economic policies are, for the most part, actually microeconomic policies, designed to improve the supply-side potential of an economy, make markets and industries operate more efficiently and thereby contribute to a faster rate of growth of real national output. If successful, such microeconomic policies have a macroeconomic effect also, through shifting the aggregate supply curve rightwards, as shown in Fig. 20.1. In turn this can lead to economic growth without additional inflationary pressure.

Supply-side policies include:

1 *Labour market measures*, including improving education and training, reducing the powers of trade unions, introducing profit-related and performance-related pay and encouraging more flexible pension arrangements.

2 *Tax reforms* including reducing the overall burden of income tax, and replacing direct taxes with indirect taxes.

3 *Reform of the welfare state* including reducing state welfare benefits to create an incentive to choose low-paid employment rather than unemployment, thereby reducing the 'unemployment trap'.

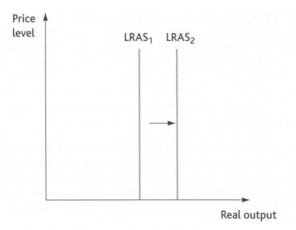

Figure 20.1 *Supply-side policies are designed to shift the long-run aggregate supply (LRAS) curve rightwards, as shown by the movement from LRAS₁ to LRAS₂*

Key terms

Supply-side policies: a range of measures designed to increase aggregate supply and hence the potential output of the economy, though many improvements may come from the private sector.

Labour market: an example of a factor market, in this case where labour is bought and sold.

Product markets: markets in which all kinds of goods and services are traded, for example the market for airline travel or for mobile phones.

4 *Industrial and competition policy measures* such as privatisation, deregulation and contracting out.

5 *Financial and capital market measures,* including deregulating financial markets and promoting greater competition amongst banks and building societies, encouraging saving with special tax privileges, encouraging wider share ownership, promoting entrepreneurship, popular capitalism and an 'enterprise culture'.

There are two broad approaches to improving the supply side. Firstly policies focused on the **labour market**, i.e. the factor market where labour is bought and sold, and secondly **product markets** where goods and services are produced and sold to consumers.

The labour market and supply-side policies

Policies aimed at the labour market are designed to improve the quality and quantity of the supply of labour available to the economy. They seek to make the UK labour market more flexible so that it is better able to match the labour force to the demands placed upon it by employers in expanding sectors, thereby reducing the risk of structural unemployment. An expansion in the UK's total labour supply increases the productive potential of an economy.

Income tax reform and improving incentives to work

One of the key aims has been to encourage more people to join the labour force, leading to an increase in total output. Underlying this particular approach is the idea that overly harsh direct taxation and generous social security benefits can actually act as disincentives to work and, through avoiding or indeed evading taxation, promote the growth of the 'hidden economy'. Whilst this relationship is not clear from empirical evidence, it is perhaps obvious in theory. Economists who support supply-side policies believe that lower rates of income tax provide a short-term boost to demand, and they improve incentives for people to work longer hours or take a new job, because they get to keep a higher percentage of the money they earn.

Mrs Thatcher firmly believed that high rates of direct taxation were a disincentive to work. When her Conservative government was elected in 1979, the top rate of income tax was a colossal 83 per cent! Over time this has been steadily reduced to 40 per cent, with the basic income

AQA Examiner's tip

■ Candidates may be asked to explain, analyse and/or evaluate the effect on macroeconomic performance of supply-side policies.

■ Candidates need an understanding of the vertical LRAS curve as presented in Fig. 20.1 as well as the Keynesian 'inverted L'. Supply-side policies lead to a rightward shift of the LRAS curve and analysis/ evaluation can focus on the impact upon macroeconomic objectives/performance.

AQA Examiner's tip

The economic effects of trade union reform, privatisation, deregulation and competition policy are A2 topics. This chapter will therefore only sketch a brief outline of these policies.

Figure 20.2 *Assessing the effectiveness of supply-side policies to boost incentives to work? Mrs Thatcher in a job centre*

tax rate at 22 per cent. Tax thresholds for low-income earners have also been revised with the objective of encouraging more people to join the labour force. Lowering income tax in this way will shift the AS curve to the right. It seems obvious that lower taxes should boost the incentive to work because tax cuts increase the reward from a job. But some people may choose to work the same number of hours and simply take a rise in their post-tax income! Millions of other workers have little choice over the hours that they work.

The Conservatives also reformed the system of unemployment benefits and social security, a process that has been continued by the Labour government since 1997. The objective is to encourage low-income earners and the unemployed to seek work rather than rely on state handouts. Because of the system, some individuals actually received more in benefits than they would be paid if they were in employment. This so-called 'unemployment trap' acts as a clear disincentive to work. The objective here, then, is to widen the gap between incomes earned by the employed or economically active and benefit payments to the unemployed or economically inactive.

Education and training

It is a fact that many unemployed people lack the skills required to secure a job. Indeed, many 16-year-old school leavers and those who have been unemployed for long periods of time do not have the skills valued by employers. Government provision of training opportunities can help to tackle wider skill shortages in the economy, leading to a more productive, mobile and flexible labour force, which will also help to improve the country's international competitiveness. Most economists agree that with the move away from industries requiring manual skills to those needing 'thinking' skills, investment in education, along with the retraining of previously manual workers, is absolutely vital. Improved training, especially for those who have lost their jobs in an 'old' industry should improve the occupational mobility of workers in the economy, which will help reduce the problem of structural unemployment. A well-educated workforce also helps to attract foreign investment. Indeed, the Irish economy is an often-used example of how supply-side reforms designed to increase the qualifications and skill level of the labour force, together with favourable tax rates for companies and workers, has encouraged a huge flow of inward investment from overseas.

A number of schemes have been used to boost the UK skills-base. Local Skills Councils provide vocational training and work placements for teenagers and unemployed adults, whilst Job Clubs, Restart schemes, Access courses and personal counselling, managed by the local offices of the Employment Services Agency, provide work opportunities for the longer-term unemployed.

Educational reform has been an active area of supply-side policy since the 1980s. The concern of government has been the relatively poor educational attainment of two-thirds of the population, when compared with other developed countries. Initiatives designed to improve overall educational standards have included the introduction of a National Curriculum, and more recently, national frameworks for literacy and mathematics. The inspection of schools by a watchdog body, Ofsted, along with targets for achievement in public examinations and the publication of school league tables are all attempts to boost educational standards.

AQA Examiner's tip

Candidates must be able to explain that supply-side policies can improve labour productivity and subsequently international competitiveness.

The importance of education and training

In a recent report on the UK economy, the OECD (Organisation for Economic Co-operation and Development) highlighted weaknesses in the UK education and training system that were hindering its growth performance. It was particularly critical of educational provision for less academic students. It said that 'much more could still be done to improve basic literacy and numeracy, thus providing a strong foundation for continued learning'. It also argued that 'continuously improving the relevance and quality of vocational programmes is as important as it is to expand their provision'. It was worried that the tax and benefits system might discourage individuals from acquiring intermediate skills. It pointed out that, whilst gross earnings of workers with intermediate skills were significantly higher than those of low skilled workers, net income was little different if those workers had children because of the tax credits that low-skilled, low-pay workers can claim. For 16–18 year olds, pilot schemes that have paid teenagers to stay in education appear to have boosted engagement in continued learning. But an alternative might be to increase the very light taxation faced by teenagers taking a job at 16.

Source: adapted from OECD Economic Surveys: United Kingdom – Volume 2005 Supplement 2, © OECD 2005

■ Activity

Read 'The importance of education and training' case study:

1 Using a diagram, explain why the quality of the labour force is so important for the long-term growth of the UK economy.

2 Suggest why improving 'basic literacy and numeracy' might be important for increasing the long-term human capital stock of the economy.

3 Explain why taxes and benefits might be a disincentive to acquire skills in the UK.

Trade union reforms

By restricting the supply of workers, **trade unions** seek to increase the wages of their members but at the cost of a decrease in numbers employed. Supply-side economists would argue that such action increases costs, reduces efficiency and reduces international competitiveness. The last Conservative government pursued a vigorous supply-side policy aimed at reducing the power of trade unions in the labour market.

■ The product market and supply-side policies

Supply-side policies in product markets are designed to increase competition and efficiency. If the productivity of an industry improves, then it will be able to produce more with a given amount of resources, shifting the LRAS curve to the right.

Privatisation and deregulation

One of the most important changes in the economy over the past few decades has been the transfer of ownership of former state-owned assets to the private sector. This is considered a supply-side policy as it is argued that privately-owned enterprises have more incentives to be efficient and competitive. Exposure to the 'discipline' of the market is argued to lead to a rightward shift of the AS curve. The UK economy has seen significant **privatisation** activity since 1979, especially for the transport and utility industries. The removal of barriers to entry into an industry, known as **deregulation**, has also taken place on a large scale, along with the contracting-out of activities previously undertaken by the public sector. This has arguably led to the creation of much more competitive markets, replacing public sector monopolies.

■ Key terms

Trade union: an organisation of workers set up to negotiate on wages, working hours and working conditions with employers on behalf of its members.

Deregulation: the process of removing government controls from markets.

Toughening up of competition policy

Most supply-side economists believe in the dynamic effects of greater competition and that competition forces business to become more efficient in the way in which they use scarce resources. This reduces costs, which can be passed down to consumers in the form of lower prices. A tougher competition policy regime includes policies designed to curb abuses of a dominant market position – in other words intervention to prevent some of the market failure that can come from monopoly power.

A commitment to free international trade

Trade between nations creates competition and should be a catalyst for improvements in costs and lower prices for consumers. The UK government is committed to an expansion of free trade within the European Single Market and also to negotiating a liberalisation of trade in the global economy as part of its membership of the World Trade Organisation. For example, it wants to see further reforms of the Common Agricultural Policy as a stepping-stone to global trade agreements between Europe, the United States and developing countries.

Table 20.1 *Selected corporation tax rates in the EU in 2004*

Country	Corporate tax rate (%)
Estonia	0.0
Ireland	12.5
Latvia	19.0
Sweden	28.0
UK	30
Italy	34.0
France	35.4
Germany	38.7

Measures to encourage entrepreneurship and capital spending

Today's small businesses can often become the larger businesses of tomorrow, adding to national output, employing more workers and contributing to innovation that can have positive spillover effects in other industries. Governments argue that they want to promote an 'entrepreneurial culture' and to increase the rate of new business start-ups. Supply-side policies include loan guarantees for new businesses, regional policy assistance for entrepreneurs in depressed areas of the country and advice for new firms.

Capital spending by firms adds to aggregate demand $(C + I + G + (X - M))$ but also has an important effect on long-run aggregate supply. Supply-side policies would include tax relief on research and development and reductions in the rate of corporation tax, which is a tax on business profits. Again, Ireland is a good example of a country inside the EU that has benefited hugely from cutting company taxes, which has led to a large rise in foreign direct investment. Estonia, one of the new countries joining the EU in 2004, cut its corporation tax rate to zero per cent in a deliberate attempt to attract new investment and stimulate economic growth and employment. As shown in Table 20.1 there are now big differences in corporation tax rates among the 27 nations of the European Union.

💡 Supply-side improvements in the economy need not necessarily rely on government policy initiatives, but may originate in the business sector independently of government, e.g. productivity improvements, innovation and investment are ways in which firms may seek to improve their competitiveness. However, there is certainly much a government can do to encourage these supply-side improvements by fostering an environment suited to business investment, utilising some of the methods outlined above.

■ Saving, investment and supply-side policies

As already outlined, the supply-side impacts of fiscal policy work by changing relative prices or incentives. So far we have examined the choice between work and leisure. Supply-side economists argue that a second choice facing individuals is between consumption and saving. Higher tax rates on investment income will also tend to reduce the return from savings. High rates of taxation on income from saving and investment thus tend to encourage consumption rather than saving. As a result, savings and investment will tend to fall. Supply-side economists argue that fiscal demand-management policies, designed to boost output and employment, lead only to rising inflation, as the aggregate supply of output fails to keep pace with aggregate demand. Further, tax cuts advocated by supply-side economists are not primarily designed to stimulate aggregate demand. Instead they are intended to produce incentives encouraging households to save rather than consume, and businesses to invest so that economic growth can continue without demand-pull inflation.

■ Case study

UK supply-side performance in 2007

The 2007 OECD Economic Survey of the UK found that our good economic performance over the past decade has been underpinned by policies that promote efficiency and economic resilience. As a result, productivity growth has remained strong, while the workforce has been boosted by immigration in recent years. Nevertheless, the productivity gap with the United States remains large, and a number of reforms should be pursued in order to further improve growth performance. Policy has focused on encouraging participation in work, although employment rates among the least skilled remain too low. A key challenge is to raise educational performance without significant further increases in expenditure, while a related key challenge is to ensure strong incentives for the least skilled to participate in the labour market and to progress in work. Finally, it remains important to ensure that the tax structure preserves the United Kingdom's position as an attractive business location.

Skill-biased technical change is changing the composition of jobs in advanced economies and raising the level of skills required to do them. This has increased the importance of educating a large proportion of the population to much higher standards than in the past. The government has responded to this challenge by raising education spending and expanding the capacity of the education system in key areas such as pre-primary education and increased participation in education beyond the age of 16. The United Kingdom has also pioneered the use of school benchmarking techniques and the use of targets to raise school quality.

The United Kingdom has recorded strong productivity growth over the past decade, surpassing the performance of many continental European countries and thereby narrowing the productivity gap. However, despite narrowing substantially since the early 1990s, the productivity gap with the United States has remained unchanged more recently. While overall the United Kingdom has some of the least restrictive product and labour-market regulations, it needs to guard against increasing red tape and tax complexities that can raise the costs of doing business. Restrictive planning regulations make entry of new firms into retailing difficult and inefficient land use raises property prices. Poor transport infrastructure is another potential factor reducing productivity growth, while R&D spending and adult training are relatively low.

Corporate tax rates have been lowered in the United Kingdom and elsewhere, while tax bases have been broadened, making corporate tax systems more efficient. While the UK was early in cutting tax rates and had strong tax competitiveness, others have caught up. And some countries now have considerably lower tax rates, even after the recent announcement to cut the UK statutory corporate tax rate from 30 per cent to 28 per cent in 2008.

💡 Supply-side policies and the AD/AS model

As already outlined, the desired effect of all the supply-side policies outlined above is to shift the AS curve to the right. An outward shift of the LRAS curve helps to increase the underlying trend rate of growth, as it represents an increase in potential GDP. Most governments now accept that an improved supply-side performance is the key to achieving sustained economic growth without a rise in inflation. But supply-side reform on its own is not enough to achieve this growth. There must also be a high enough level of aggregate demand so that the productive capacity of an economy is actually brought into play. As shown in Fig. 20.3, a rightward shift of the LRAS curve alone will not necessarily lead to a substantial increase in equilibrium real GDP. Only when combined with an increase in AD will a substantial increase in actual output (Y_1 to Y_2) result.

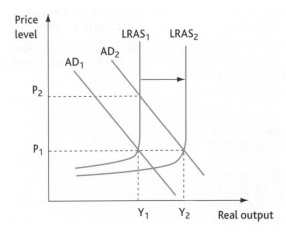

Figure 20.3 *A rightward shift in aggregate supply and aggregate demand*

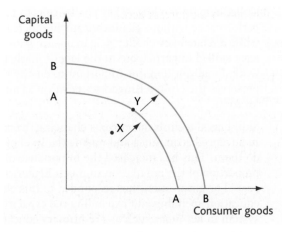

Figure 20.4 *An increase in the economy's potential output as a result of improvements in the supply-side*

Supply-side improvements can also be shown using a production possibility boundary. As shown in Fig. 20.4, an increase in labour productivity or a rise in the economy's stock of capital or labour will cause an outward shift in the PPB (*AA* to *BB*). This means that the potential output of capital and consumer goods has increased. Note that this is different to simply moving from point *X*, which is inside the original PPB to point *Y*, on the boundary itself. This implies an improvement in the productive efficiency with which existing resources are used or that previously unemployed resources are now being used. Supply-side improvements can, of course, have both effects.

Supply-side policies and the government's macroeconomic objectives

As outlined in Chapter 14, the government has four main macroeconomic objectives: strong, steady growth, low inflation, low unemployment, and balance of payments equilibrium on the current account. Supply-side policies, when combined with effective policies to boost aggregate demand can help to achieve these macroeconomic objectives.

In Fig. 20.3, an increase in aggregate demand, from AD_1 to AD_2 would result in demand-pull inflation (P_1 to P_2) if there was not also an increase in the productive capacity of the economy. An associated increase in aggregate supply of $LRAS_1$ to $LRAS_2$ would lead to an increase in the equilibrium level of real GDP, with little extra inflationary pressure, as the equilibrium price level remains at P_1 in the diagram. Thus a government that makes use of both demand-management and supply-side policies can achieve growth and low inflation. Assuming accurate use of economic policies, the government can also achieve low unemployment. We have seen that one of the underlying principles of supply-side policies involves strengthening incentives to work and provide individuals with appropriate skills for a changing pattern of economic activity.

💡 Supply-side policies designed to boost productivity, especially of labour, and make firms more competitive should, other things being equal, make UK goods and services more price competitive internationally. This in turn should provide a boost to the balance of payments. Whether supply-side policies are sufficient to restore equilibrium to the current account remains to be seen.

Activity

Stretch and challenge

Both Conservative and Labour governments claim success for the improved performance of the UK economy in recent decades. Since the early 1990s, the combination of rising living standards, high levels of employment and economic stability has been unmatched by any other developed nation. The statistics make impressive reading:

- 2 million more are employed than in 1997.
- 75 per cent of the potential UK labour force is now in work.
- Unemployment levels in recent years have been lower than any time since 1975.
- Productivity growth has risen since 1997 at a greater rate than France, Germany, Japan and the USA, though our absolute levels are still considerably lower.
- We have enjoyed over 60 successive quarters of positive growth since the last recession.

To what extent, do you think, are recent improvements in the UK economy the result of effective supply-side policy?

Activity

For each of the following policies, identify whether it is an example of fiscal, monetary or supply-side policy. Discuss how each policy affects either aggregate demand or aggregate supply (or both), and examine its effects on equilibrium real output and the overall price level:

1. An increase in government expenditure.
2. A decrease in the rate of unemployment benefit.
3. A fall in the rate of interest.
4. Legislation limiting the power of trade unions.
5. Financial incentives to encourage more students to attend university.
6. Provision of retraining in the form of adult education.
7. A reduction in the highest rate of income tax.
8. Measures to break up a concentrated market.
9. An increase in the Bank of England's base interest rate.

✓ *After completing this chapter you should:*

- be able to define supply-side policies and give examples
- be able to analyse the impact of supply-side policies using AD/AS analysis

■ understand the role of supply-side policies in influencing the underlying trend rate of economic growth and the potential output of the economy, the level of unemployment, the rate of change of prices, and UK external performance as reflected in the balance of payments on current account.

AQA Examination-style questions

1 Which one of the following is a supply-side policy aimed at reducing unemployment?
(a)   a cut in interest rates
(b)   an increase in the money supply
(c)   an increase in unemployment benefits
(d)   a cut in the rate of income tax.

2 The diagram below shows aggregate demand and supply curves for the UK economy.

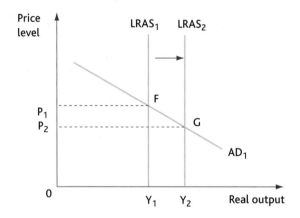

The move of the economy from equilibrium at F to G could be explained by an increase in
(a)   the level of taxation
(b)   the level of interest rates
(c)   government expenditure on education and training
(d)   the level of welfare benefits.

UK TRADE (adapted from June 2006, ECN 2/2)

Study Extracts A and B, and then answer all parts of the question that follows.

Extract A: UK trade in goods, August 2003 – June 2004 (£bn)

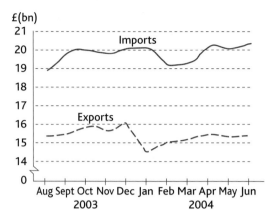

Extract B: The deepening deficit

Data on the UK trade balance in goods and services make depressing reading, with the deficit likely to continue to deepen. The trade in goods shows the severest problems. There are various factors that can help explain this weakness. The sterling exchange rate continues to be high, generating greater pressure on manufacturers in export markets and causing home producers to face stiffer competition from imports. The increases in interest rates in 2004 might push the exchange rate even higher. Exporters will argue more strongly than ever that a fall in the exchange rate is needed for an improved balance of payments on current account, as well as for growth and jobs. In May, another ten countries joined the existing fifteen members of the European Union (EU). This will lead to an intensification of competition as all the member countries attempt to improve their trading position inside the EU. The UK needs to improve its competitiveness and this is reliant on further improvements to the supply side of the economy such as productivity, skills and investment. Thus the conclusion seems inescapable that 2004 is going to see a substantial deficit.

Source: adapted from Michael Morris, *British Economy Survey*, Vol 34 (1), Autumn 2004, © British Economy Survey 2004

1 Using Extract A, compare the changes in UK exports and imports of goods for the period August 2003 to June 2004. *(5 marks)*

2 Outline two determinants of a country's exchange rate. *(8 marks)*

3 Explain why a fall in the exchange rate of the pound sterling is 'needed for an improved balance of payments on current account, as well as for growth and jobs'(Extract B, lines 7–8). *(12 marks)*

4 Using the data and your economic knowledge, evaluate the effects on the UK trade balance in goods and services of 'further improvements to the supply side of the economy' (Extract B, lines 12–13). *(25 marks)*

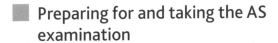

Examination skills

Preparing for and taking the AS examination

Throughout this book we have given you examiner's tips that should assist you with the examination and the knowledge that you require in order to be successful. In this chapter the mechanics of the examination are explained, together with the knowledge and skills you need to demonstrate in order to succeed.

Setting and marking the exam

Questions are set by the chief or principal examiner about 18 months to 2 years ahead and are considered by a committee of teachers in order to ensure that they comply with the specification and are at the correct level. When the paper has been taken examiners attend a coordination meeting to ensure that all are marking to the same standard and assistant examiners have to send a proportion of their scripts to a team leader who will check that their marking is at the right standard. The team leaders in turn have to send scripts to the chief examiner.

When all marking has been completed team leaders and the chief examiner attend meetings at the exam board to consider any scripts where there might be a particular problem. Finally, students, after the results have been announced, can have their script re-marked by a team leader.

Mark schemes

All examinations are marked on the basis of a mark scheme that is drawn up by the chief examiner when the papers are set. The mark scheme is not rigid but will be adapted to account for the way that candidates have answered the questions. The AQA mark scheme makes it quite clear that 'Where the candidate's response to a question is such that the mark scheme permits full marks to be awarded, full marks *must* be given. A perfect answer is not necessarily required for full marks.'

The format of the AS paper for Units 1 and 2 is as follows:

- Time allowed 1 hour 15 minutes
- 25 multiple choice questions
- One data response question from a choice of two – you are advised to spend at least 50 minutes on this section

- Each piece of data has four questions to it – the mark allocation is 5, 8, 12 and 25.

Two approaches are used in the construction of the mark scheme: an issue-based approach and a levels approach.

An issue-based approach

The mark scheme for parts (a), (b) and (c) of the data response questions adopts this approach. With this type of mark scheme marks are awarded for discussing and possibly developing certain issues. An example taken from Unit 1 Specimen Mark Scheme part (b) is shown below:

'Define income elasticity of demand and explain why a knowledge of income elasticity of demand for housing would be useful to an economist wishing to study the housing market (8 marks)'

Marks are awarded as follows – for candidates who:

Give a definition of income elasticity of demand, or a formula, or a description of what income elasticity of demand attempts to measure (*up to 3 marks*).

Give reasons why a knowledge of income elasticity would be useful, for example:

- Affordability depends on both price and income
- Most houses are bought with borrowed money
- Loans are closely linked to incomes
- Income elasticity is likely to be more influential than price elasticity of demand

Award up to *3 marks* for each valid point made (*1 mark* for mention/ identification, up to *2 marks* for elaboration).

Since a definition is required in the question, there is a maximum of *6 marks* if there is no formal definition or formula or description of what it is that income elasticity attempts to measure.

A levels approach

This is used for marking part (d) of the data response questions. The Levels Mark Scheme identifies five levels representing differences in the quality of work. A range of marks is allocated to each level and examiners are instructed to choose the level that best fits the candidate's answer. Answers do not have to satisfy every statement in the level description. In part (d) of the data response questions approximately half the marks are available to award to candidates who demonstrate that they can 'evaluate economic arguments and evidence, and make informed judgements'. An answer showing no evidence of evaluation, however good the analysis, would not be awarded more than 13 marks (in Level 3). The quality of evaluation should be the sole distinction between a Level 4 and Level 5 answer.

The levels and their descriptors are as follows:

Level 1: A very weak answer

Few, if any, relevant issues are recognised. Economic concepts and principles are not adequately understood or applied to the question. No satisfactory analysis or evaluation. There might be some evidence of organisation in the answer but generally it fails to answer the question. Descriptions and explanations lack clarity. Spelling, punctuation and grammar may be poor. There is little use of economic terminology.

0 to 6 marks

Level 2: A poor answer but some understanding is shown

One or more relevant issues are recognised. An attempt is made to use basic economic concepts to answer the question but the candidate's explanation may become confused and analysis will therefore be very limited. There may be some attempt to present alternative points of view but any attempt at evaluation is limited or superficial. There is some logic and coherence in the organisation of the answer. The candidate demonstrates some ability to spell commonly used words and to follow the standard conventions of punctuation and grammar. Some use of economic terminology is made but this is not always applied appropriately.

7 to 11 marks

Level 3: An adequate answer with some correct analysis but very limited evaluation

Two or more relevant issues are recognised. The candidate has made a reasonable attempt to apply economic concepts and ideas. A satisfactory understanding of some basic economic concepts and theories is demonstrated and there is some evidence that the candidate can analyse issues. There will be some attempt to present alternative points of view and to evaluate the issues, arguments and/or data. There is some logic and coherence in the organisation of the answer. The candidate is generally able to spell commonly used words and usually follows the standard conventions of punctuation and grammar. Some descriptions and explanations are easy to understand, but the answer may not be expressed clearly throughout. There is some evidence of the correct use of relevant economic terminology. *12 to 16 marks*

Level 4: Good analysis but limited evaluation

Two or more relevant issues are identified. Good understanding of basic economic concepts and models

is demonstrated. The candidate is able to apply these concepts and models to answer the question. Some appreciation of alternative points of view is shown. Satisfactory use is made of evidence and/or theoretical analysis to evaluate the issues/arguments/economic models identified and to support conclusions. Spelling is generally accurate and the standard conventions of punctuation and grammar are usually followed. The answer is well organised. Descriptions and explanations are clearly expressed. Appropriate use is made of relevant economic terminology.

17 to 21 marks

Level 5: Good analysis and evaluation

Two or more relevant issues are identified. Good understanding of basic economic concepts and models is demonstrated. The candidate is able to apply these concepts and models to answer the question. Clear understanding of alternative points of view is shown. Good use is made of evidence and/or theoretical analysis to evaluate the issues/arguments/economic models identified and to support conclusions. A clear final judgement is made. Spelling is generally accurate and the standard conventions of punctuation and grammar are usually followed. The answer is well organised. Descriptions and explanations are clearly expressed. Appropriate use is made of relevant economic terminology. *22 to 25 marks*

What skills do you require?

You will have noted from the mark scheme that certain skills are being tested by the specification:

- Knowledge of the subject.
- Application of knowledge to the problem set.
- Analysis of the problem or issues.
- Evaluating the evidence and making judgements.

Knowledge

Knowledge requires candidates to show that they can understand what is meant by the question and use the correct economic terms to explain it. A question that asks 'what is inflation?' requires you to explain inflation and recognise the concept and in this way show that you have the required knowledge of inflation to explain. If you are asked to draw an AD/AS diagram you show knowledge by putting in the correct curves, labelling them and labelling the axis correctly. You show knowledge by distinguishing between the axis for AD/AS and the axis for demand and supply.

Application

Knowledge is essential for any economist, but the knowledge must be applied to economic problems to be of use. For instance, knowledge of how the Monetary Policy Committee changes the interest rate may need to be applied in a question. Candidates would be expected to apply their knowledge and suggest how an increase in the rate of interest would affect the economy. Chief examiners set wide-ranging questions and candidates are expected to be able to apply their knowledge to a wide range of situations. The country referred to in the question may be unfamiliar but a student who has understood how interest rates affect the economy would be expected to be able to use this knowledge. Similarly in terms of a diagram the student may be familiar with the production possibility boundary and understand the analysis in terms of consumption goods and capital goods. Application of this knowledge in a different context like a choice faced by a hospital performing specialised heart operations or general surgery would be an example of application.

Analysis

By analysis we mean dissecting information and using it to explain a problem or issue. Quite often chief examiners ask you to explain data trends from information provided and then link it with other information. Analysis can also be shown graphically where a diagram is used to explain a situation or the result of a particular economic policy. An example could be 'with the aid of an AD/AS diagram analyse the effect of a large balance of payments surplus on the macro economy'. Your diagram would show what you expected to happen and the text would analyse the relationship between the balance of payments surplus and the macroeconomy.

In economics analysis is usually:

- written explanation of a theory
- a diagram to enhance explanation
- some equation or use of mathematics when, e.g. analysing elasticity.

Evaluation

Evaluation requires candidates to draw conclusions from what they have previously explained or to suggest a particular course of action and argue which courses of action might be most appropriate in a situation. While drawing a simple conclusion a candidate may show some degree of judgement. At AS and A2 Level examiners expect more involved evaluation. This can be seen in the essays of students who read widely and are knowledgeable about current economic affairs. Often economic columnists in the quality newspapers will evaluate a particular course of action that the government is taking and reading such comments assists students in making more valid judgements.

Any essay question in economics will require a number of issues to be discussed. For example, in the question 'Outline the main disadvantages of the price mechanism as a means of allocating resources', some of the issues that might be discussed are: that no account is taken of external costs or benefits; might lead to the

development of monopolies; uneven distribution of income. If each of these issues is discussed the drawing of a conclusion or evaluation of the importance of the point needs to take place.

There are a number of ways in which evaluation can be undertaken:

- While this can be written at the end of the essay candidates are more likely to be successful if the evaluation occurs after the relevant issue has been discussed and analysed. This does not preclude a final conclusion at the end of the essay.
- Leaving all evaluation until the end of the essay may lead to the student forgetting what has previously been analysed, leading to a lower level of evaluation than would have occurred had it been continuous.
- Many years' experience as an examiner suggests that the more organised and focused candidates, who achieve high marks, tend to evaluate throughout and as a final conclusion.
- Evaluation to be sound must be based on the theory or material that you have previously analysed. The marks will be for the quality of the evaluation and not for a statement of personal opinions.

Evaluative statement

A frequently asked question from new students of economics is how to introduce or begin an evaluative statement. One way *not* to begin is to start the sentence with the words 'I think'. For those who are unsure the following terms can be used to introduce evaluative statements, bearing in mind that this is not an exhaustive list:

- As a result of
- Because of
- In the light of
- The advantages/disadvantages of this
- As a result of the analysis the best solution would be to

Evaluation is what is described as a higher-order skill and can be seen at a number of different levels. At a basic level the student may just draw a conclusion from the analysis. In terms of the example given above the student may decide that as no account of external costs takes place that pollution will result. A more sophisticated conclusion may be that pollution will result but the authorities will deal with this by other methods because the overall advantages of the price system greatly outweigh the disadvantage that it ignores external costs.

Evaluation may require the student to consider the importance of competing theories where assumptions are likely to be stated and considered. For example, a candidate might discuss both the benefits of and the disadvantages of economic growth to an economy and then evaluate the outcome. The student might decide that growth is beneficial but it will cause certain problems but the problems can be overcome by the increasing wealth that is generated by the growth. On the other hand, evaluation could consist of the student stating that growth impacts unfavourably on the environment and that growth should be slowed. A further conclusion might be that at present it is too early to tell as there is still a large amount of disagreement among experts. Any of these responses would count as evaluation and be rewarded by examiners.

Evaluation may occur when considering the likely results of policies and their wider ramifications on the economy. For example, an increase in the levels of income tax is likely to reduce disposable income that may lead to a fall in aggregate demand. It may also cause a fall in the demand for imports and lead to less effort and participation supplied by the working population; a disincentive effect. Discussion of these and drawing conclusions about them as a result of a change in policy would count as evaluation.

Empirical evidence may also be considered and evaluated and wide reading and knowledge of what is going on in the economy and the world will help improve your evaluation of policies and their effects.

■ The quality of written communication

The specification in economics at both AS and A2 Level assess candidates on the level of the quality of written communication. The levels mark scheme says 'Spelling is generally accurate and the standard conventions of punctuation and grammar are usually followed.' The standard conventions mean that candidates must be able to use a style of written English that is appropriate for the subject, which includes familiarity with the key terms.

Organise the essay in paragraphs, which should be structured in a logical order – you will note that the levels mark scheme refers to 'organisation'. A badly organised essay is unlikely to get beyond level 1 or 2 as you will not convince the examiner of your understanding of the subject.

Writing needs to be legible – if the examiner cannot read it you cannot receive credit for it. Do not write in faint pens that are difficult to read and pay attention to the conventions of spelling – no text language or arrows that you may have used in your notes. Write out full names the first time you use them, e.g. the Monetary Policy Committee (MPC); thereafter initials will be acceptable.

■ Examination instructions

The examination paper will tell you exactly what is required in the way of questions to be answered – do not answer extra questions in the hope that you will obtain extra marks – infringement of the rubric (instructions) in doing extra questions means that you are spreading the available time over too many questions and as a result your answers will lack sufficient depth.

Each question will have within it a command word that tells you what approach the question requires in terms of the skill you need to use to answer it. If the question says evaluate and the candidate only analyses the problem without drawing conclusions marks will be lost.

Command words

Looking through past papers, command words for different skills are as follows:

Knowledge

- ■ Define, e.g. define price elasticity of demand
- ■ State, e.g. the determinants of supply

Application

- ■ Identify, e.g. the cause of unemployment
- ■ Explain, e.g. what you understand by the consumer price index

Analysis

- ■ Analyse, e.g. analyse the possible effects of a government decision to impose a maximum price
- ■ Compare, e.g. compare the inflation rate of France with that of the UK
- ■ Describe, e.g. describe what you understand by market failure
- ■ Predict, e.g. predict the likely outcome of an increase in the UK interest rates

Evaluation

- ■ Evaluate, e.g. evaluate the result of an increase in the rate of interest
- ■ Discuss, e.g. discuss the likely results of a severe inflation in the UK
- ■ Justify, e.g. do you agree that the price of oil should be determined by free-market forces rather than through the intervention of government. Justify your answer
- ■ Assess, e.g. assess the effect of a strike by railway workers

■ Multiple choice questions

AQA at AS Level uses multiple choice questions as a technique of assessment. They are used mainly to test knowledge and application and can cover any aspect of the course. Quite often they are diagram based so it is important that you are familiar with the standard diagrams. They can also be based on definitions and understanding the meaning of economic terms is basic to a further appreciation of the subject. Usually all multiple choice questions on the paper need to be answered; there is no choice as in data response and essay papers. Skill in multiple choice papers requires practice and your college or school is likely to have a collection of past papers or alternatively they are available from the AQA website.

Answers are right or wrong and candidates either know the correct answer or need to eliminate those that are incorrect. If you find a question very difficult leave it out, carry on with the questions and come back to it at the end. One final word of advice – at the end of the paper do not go over it again and change your answers as studies have proved that students are more likely to be right in their first choice and changing their answers reduces the marks.

■ Data response questions

Data response questions are based either on graphs, tables or text and they may be on areas that are relevant to but not familiar to the student, for example the French balance of payments figures. Questions are based around the data and as with the data response questions in this book, they will contain prompts to point you in the right direction when writing your answer. Typically they start with a definition or application to give you an easy start to the examination. Other questions are highly likely to contain the command words 'with the aid of a diagram analyse...'. Some questions, e.g. elasticity, may require calculations – show your working out; do not just jot down an answer. The final question will require evaluation and will be based on the material in the passage but will require you to draw on your own knowledge and analyse and evaluate issues that you have studied in the course. These final questions are marked out of 25 marks and require the use of the higher-order skills of analysis and evaluation.

The AS examination has a combination of both multiple choice and data response and you are advised to spend at least 50 minutes on the data response. You must read the material thoroughly and give yourself time to do this. You may decide to underline key points or parts that you consider to be important.

As the data response element has 50 marks this gives one minute per mark, which gives a guide of how long to spend on each question. Many candidates write far too much on low-mark questions, which limits the amount of time that they have available for the more valuable questions.

There are 25 multiple choice questions to be completed in 25 minutes, which should give a well-prepared candidate ample time.

Glossary

A

Accelerator effect: the relation between the change in new investment and the rate of change of national income.

Actual supply: the amount that producers in fact produce. This may differ from planned supply for a variety of reasons such as breakdowns in production, staff absences, etc.

Aggregate demand: total planned expenditure in the economy. Known by the identity $C + I + G + (X - M)$.

Aggregate supply: the total value of goods and services supplied in the economy.

Allocative efficiency: this is achieved in an economy when it is not possible to make anyone better off without making someone worse off, or you cannot produce more of one good without making less of another.

B

Balance of payments: exports minus imports – a deficit means more is imported than exported.

Balance of trade: visible exports minus visible imports.

Balanced budget: where government receipts equal government spending in a financial year.

Boom/bust policy: the government using macroeconomic tools to stimulate and then contract the economy.

Broad money: money that is held in banks and building societies but that is not immediately accessible.

Budget deficit: where government spending exceeds government receipts in a financial year (PSNCR).

Budget surplus: where government receipts exceed government

spending in a financial year (PSDR).

Buffer stock: an intervention system that aims to limit the fluctuations of the price of a commodity.

C

Capital spending: government spending to improve the productive capacity of the nation, including infrastructure, schools and hospitals.

Central bank: the financial institution in a country or group of countries typically responsible for issuing notes and coins and setting short-term interest rates.

Classical view: economists who believed that recessions and slumps would cure themselves.

Commodity: a good that is traded, but usually refers to raw materials or semi-manufactured goods that are traded in bulk such as tea, iron ore, oil or wheat. Often they are unbranded goods (homogeneous) where all firms' products are very similar and undistinguishable from each other.

Competition: a market situation in which there are a large number of buyers and sellers.

Complementary products: goods that are consumed together, for example bread and butter, or DVDs and DVD players.

Complete market failure: where the free market fails to provide a product at all, i.e. the case of public goods.

Composite demand: a good that is demanded for more than one purpose so that an increase in demand for one purpose reduces the available supply for the other purpose, typically leading to higher prices, e.g. milk used in butter and cheese.

Contraction in supply: when the amount offered for sale is reduced because the price level has fallen.

Contractionary fiscal policy: increasing levels of tax revenue relative to government spending, appropriate during a boom in economic activity.

Contractions in demand: falls in the quantity demanded caused by rises in prices.

Cost push inflation: where increased costs of production result in firms increasing their prices leading to an increase in the general price level.

CPI (Consumer Price Index): a measure of the price level similar to the HICP (Harmonised Index of Consumer Prices) used widely in the Eurozone. Used since 2004 as the target measure for inflation by the government and MPC.

Credit crunch: where borrowing becomes more expensive or unavailable.

Current account equilibrium: where the current account exercises no effect on the domestic macroeconomy.

Current spending: government spending on the day-to-day running of the public sector, including raw materials and wages of public sector workers.

Cyclical unemployment: demand deficient unemployment that occurs as a result of the economic cycle.

D

Deflation: a situation where prices persistently fall.

Deindustrialisation: a fall in the proportion of national output accounted for by the manufacturing sector of the economy.

Demand: the amount that consumers are willing and able to buy at each given price level.

Demand deficient unemployment: insufficient aggregate demand in the economy to employ the available labour.

Demand pull inflation: where aggregate demand exceeds aggregate supply leading to an increase in the level of prices.

Demand-side fiscal policy: changes in the level or structure of government spending and taxation aimed at influencing one or more of the components of aggregate demand.

Demerit good: a good that would be over-consumed in a free market, as it brings less overall benefit to consumers than they realise.

Deregulation: the process of removing government controls from markets.

Derived demand: when the demand for one good or service comes from the demand for another good or service. The demand for cars stimulates the demand for steel, therefore the demand for steel is derived demand.

Discouraged workers: workers who leave the labour market because despite numerous attempts they are unable to find a job.

Discretionary fiscal policy: the deliberate manipulation of government spending and taxation to influence the economy.

Diseconomies of scale: where an increase in the scale of production leads to increases in average total costs for firms.

Disequilibrium: a situation within the market where supply does not equal demand.

Disposable income: income available to households after the payment of income tax and national insurance contribution.

Division of labour: breaking the production process down into a sequence of tasks, with workers assigned to particular tasks.

Economic goods: goods that are scarce and therefore have an opportunity cost.

Economic growth: the capacity of the economy to produce more goods and services over time.

Economic indicators: economic statistics that provide information about the expansions and contractions of business cycles.

Economic models: these are used to show the essential characteristics of complicated economic conditions in order to analyse them and predict the result of changes of variables.

Economic welfare: refers to the benefit or satisfaction an individual or society gets from the allocation of resources. We can attempt to measure the welfare of individuals but really we want to understand the overall effects on society as a whole. This will include how well off people feel, how much they have but also might consider other factors such as their environment and standard of living – their physical well-being, although this is hard to define.

Economies of scale: where an increase in the scale of production leads to reductions in average total cost for firms.

Effective demand: demand supported by the ability to pay for a good or service.

Employment: where labour is actively engaged in a productive activity usually in exchange for payments such as wages.

Equilibrium: the price at which demand is equal to supply and there is no tendency for change.

Ex ante: a term that refers to future events.

Ex post: a term that refers to after the event.

Excess demand: when demand is greater than supply at a given price.

Excess supply: when supply at a particular price is greater than demand; this should signal to producers to lower prices.

Exchange rate: the price at which one currency, e.g. the pound, exchanges for another, e.g. the US dollar.

Expansionary fiscal policy: increasing levels of government spending relative to tax revenue, appropriate to stimulating aggregate demand during a downturn in economic activity.

Exporting: the sale of goods or services to a foreign country – generates income for the home country.

Exports: goods or services sold abroad.

Extension in supply: when there is an increase in supply because the market price has risen.

Extensions in demand: increases in demand caused by changes (falls) in price.

Externalities: costs or benefits that spill over to third parties external to a market transaction.

Factor market: the market for the factors of production that make other goods and services such as labour or raw materials.

Failure of information (or information failure): where economic agents do not properly perceive the benefits or disadvantages of a transaction.

Fiscal policy: the policy of the government regarding taxation and government expenditure.

Fixed costs: costs of production that do not vary as output changes.

Flow: measured over a specified period of time.

Free goods: goods that have no opportunity cost, for example air.

Free-market economy: one in which there is very limited government involvement in providing goods and services. Its main role is to ensure that the rules of the market are fair so that, for example, people cannot steal each other's property.

Free-rider problem: where some consumers benefit from other consumers purchasing a good, particularly in the case of public goods.

Frictional/search unemployment: people between jobs.

GDP per capita: GDP divided by the population – a measure of living standards.

Geographical immobility: where workers find it difficult to move to where employment opportunities may be, due to family ties and differences in housing costs.

Globalisation: the ability to produce goods anywhere in the world and sell them in any country.

Goods and services: goods are considered to be tangible products that we can touch such as CDs or a car. These are distinct from services, which are not tangible (touchable) such as a trip to the cinema or a train journey. We do not buy the train or the cinema but do receive intangible benefits from watching the film or travelling.

Government failure: when government intervention to correct market failure does not improve the allocation of resources or leads to a worsening of the situation. The costs of government intervention may therefore exceed the benefits.

Gross domestic product: the total value of goods and services produced in the economy.

Hot money: money that is liable to rapid transfer from one country to another.

Human capital: the skills, abilities, motivation and knowledge of labour. Improvements in human capital raise productivity and can shift the PPB to the right.

Importing: the purchase of goods and services from abroad – leads to expenditure for the home country.

Imports: goods or services purchased from abroad.

Incidence of tax: the proportion of a tax that is passed onto the consumer. If most of a tax rise is added to the consumer then the incidence of tax is said to be 'high'. When demand is price inelastic then the incidence of tax tends to be high.

Income: a flow of earnings to a factor of production over a period of time, e.g. wages or salaries.

Income elasticity of demand: the proportion to which demand changes when there is a change in income.

Income induced: will increase as income increases and decrease as income decreases.

Index numbers: a weighted average of a group of items compared to a given base value of 100.

Indirect tax: a tax on spending.

Inferior goods: goods or services that will see demand fall when income rises.

Inflation: a persistent increase in the level of prices.

Inflationary pressure: occurrences that are likely to lead to increased prices.

Injections: money that originates outside the circular flow and so will increase national income/ output/ expenditure.

Interest rate: the cost of borrowing or the reward for saving.

Investment (I): spending by firms on buildings, machinery and improving the skills of the labour force.

Investment good: a product that will increase in value over time.

Invisibles: intangibles such as the provision of insurance or banking services.

Joint supply: when the production of one good also results in the production of another.

Keynesian: the view of John Maynard Keynes, a very influential UK economist (1883–1946) who suggested how governments could cure mass unemployment.

Labour market: an example of a factor market, in this case where labour is bought and sold.

Law of unintended consequences: when the actions of consumers, producers and governments have effects that are unanticipated.

Long-run aggregate supply: the economy's productive capacity.

Marginal external benefit: the spillover benefit to third parties of an economic transaction.

Marginal external cost: the spillover cost to third parties of an economic transaction.

Marginal private benefit: the benefit to an individual or firm of an economic transaction.

Marginal private cost: the cost to an individual or firm of an economic transaction.

Marginal social benefit: the full benefit to society of an economic transaction, including private and external benefits.

Marginal social cost: the full cost to society of an economic transaction, including private and external costs.

Market-clearing price: the price at which all goods that are supplied will be demanded.

Market demand: total demand in a market for a good, the sum of all individuals' demand, at each given price.

Market failure: where the market fails to produce what consumers require at the lowest possible cost.

Market supply: the sum of all individual firm's supply curves at each given price.

Maximum price: a price ceiling above which the price of a good or service is not allowed to increase.

Merit good: a good that would be under-consumed in a free market, as individuals do not fully perceive the benefits obtained from consumption.

Minimum price: a price floor below which the price of a good or service is not allowed to decrease.

Monetary policy: controlling the macroeconomy via changes in monetary variables such as the money supply or interest rates.

Monetary Policy Committee: a committee of economists and central bankers who meet monthly and decide whether or not to change the rate of interest.

Money supply: the total amount of money in an economy.

Monopoly: a market structure dominated by a single seller of a good.

Multiplier effect: where an increase or decrease in spending leads to a larger than proportionate change in the national income.

Narrow money: notes, coins and balances available for normal transactions.

Natural rate of unemployment: (NB this is an A2 topic) the rate of unemployment that is consistent with a stable rate of inflation.

Negative expectations: businesses expect future sales and profits to be less due to factors like falling aggregate demand.

Negative externalities: costs imposed on a third party not involved with the consumption or production of the good.

Negative output gap: where the economy is producing less than its trend output.

Net government spending: the difference between government spending and taxation.

Nominal GDP/nominal national income/nominal output: GDP/income/output figures not adjusted for inflation.

Normal goods: goods or services that will see an increase in demand when incomes rise.

Normative statements: opinions that require value judgements to be made.

Occupational immobility: as patterns of demand and employment change, many workers may find it difficult to easily secure new jobs, since they may lack the necessary skills.

Opportunity cost: the next best alternative forgone (given up) when an economic decision is made. Note: it is only the next best alternative not a range of alternatives.

Partial market failure: where the free market provides a product but with a misallocation of resources.

Participation rates: proportion of the country's population that makes up the country's labour force.

Planned supply: the amount producers plan to produce at each given price.

Policy instrument: techniques used to achieve policy objectives.

Policy objective: government's major macroeconomic objectives.

Pollution permit: a permit sold to firms by the government, allowing them to pollute up to a certain limit.

Positive expectations: businesses expect the future sales and profits

to improve due to factors like increased aggregate demand.

Positive externality: a positive spillover effect to third parties of a market transaction.

Positive output gap: when actual GDP exceeds trend GDP increasing inflationary pressure.

Positive statements: statements that can be tested against real-world data.

Price ceiling: see maximum price.

Price elasticity: the responsiveness of demand to a change in the price level. The formula is percentage change in quantity demanded divided by percentage change in price.

Price floor: see minimum price.

Private good: a good that is both excludable and rival in consumption.

Privatisation: sale of government-owned assets to the private sector.

Product markets: markets in which all kinds of goods and services are traded, for example the market for airline travel or for mobile phones.

Production: the process that converts factor inputs into outputs of goods and services.

Production possibility boundary: the PPB indicates the maximum possible output that can be achieved given a fixed set of resources and technology in a particular time period.

Productive efficiency: when a firm operates at minimum average total cost, producing the maximum possible output from inputs into the production process.

Productivity: a measure of efficiency, measuring the ratio of inputs to outputs; the most common measure is labour productivity, which is the output per worker.

Profit: when total income or revenue for a firm is greater than total costs.

Public good: a good that possesses the characteristics of non-excludability and non-rivalry in consumption.

 Q

Quasi-public good: a good that has some of the qualities of a public good but does not fully possess the two required characteristics of non-rivalry and non-excludability.

R

Real GDP/real national income/ real output: GDP/income/output figures adjusted for inflation.

Real interest rate: the money rate of interest minus the rate of inflation.

Recession: when an economy is growing at less than its long-term trend rate of growth.

Renewable resources: resources that are able to be replenished over time, whereas non-renewables such as oil and gas are likely to run out.

Repo rate: the interest rate that is set by the Monetary Policy Committee of the Bank of England in order to influence inflation. Short for 'sale and repurchase rate'.

RPIX: a measure of the price level that excludes payments to service mortgage interest from the Retail Price Index measure. Used as the target measure for inflation by the government and MPC until the end of 2003.

 S

Savings (S): a withdrawal from the circular flow.

Specialisation: the production of a limited range of goods by an individual factor of production or firm or country, in cooperation with others so that together a complete range of goods is produced.

Stock: a quantity measured at a particular point in time.

Structural unemployment: unemployment caused by a change in the demand side or supply side of the economy.

Subsidies: payments by government to producers to encourage production of a good or

services. Often subsidies are found in farming where farmers receive funds from government per tonne or unit of output. This typically means that prices can be lower than would otherwise be the case.

Substitutes: goods that can be used as alternatives to another good, for example bus and rail services or Mars Bars and Snickers. Close substitutes are good alternatives, whereas weak substitutes are not very good or likely alternatives, such as gas-fired power in the UK and hydroelectric power.

Supply: the amount offered for sale at each given price level.

Supply-side fiscal policy: changes in the level or structure of government spending and taxation designed to improve the supply side of the economy through influencing incentives to save, to supply labour, to be entrepreneurial, and to promote investment, which are largely microeconomic in nature.

Supply-side policies: a range of measures designed to increase aggregate supply and hence the potential output of the economy, though many improvements may come from the private sector.

Supply-side shock: something that will increase or reduce the costs, hence supply side of all firms in the economy, e.g. a large increase in the price of oil.

Sustainable: an activity carried out today that does not stop future generations maximising their welfare.

 T

Tight labour market: where firms have to increase wages to attract the labour that they require.

Total factor productivity: the overall productivity of inputs used by a firm in producing a particular level of output.

Trade union: an organisation of workers set up to negotiate on wages, working hours and working

conditions with employers on behalf of its members.

Trade-off: where one macroeconomic objective has to be curtailed in favour of another objective.

Transfer payments: government payments to individuals for which no service is given in return, e.g. state benefits.

Transmission mechanism of monetary policy: how changes in the base interest rate influence the components of aggregate demand.

 U

Unemployment: those without a job but who are seeking work at current wage rates.

Unemployment trap: where individuals receive more in benefit payments than they would be paid if they were in a job.

 V

Value judgements: statements or opinions expressed that are not testable or cannot be verified and depend very much on the views of the individual and the values they hold.

Variable costs: costs of production that vary with output.

Visibles: exports or imports that are tangible, that you can see and touch as it crosses international boundaries.

Voluntary unemployment: workers who are not prepared to take a job at current wage levels.

 W

Wealth: a stock of owned assets, e.g. housing property or a portfolio of shares.

Weighting: where a commodity is given a weighting proportional to its importance in the general pattern of consumer spending.

Withdrawals: any money not passed on in the circular flow and has the effect of reducing national income/output/expenditure.

Index